The Primacy of Resistance

Also Available from Bloomsbury

Force and Understanding: Writings on Philosophy and Resistance,
Howard Caygill, ed. Stephen Howard
The Ethics of Resistance: Tyranny of the Absolute, Drew M. Dalton
Resistance, Revolution and Fascism: Zapatismo and Assemblage Politics,
Anthony Faramelli
Hegel and Resistance: History, Politics and Dialectics, ed. Bart Zantvoort
and Rebecca Comay
On Resistance: A Philosophy of Defiance, Howard Caygill

The Primacy of Resistance

Power, Opposition and Becoming

Marco Checchi

BLOOMSBURY ACADEMIC
LONDON • NEW YORK • OXFORD • NEW DELHI • SYDNEY

BLOOMSBURY ACADEMIC
Bloomsbury Publishing Plc
50 Bedford Square, London, WC1B 3DP, UK
1385 Broadway, New York, NY 10018, USA
29 Earlsfort Terrace, Dublin 2, Ireland

BLOOMSBURY, BLOOMSBURY ACADEMIC and the Diana logo
are trademarks of Bloomsbury Publishing Plc

First published in Great Britain 2021
This paperback edition published in 2022

Copyright © Marco Checchi, 2021

Marco Checchi has asserted his right under the Copyright,
Designs and Patents Act, 1988, to be identified as Author of this work.

For legal purposes the Acknowledgements on p. x constitute an
extension of this copyright page.

Cover design by Charlotte Daniels

All rights reserved. No part of this publication may be reproduced or
transmitted in any form or by any means, electronic or mechanical, including
photocopying, recording, or any information storage or retrieval system,
without prior permission in writing from the publishers.

Bloomsbury Publishing Plc does not have any control over, or responsibility for,
any third-party websites referred to or in this book. All internet addresses given in
this book were correct at the time of going to press. The author and publisher
regret any inconvenience caused if addresses have changed or sites have
ceased to exist, but can accept no responsibility for any such changes.

A catalogue record for this book is available from the British Library.

Library of Congress Cataloging-in-Publication Data

Names: Checchi, Marco, author.
Title: The primacy of resistance: power, opposition and becoming / Marco Checchi.
Description: London; New York: Bloomsbury Academic, 2021. |
Includes bibliographical references and index. | Summary: "What is at the heart
of political resistance? Whilst traditional accounts often conceptualise it as a reaction
to power, this volume (prioritising remarks by Michel Foucault) invites us to think of
resistance as primary. The author proposes a strategic analysis that highlights how our efforts
need to be redirected towards a horizon of creation and change. This text combines
a range of political and philosophical scholarship and provides an innovative rethinking of
Foucault's model of power relations that leads towards a new autonomism for the
21st century"– Provided by publisher.
Identifiers: LCCN 2020039506 (print) | LCCN 2020039507 (ebook) | ISBN 9781350124455 (hardback) |
ISBN 9781350214354 (paperback) | ISBN 9781350124462 (ebook) | ISBN 9781350124479 (epub)
Subjects: LCSH: Government, Resistance to. | Opposition (Political science) |
Political science–Philosophy. | Foucault, Michel, 1926-1984–Political and social views.
Classification: LCC JC328.3 .C4734 2021 (print) | LCC JC328.3 (ebook) | DDC 320.01–dc23
LC record available at https://lccn.loc.gov/2020039506
LC ebook record available at https://lccn.loc.gov/2020039507

ISBN: HB: 978-1-3501-2445-5
PB: 978-1-3502-1435-4
ePDF: 978-1-3501-2446-2
ePUB: 978-1-3501-2447-9

Typeset by Integra Software Private Limited

To find out more about our authors and books visit
www.bloomsbury.com and sign up for our newsletters.

To Maddalena

Contents

Acknowledgements	x
Introduction: Resistance against the against	1
Against the traditional understanding of resistance	3
The oppositional tradition	6
The reactive tradition and the primacy of power	8
Rethinking resistance	13
'A third kind of affect'	15
Why the primacy?	18
Overview of chapters	20
1 'Resistance comes first': Metamorphoses, change, creation	25
Points, forces and relays: A microphysics of resistance	27
From resistance to resistance-and-its-possibility	31
Antagonistic metamorphoses	33
Strategies of resistance	40
The primacy of resistance with and beyond Foucault	42
Resistance, creation and becoming	46
2 Human nature and resistance. From La Boétie's companionship to the liberal closure	51
Towards an art of voluntary inservitude	55
The contract's evil twin: The misfortune of servitude	56
La Boétie's Leviathan	59
Spotting freedom among denatured beings	60
'We are all comrades'	63
A cooperative state of nature	66
The liberal closure: Securing the necessity of power despite natural freedom	69

Comradeship as self-betrayal	70
Where there is non-resistance, there is power	73
Hobbes's Leviathan: A body without bodies?	75
The right to resist	76
From the primacy of resistance to the necessity of power	78
Towards the edge, never beyond the edge	81

3 The primacy of labour: Processes of expansions and scenarios of extinction — 83

Arendt's (unwanted) primacy of labour	87
The modern victory of labour	91
Warning against extinction	94
The trajectory of Italian autonomist Marxism	98
The Copernican inversion of *operaismo*	100
Working-class becomings	107
Expansion and extinction	110
The cooperativist principle of the sovereignty of labour	114
The sovereignty of labour	119
Neoliberal closures	122
Extending labour to the whole of life: Human capital	123
Biofinancialization	128
Scenarios of extinction	132

4 Power as interruption and the affirmation of potentia: Politics and resistance between Rancière and Negri — 135

Openness and creation	137
The primacy of politics in Rancière	138
From equality to obedience	141
Obedience as accidental misfortune	143
Interruption comes first	146
Political resistance creates worlds	149
A physics of resistance: Potentia and being in Negri's Spinoza	152
The dangerous process of the construction of being	154
Corrupt imagination creates worlds too	157
The self-organization of the multitude	161

Potentia: Resistance – counter-power – constitution	164
De-stat-ic-ization: The real urgency of the inexistent	166
The primacy of *potentia* qua resistance	168
Constitutive affirmation and accidental opposition	171
An eternal age of resistance	174

5   Re-existence: The materialist ontology of resistance and becoming — 177

A transversal line	179
How many diagrams?	185
The unified abstract machine	191
Deleuze's lectures on Foucault	195
Active and reactive singularities	197
Diagrams and mutation	200
A third kind of singularity	203
Resistance as the outside of the outside	206
From history to becoming	208
Resistance, dice-throws and optional rules	213
Material openings	216

A conclusive opening: At last resistance comes first — 219

Notes	224
References	232
Index	243

Acknowledgements

Many thanks to all friends, comrades and colleagues who have helped me throughout the writing of this book and in particular to my partner Maddalenina, Matteo, Andrea, Martina, Leandros, George, Margherita, Lele, Thomas. I am deeply thankful to Stephen Dunne and Dimitris Papadopoulos for their continuous help and dedication at every stage of this long process. Thanks to my family for their encouragement and support.

The author and publisher gratefully acknowledge the permission granted to reproduce the copyright material in this book. Every effort has been made to trace copyright holders and to obtain their permission for the use of copyright material. The publisher apologizes for any errors or omissions in the above list and would be grateful if notified of any corrections that should be incorporated in future reprints or editions of this book.

Introduction:
Resistance against the against

The dearest memory of my childhood is when we moved to our new house. … This gave me the chance to regularly attend … the Circle for the socialist childhood, where young socialists introduced us to class struggle and on how to build a better society, with no classes and no exploitation.

A young couple was not allowed to have a walk together without the presence of a family member … We discussed on the backwardness of this custom. We decided to challenge it … going out hand in hand with our girlfriends.

[In 1943] I founded the – provisional – National Liberation Committee for the Castelli Romani, to which I participated in my capacity of president.

(Capogrossi 2018) *[my translation]*[1]

Those are flashes of a resistant life in the age of Resistance par excellence, one of the dispersed accounts of Resistance to Nazi-fascism during the Second World War. Salvatore Capogrossi has not drawn much historical commentary. Nevertheless, his memoirs meticulously describe the everyday struggles that marked his life, including those years in which local fascist authorities and then Nazi occupiers tried to domesticate his rebellious little town, Genzano,[2] situated on the outskirts of Rome (Castelli Romani) and better known as 'little Moscow'.

Yet the pages of his book where disillusion and bitterness prevail are not those that describe the infamous injustices of Nazi-fascism. Once weapons are silent, it is time for reflections and also for recognition. In the aftermath of the Second World War, Resistance becomes material to be codified – on the one hand, the works of historians that reconstruct the crucial battles, the main characters, the acronyms and the political parties; on the other hand, the formal recognition of the state that distributes the honour (and the pension) of 'Resistance partisan' to those who participated to at least three armed conflicts between 1943 and 1945. For Capogrossi, both these processes are not only incorrect, but also dangerously reductive. He thinks of historians who attributed to the Allies the successful sabotage of Nazi trains directed to Cassino[3] conducted instead by his brigade. He thinks of those young women who risked their lives transporting weapons for the partisans hidden in the countryside, whose crucial contribution will be ignored and forgotten by the processes of official recognition. But, more generally, he thinks of his own life, his lifetime engagement that cannot be restricted to the years of war. Sadder but wiser, he concludes: 'As I was able to show in this book, Resistance to fascism in Genzano actually started in 1919' (Capogrossi 2018: 246).[4] Before armed struggle, even before fascism in Italy came to power (1922), his Resistance was already there. But what is this Resistance that Capogrossi describes then? Can his Resistance still have the capital letter? Perhaps Capogrossi's memoirs are more about resistance*s*, without capital letter and in the plural. It is in the hiatus that separates those resistances from Resistance that we need to find a trajectory for problematizing the concept of resistance. That will be the task of this book.

The problem, though, is whether there is actually room to think resistance outside the historic memory of the Resistance during the Second World War. Jacques Derrida probably summarizes the general feeling of his generation when he defines resistance as a 'word loaded with all the pathos of my nostalgia, as if, at any cost, I would like not to have missed blowing up trains, tanks, and headquarters between 1940 and 1945' (Derrida 1998: 2).[5] This sense of overloading and conflation can partly explain a certain reluctance to the conceptualization of resistance in political and theoretical debates. Michel Foucault's engagement with resistance is quite emblematic in this sense. Although I aim to unveil his engagement with resistance throughout the whole of his work, Foucault's explicit use of the term is soon abandoned in favour of other germane, but perhaps less historically laden, concepts. As Judith Butler notes, in his 'What Is Critique?', 'one might be tempted to think that Foucault is simply describing resistance, but here it seems that [critique as] virtue has taken the place of that term. ... We will have to ask why' (Butler

2001: 218). Michael Hardt (2010) attempts to answer this question in the frame of Foucault's refusal to sign a petition in defence of the Red Army Faction's attorney Klaus Croissant, in which the West German state was accused of becoming fascist. His hypothesis is that the historical legacy of Resistance has somehow managed to impose precise theoretical implications on any possible conceptualization of resistance. Resistance was somehow bound to be stuck with its own enemy (fascism), but also with those specific modalities (armed struggle and clandestine bands). Especially in the late 1970s, Resistance and fascism come to form a political and theoretical compound – when there is fascism, there *must* be Resistance: 'in groups like the Red Army Faction and the Italian Red Brigades, the claim [of a "fascist state"] carried specific political consequences: since the state was fascist, the only effective means to oppose it was armed struggle organized in highly disciplined, clandestine bands' (Hardt 2010: 154).

A similar hypothesis has also been advanced by Howard Caygill to justify the striking absence of a theoretical engagement with the concept of resistance in the works of Italian autonomia, particularly in the work of Antonio Negri and Mario Tronti. Caygill wonders 'whether the avoidance of the term "resistance" was an allergic response to the mythology of Resistance in Italy and its ideological role in the post-war Italian constitution or to the Red Brigades' description of themselves as partisans of a "New Resistance"' (Caygill 2013: 219).

Against the traditional understanding of resistance

Away from the monolithic couple Resistance-fascism, resistance has received a growing attention after the cycle of struggles in 2011, ranging from the Arab spring to the Spanish *indignados*, the Greek *aganaktismenoi* occupations, the Occupy movement and the UK riots. Instead of blocking a theoretical engagement with the concept of resistance, the streets of Athens, Tunis, Madrid, Cairo, New York and London have been more than an inspiration for a much-needed theoretical analysis of resistance and political struggle. Several publications have alimented a growing debate whose urgency reaches far beyond the necessity of filling a theoretical lacuna in virtue of its own embodiment into concrete practices of resistance (Hardt and Negri 2012, Mason 2012, Žižek 2012, Caygill 2013, Douzinas 2013, Worth 2013, Bloom 2016, Fishwick and Connolly 2018). In these works, there has been a significant advancement in conceptualizing resistance well beyond the couple Resistance-fascism: each resistance has its own enemy and this does not have to be necessarily fascist. By the same token, each resistance has its own modality and does not necessarily involve neither armed struggle, nor secrecy or clandestinity.

Yet what persists, more or less implicitly, is a certain identification of resistance with rare and spectacular events of struggle. Resistance involves masses, barricades, occupations, clashes, a certain degree of violence and febrile enthusiasm. These coordinates define a circumscribed moment in history that momentarily disrupts the ordinary stability of power. This appears prominently in Costas Douzinas's proclamation that the recent uprisings suggest that 'ours is an age of resistance' (Douzinas 2013: 9). Douzinas looks at resistance through Alain Badiou's concept of event: 'a pure break with the becoming of an object of the world, ... an intemporal instant which renders disjunct the previous state of an object (the site) and the state that follows' (Badiou 2007: 39). The event of resistance marks a rupture, an absolute separation with the rest of history given in its isolation and circumscription. But when did our age of resistance actually begin? Is it still on? And what happens to resistance in the age that precedes an age of resistance?

Capogrossi's assertion of the continuity of his resistance poses a radical challenge to these questions. Against Badiou's concept of event, Daniel Bensaïd highlights the theoretical and strategical problems that this account of resistance implies: '[d]etached from its historical conditions, pure diamond of truth, the event ... is akin to a miracle. ... Its rarity prevents us from thinking its expansion' (Bensaïd 2004: 101). On the one hand, there is power in its ordinarity; on the other hand, there is resistance in its miraculous exception, always already on the verge of vanishing to leave room for another age of non-resistance. Despite the assonance, this account of the event does not capture the theoretical potential of Foucault's relationality between power and resistance: 'Where there is power, there is resistance' (Foucault 1978: 95). Not only resistance as event undermines the contemporaneity and coextesiveness of power and resistance, but it also reduces the crucial contributions of a multiplicity of resistant practices (e.g. Capogrossi's resistances before 1943–5) that precede the miracle of the age of resistance. The notion of rarity has the effect of closing off the possibility of thinking the expansion of resistance (as continuous multiplicity of practices), but also the possibility of thinking resistance *as* expansion: proliferation, creation, openings, becomings. The exploration of this possibility defines the trajectory of this book.

Foucault's concept of resistance serves here as the overarching theoretical framework. His intuition that 'resistance comes first, and resistance remains superior to the forces of the process' (Foucault 1997a: 167) hints towards a conceptualization of resistance that fully accounts for its creative and affirmative character. The primacy of resistance operates a Copernican revolution of traditional understandings of the relation between power and resistance. The latter has often been conceptualized as subordinated, reactive, negative and bound to defeat. This is not only the result of explicit theorizations, but it also reflects a certain sedimentation in the ordinary use of the word 'resistance'. Within this traditional understanding of resistance, it is possible to distinguish two main axes: one focuses on the oppositional stance of resistance; the other on its reactive character. These axes represent trajectories defined by the convergences of multiple conceptual lines on which distinct understandings of resistance install themselves. The two trajectories often tend to overlap as the reactive tradition necessarily rests on the oppositional understanding of resistance. Yet recent attempts of challenging the reactive tradition have nevertheless maintained the oppositional trajectory, de facto demonstrating their distinction. The task is to show how the primacy of resistance can successfully reject the reactive understanding of resistance through the problematization of its oppositional stance, by subordinating the latter to the creative and transformational character of resistance. The hypothesis is that opposition does not constitute a defining feature of resistance, but its accidental destiny. The idea is to problematize the relation of resistance and creation (against the reactive tradition) through the problematization of the relation between resistance and struggle (against the oppositional tradition). There is no intention to claim that resistance does not imply a moment of opposition. Rather, we need to wonder whether and how to bracket this moment of opposition in order to fully appreciate the creative dynamics that resistance sets in motion. If resistance needs to be against something, it is primarily against the against that follows it.

The oppositional tradition

The oppositional tradition sets resistance always against another force or agent. The latter is usually given as more powerful or in a position of domination. Resistance is never presented in its independence but needs its opposite or its enemy as its own qualification: resistance to what? Against what? This is deeply embedded in everyday language, but it also constitutes the bulk of the various possible conceptualizations of resistance so far available. Following the typological account provided by Christine Chin and James Mittelman (2000), Owen Worth lists and analyses the different possible frameworks through which resistance can be understood: 'through Gramsci's uses of counterhegemony, through Polanyi's understanding of the counter-movement, and through James C. Scott's bottom-up understanding of hidden transcripts or infrapolitics' (Worth 2013: 34). All the different accounts converge on this oppositional logic: *counter*hegemony, *counter*-movement, bottom-up.

The enemy represents the essential condition of possibility of resistance. It is the very moment of struggle and opposition that circumscribes the emergence and the duration of resistance. Resistance lasts as long as its enemy fights back and its existence is not given outside the context of warfare or confrontation. This enemy is usually identified with a precise entity that constitutes its defining qualification: Resistance to Nazism, anti-capitalist resistance, resistance against austerity. Whenever resistance is successful in overthrowing the singular target of its opposition, even its own existence loses its significance. The end of the adversary turns to be the end of resistance as well. This is quite ironic from a conceptual perspective: by entering a conflict, resistance seems to proceed towards its own extinction. Either repressed and erased under the blows of its enemy or exalted by the triumphant trumpets of victory, the end of the conflict always implies the end of resistance. We bizarrely move from the uncertainty of struggle to the absolute certainty of the extinction of resistance.

The same does not seem to apply to power. Confrontations and oppositions are often only marginally mentioned in the discourses of power. For instance, global capitalism seems always concerned with its own dynamics (how to promote competition, how to foster the circulation of goods and capitals), but not with anti-capitalist resistances. Confrontation is (strategically) ignored in these discourses: power presents itself as an already accomplished pacification, casting opposition to its outside. Hardt and Negri place this conception of power in direct connection with the tradition that, from Hobbes to Rousseau, defines 'the dominant stream of modern European thought': 'Modern sovereignty is meant to put an end to civil war. ... [T]he sovereign power [Hobbes] proposes will be constituent, producing and reproducing the people as a peaceful social order and bringing an end to the war of all against all that is synonymous with social and political chaos' (Hardt and Negri 2004: 238–9). The dualism (pacified civil order vs. natural state of war; the people vs. the multitude) is not resolved, but effaced, mediated and reproduced in 'the *transcendence* of the sovereign ... over the social plane', embodied by Hobbes's 'unitary Leviathan that rises above and overarches society and the multitude' (Hardt and Negri 2000: 325).

Power becomes insulated from resistance. The boundaries of civil order impose a closure through which the opposition of resistance is cast outside. This subordinates the oppositional stance of power to the problem of government. In turn, resistance is reduced uniquely to a mere opposition. In the process of posing the people as constitutive synthesis within the unitary order of Leviathan, 'the multiplicity of difference', which is proper of the multitude, is relegated to 'binary oppositions' (Hardt and Negri 2000: 140): the multitude against the people, the state of nature against civil order, resistance against power. To the unity of sovereign power corresponds the unity of resistance. Once again, resistances become Resistance. This reduction is at once the reduction of resistance to its oppositional stance.

The oppositional tradition needs to be thought as a reaction to the other tradition of modernity that, from Étienne de La Boétie to Spinoza, founds itself on 'the discovery of the place of immanence and the celebration of singularity and difference' (Hardt and Negri 2000: 140). The binary scheme of the oppositional stance is exploded in an absolute multiplicity. Resistance has to resist the centralization of the multiplicity of its difference. When resistance is understood as against a single enemy (e.g. against Leviathan), it undergoes a process of centralization that betrays its constitutive multiplicity. 'As Spinoza says, if we simply cut the tyrannical head off the social body, we will be left with the deformed corpse of society' (Hardt and Negri 2000: 204).

Prolonging the lines of this tradition, this resistance against the centralization of resistances finds a consistent conceptualization in the idea of transversality. Gilles Deleuze sees the emergence of this theme of the transversality of resistance in the theoretical and practical experiences of Milovan Djilas's model of workers' self-management in Tito's Yugoslavia, Tronti's Autonomist reinterpretation of Marxism in Italy and Sartre's involvement with the struggle against the Algerian War – a turning point where anti-colonial struggles force French intellectuals to rethink resistance (Deleuze 2018b). These experiences express the transversal conjunction of multiple resistances: against capitalism, against Stalinism, against Marxist dogmatism. This series of 'against' radically challenges the binary scheme of the oppositional tradition: which is the defining 'against'? At the same time, Deleuze notes how these transversal struggles are immediately projected towards a creative aspect: 'this theme of transversal struggles, of non-centralized struggles, inspired first by Yugoslavian self-determination, then by Italian autonomy, had been mingled with a question that was more unclear, more difficult, which was what? Something like: toward a new subjectivity' (Deleuze 2017a). For Deleuze, Foucault's primacy of resistance responds to the problem of accounting for both this transversality of struggle and the creation of new subjectivities. Resistance subordinates its oppositional moment by fully affirming its multiplicity (against this, against that, against that other) and immediately discovers its relation with creation and transformation. We will have to wonder whether resistance is not only against something, but also against its reduction to its enemies: is resistance also against this tendency of necessitating an against that follows? Can resistance be against the 'against'?

The reactive tradition and the primacy of power

The other tradition that generally follows the oppositional understanding of resistance relates to its qualitative modality of operation. The enemy is generally charged with a variety of features that decree its ultimate primacy. From a chronological perspective, resistance always seems to be against something that precedes it, something that is there before the emergence of resistance. Although the anecdote on Capogrossi invites us to do so, we can hardly think of Resistance to Nazism before the actual Nazi occupation. As for any colonial occupation, enclosure of commons or dispossession of natural resources, although those that will then resist are actually there before by definition (the natives, the indigenous), the invasion has the quasi magical effect to come before the resistance that will then follow. Also in terms of force, there is a differential in strength that establishes a certain hierarchy between resistance and its antagonist. The latter is more powerful and qualitatively superior in terms of (military) means and capacity of struggle. Resistance starts from a position of inferiority and weakness. And this position is often radicalized to the point in which resistance seems to vanish into complete powerlessness (Adorno 2005).

From this chronological priority and this superiority in strength, power affirms its conceptual (or even ontological) primacy. Resistance is reduced to a mere response, a reaction to something that comes first and that would have been there with or without the presence of resistance. This way of understanding resistance defines the reactive tradition. Power is understood as active insofar its affirmation is autonomous and independent. Resistance is instead given as reactive insofar its own emergence, its existence, its modality of operation and even its temporal trajectory (its duration) rest on its opponent. This differentiation evokes Friedrich W. Nietzsche's distinction, then elaborated by Deleuze (2006b), between active and reactive forces, where the former are 'superior forces that dominate', while reactive forces are 'conditioned or constrained by superior forces' (Patton 2000: 60). By the same token, the active character that defines power implies that those forces are creative, affirmative, transformative and self-directed, whereas resistance is considered as a force of reaction, adaptation and conservation.

Nevertheless, Deleuze's account of Nietzsche's distinction is complicated by the fact that 'the reactive forces of the slave who hates not only all others, but also himself, become the dominating forces in a regime of reactive forces. ... In a regime of reactive forces, the world thus becomes inverted, and the weak rule the strong' (Hoy 2004: 27). Neither is any power active, nor is any resistance reactive. The reference to this Nietzschean distinction helps challenge the reactive tradition in the understanding of resistance. But even in these approaches, there seems to be an inevitable tendency to fall back into a conception that does not move fully beyond the reactive tradition. In order to explore 'the possibility of resistance that is not merely reactive' (Hoy 2004: 6), David Houzens Coy proposes a further distinction: 'The word "resistance" does not of itself distinguish between emancipation and domination. That is why I speak of *critical* resistance. Critique is what makes it possible to distinguish emancipatory resistance from resistance that has been co-opted by the oppressive forces' (Hoy 2004: 2). As such, Hoy seems to be subtly trapped once again in the reactive paradigm, although in a slightly different form. In fact, this critical resistance does not seem to set forth the idea of an affirmative and self-directed force. It ends up subordinating resistance to emancipation, de facto implying that power comes still first and emancipation will follow.

A similar ambivalence survives in Douzinas's attempt to reject an exclusively reactive understanding of resistance. 'Resistance is a mixture of reaction and action, negation and affirmation. ... Reactive resistance conserves or restores a state of things power has disturbed. Active resistance deconstructs the adversary's arms, and borrows, mimics or subverts their components' (Douzinas 2014: 90). The mixture that Douzinas proposes is indeed a repetition of the same ingredient: reaction. Even when he calls it active, resistance finds already an adversary that seems to come first. Although Douzinas rightly recognizes the creative and affirmative character of resistance, the reactive tradition ultimately persists: 'every force affected by another provokes a resistance, which thwarts the first without stopping it' (Douzinas 2014: 89); 'Resistance is the bodily reaction to an overwhelming sense of injustice, an almost irrepressible response to hurt, hunger and despair' (Douzinas 2014: 93).

In his *On Resistance*, Caygill (2013) challenges the reactive tradition by framing the conceptualization of resistance through an approach that focuses on the strategical interplay of forces. Resistance confronts itself with counter-resistances that emerge in a complex sequence of interactions in which the defining factors are the seizure of the initiative and the purpose of the struggle. In particular, by establishing a dialogue between Nietzsche and Karl Marx on the events of the Paris Commune, Caygill problematizes this understanding of resistance as reactive in connection with *ressentiment* and with slave morality:

Marx's emphasis on the affirmative character of the Commune places the purity of Nietzsche's genealogy of *ressentiment* into question. There is never a pure noble morality free of *ressentiment*, nobility consists not in innocent creation, but in overcoming a predicament of *ressentiment*. In Marx's scenario, the proletariat in its struggle against Empire finds affirmation in the struggle for a new political form.

(Caygill 2013: 39)

With Marx, Caygill holds that resistance is never only a struggle against something. It is never only a revenge, a reaction. Resistance implies the emergence of an affirmative moment in which the struggle is projected towards (or even subordinated to) the creation of a future to come: 'It becomes less the spectre haunting the old capitalist world than a sphinx inhabiting the borderlands of the new' (Caygill 2013: 39). There is a complex interplay of these two distinct moments of affirmation and reaction, noble and slave morality, repression and expansion. Any confrontation involves therefore two opponents which are neither active nor reactive, as they both share a fluid and varying combination of these two approaches. As such, antagonism can be rephrased in terms of resistances and counter-resistances without relying on the reactive tradition: 'There is never a moment of pure resistance, but always a reciprocal play of resistances that form clusters or sequences of resistance and counter-resistance corresponding to each other in surrendering or seizing initiative' (Caygill 2013: 5).

Caygill's analysis is crucial for debunking the problematic aspect of resistance as merely reactive and its implicit corollary of the primacy of power over resistance. This rescues the affirmative and creative character of resistance which has been traditionally locked up by the reactive tradition. What Caygill ultimately achieves is a more balanced distribution of this affirmative and creative character to power and resistance. Affirmation is not only power's business. What has been traditionally denied to resistance and attributed exclusively to power, it is finally extended to both the warring parties. Resistance is not only reactive, but also active. At the same time, we discover that power is not only active, but also reactive. This creates a sort of equivalence between the two. But to what extent can this equivalence suffice to reject the traditional primacy of power? To what extent is power conceptually affected by this rethinking of resistance? Insofar as the oppositional logic is concerned, the conceptual equivalence of power and resistance in relation to the problem of affirmation and reaction leaves the strategic differential between the two quite intact. Power still comes first, even though it is not as creative as we thought it to be. Resistance is still in a position of inferiority, even though it is not as reactive as we thought it to be. Have we actually got rid of the reactive tradition that affects and has affected our understanding of resistance?

The problem amounts to the persistence of the other axis that defines the traditional understanding of resistance. By insisting on the moment of struggle and opposition, the reactive tradition does not seem to be completely rejected but only weakened. The question is whether we can actually get rid of the reactive tradition while maintaining an understanding of resistance based on an oppositional logic. To an extent, Peter Bloom (2016) produces a similar critique, but he ends up getting rid of resistance altogether. In *Beyond Power and Resistance*, Bloom proposes to overcome the paradigm of power and resistance for a radical politics where social change revolves around possibility rather than opposition. He traces the history of the power/resistance discourse from its modern origin in the Enlightenment where power and resistance represent a continuous struggle for sovereignty. In turn, Bloom looks at contemporary social movements pursuing social change through non-resistance-based transformational politics.[6] Their main purpose is not to resist power, but to create alternative arrangements and way of living. According to Bloom, there is a historical divide between social and political movements that have tried to seize power through struggle and opposition and those that have instead explored alternative possibilities breaking with the paradigm of power and resistance. But to what extent can these two types of social and political movements be made into an opposition? Is there no creative side in those who oppose power? In creating alternative arrangements and ways of life, is there not an extent of opposition, although accidental? As proposed throughout the book, resistance is primarily a matter of creative affirmation and exploration of possibilities, but opposition can accidentally emerge when these possibilities are blocked or obstructed by reactive forces. Opposition is not constitutive, but accidental. By understanding resistance as prior to power, by posing opposition as constitutive of power and as accidental for resistance, we do break away from the sovereign paradigm of power and resistance. Why should we maintain that there is a mutually exclusive choice to be made, that is either resist or build the new? Why cannot these two moments be thought together within practices that we have always defined as resistant? Why should resistance stop and something creative begin straight after that? Is not this as well a closure of possibilities for which only one possibility can be actualized per time?

In his *Experimental Practice*, Dimitris Papadopoulos (2018) highlights how new contemporary forms of resistance are characterized by an 'insurgent posthumanism': movements that operate on the continuum between the human and the non-human, creating alliances and interconnections that transform both society and the world in general at the level of matter, in the materiality of the practices that they create and foster. These more-than-social movements craft alternative and autonomous forms of life (alterontologies) affirming ecological, social and economic justice. Opposition becomes necessary only when power stumbles upon their trajectory. And yet, even then, the affirmative and creative character of resistance persists. From forest defenders and indigenous struggles against dispossession and ecological destruction to local movements rejecting intrusive infrastructures (Greyl, Healy et al. 2012), resistance constructs the ontological conditions of autonomous creative becoming.

Rethinking resistance

The challenge is to set forth an understanding of resistance that acknowledges the microphysics of forces, to say it with Foucault, and the complexity of their strategical interactions. Resistance with a capital letter is nothing but the strategical coding of a multiplicity of local, more or less dispersed and transversal resistances. These resistances are the material fabric that is somehow condensed into a revolution, an occupation, an exodus. Effacing the constituent power of resistance helps power to claim for the benefit of the ordinary, its tranquillity, that reassuring sense of security and certainty. Paraphrasing J. K. Gibson-Graham's (2006) analysis of capitalism and Peter Kropotkin's idea of mutual aid (O'Hearn and Grubačić 2016), we need to recognize that it is precisely upon the effacement of the presence of resistance and of its already actual strength that power reactively reproduces itself. 'Whereas Machiavelli proposes that the project of constructing a new society from below requires "arms" and "money" and insists that we must look for them outside, Spinoza responds: Don't we already possess them? Don't the necessary weapons reside precisely within the creative and prophetic power of the multitude?' (Hardt and Negri 2000: 65). Resistance is already the ordinary, resistance is always present. Resistance is what actually constitutes the thickness of the present and its opening towards the future (Ghelfi 2016). Any apparatus or dispositive of power is always already a backward past, it is the parasitical clinging of a past that does not want to pass.

This does not mean that a moment of destruction and opposition is never given. But this moment occurs in the midst of a multiplicity of processes of affirmation and creation which are primary despite their traditional subordination. In the rare instances in which a constitutive role has been recognized to resistance, this moment has always been depicted as the step that follows a successful confrontation: 'Unforeseeable, unexpected, sudden, the process of protest and resistance turns into a moment of innovation' (Negri 1999: 147). After the defeat of power, resistance is supposed to abandon its oppositional stance (and even its qualification as resistance) and to finally engage with a process of creation. This duality persists even when resistance is identified exclusively as creative: 'Disobedience negates, resistance creates' (Douzinas 2013: 98). From a theoretical perspective, the attention should then be focused on this exact instant of passage, this turning point that signals a quasi-metaphysical transformation: '[what] constitutes political society [is] the active resistance that is rationally transformed into a counter-Power, the counter-Power that is collectively developed in active consensus, the consensual praxis that is articulated in a real constitution' (Negri 1991: 112). But this point of transformation has never been fully problematized. Perhaps there is no such a turning point because resistance is affirmative and creative from the outset. In any struggle, there are already practices of affirmation and creation that are primary: new modalities of organization, new social relations, new forms of solidarity and bonding, new techniques of warfare.

What is urgent is therefore an inversion that turns these subordinations (to power, to opposition) upside down. In order to affirm the creative, constitutive and transformational aspect of resistance, we need to engage with a Copernican revolution (Toscano 2009) in political philosophy. But this inversion needs to be accounted for in its contingency. More than an inversion, we need a re-inversion: the inversion of something that was already inverted that was already upside down in relation to the ontologically materiality from which it necessarily emerges. The subordination of resistance is already a strategical inversion, an effacement that aims to destroy or annihilate the very capacity of resistance. Inverting this subordination though is not only strategical. Evading the oppositional tradition means also to understand this inversion as beyond strategy, as the tuning with ontology in its materiality.

'A third kind of affect'

This requires a move beyond the distinction between active and reactive. Although the inversion seems to draw resistance towards the active side of the relation with power (Checchi 2014), with Deleuze (or with Deleuze's interpretation of Foucault) we find resistance attached to a kind of affect that escapes the binary partition of active and reactive. Resistance constitutes a kind of affect on its own. A third kind of affect: 'I can no longer say, as I was happy to do up until now, that there is a fundamentally a double power in relation, namely, a power to affect and a power to be affected. Now I must link it up with a third power: the power to resist. The power to resist is a third sort of affect, irreducible to the active affects and to reactive affects. It is a third kind of singularity' (Deleuze 2018d). We move beyond the Nietzschean distinction and even beyond Deleuze's characterization in his work on Nietzsche. The modes of operation of active and reactive forces are qualitatively distinct. But Deleuze attributes these two modes to the poles that constitute a relation of power. Through Foucault's definition of power as 'an action upon an action' (Foucault 2001: 340), the two poles that constitute a power relation are respectively active and reactive. None of these poles exerts resistance though. Resistance affirms itself outside this relation.

This offers an avenue to rethink resistance and its relation to the oppositional tradition. Resistance can be understood as a third affect to the extent that it draws a trajectory that runs through a liminal and subtle line between its contemporary affirmation and negation. The ultimate dream of resistance is modulated upon the undecided negotiation of its appearance and disappearance (Checchi 2015). The oppositional tradition recognizes only one side of this ambivalence. Resistance fights for a change or a transformation and, in turn, acquires its own significance through the struggle that might possibly bring this transformation. This is arguably a crucial component that animates resistance and its will to change and transform the existent. But this postulates once again its traditional subordination to power. Although resistance might often seem necessary or even a moral duty, this does not erase its defining posture: resistance aspires not to fight, it would have preferred not to engage in confrontations or struggles. This marks the affinity of resistance with Deleuze and Guattari's war machine: 'war represents not at all the supposed essence of the war machine ... The other pole seemed to be the essence; it is when the war machine ... has as its object not war but the drawing of a creative line of flight, the composition of a smooth space and of the movement of people in that space' (Deleuze and Guattari 1987: 422). By understanding the primary character of creation and transformation, the opposition that resistance encounters needs to be understood as an accidental and tedious burden: a misfortune.

This is brutally evident in the history of colonialism: the native does not want to be forced to fight the settler – the native does not want the settler at all, even before the settler arrives. Its arrival is a tragic misfortune, an unnecessary disruption that should have not taken place. As between the native and the settler 'no conciliation is possible, for of the two terms, one is superfluous' (Fanon 2001). Likewise, Capogrossi's resistance mentioned at the beginning of this introduction would have gladly done without fascism and its capitalist allies. The process of affirmation that resistance brings about is halted and obstructed by the moment of opposition that often (but perhaps not inevitably) arises. Resistance does not seem to emerge for the sake of resisting. Resistance affirms itself dreaming that the obstacle of power will never emerge on its path. The opposition is only accidental. When resistance is understood as exclusively oppositional (as Resistance with the capital R), the paradox is that its final objective is its own end. Resistance to Nazi-fascism dreams that the latter will be defeated and that Resistance will no longer be needed. Resistance shows a paradoxical suicidal aspiration. Its existence is oriented towards its own annihilation.

In order to escape this paradoxical trap, resistance needs to be followed along its trajectories of creation and affirmation. Rather than an oppositional stance, resistance shows an affinity to becoming. This trajectory of continuous motion moves away from the subordination of resistance to power and from the traditional account that has more or less overtly supported the primacy of power over resistance. On this trajectory we discover the (re-)inversion that poses resistance as prior to power: the primacy of resistance not as the arrival point of this trajectory, but as the trajectory itself in its multiplicity of lines, its paths of creations, its closures and its new openings. The primacy of resistance affirms a movement and a dynamic that is beyond opposition, a material or materialist politics of movement, kinopolitics: 'instead of analysing societies as primarily static, spatial, or temporal, kinopolitics or social kinetics understands them primarily as regimes of motion. Societies are always in motion' (Nail 2015: 24).

This dynamic trajectory rejects and transforms the pretence of stasis and equilibrium that power strategically attempts to impose. Power operates for the reproduction of the existent or for the reinforcement of the structures that support the strategic mapping of its present social field. The state, one of the traditional and long-standing centres of power, reveals in its etymology a sheer relation with the absence of movement: stasis. What the primacy of resistance affirms instead is a process of *de-stat-ic-ization*, the eruption of a movement that, although accidentally, affirms dynamism over any attempt of crystallization of the existent, over any attempt of presenting a static ontology, of which the state is a quintessential expression. Hence, even the etymology of resistance can be reinvented. That resistance comes from re-sistere (a clear appeal to stasis) is a strategic effacement perpetrated by the combination of the traditional accounts that have tried to impose the subordination of resistance to power. The primacy of resistance instead reinvents its own etymology: rather than re-sistere, *re-existere* – renovating existence, change, transformation, becoming.

The failure of the traditional understanding of resistance lies in fact in a conception of power that is unable to account for change. As Deleuze puts it, the primacy of resistance cannot be thought as an additional or alternative way of problematize resistance in relation to power: the primacy of resistance is a conceptual necessity.[7] Resistance cannot be thought otherwise than as prior to power.

Why the primacy?

Why does resistance come first? Once we get rid of the oppositional and reactive traditions, power is unveiled as constitutively reactive and parasitical. The existence of power rests exclusively upon the anticipation of an autonomous affirmation that is likely to diverge from a desired course of action. No force is exerted upon another unless the latter is expected to affirm itself in a way that does not correspond to a precise objective. Power is exerted only when resistance is anticipated to occur. As such, resistance is the condition of possibility of power, its raison d'être. The reverse is valid only to a limited extent. In fact, although there is a contemporaneous emergence of power and resistance, the latter might be already there under the guise of practices that only at a later stage will determine an opposition to power. These practices often emerge autonomously without necessarily intending to constitute a resistance to a given power. This once again shows that resistance is not oppositional per se, but only accidentally oppositional. The contrary is valid for power, whose operational modality is necessarily oppositional.

The second problem with power is its tendency towards conservation and stasis. This does not imply that power is exclusively repressive. Although with Foucault it is necessary to acknowledge the productive character of power, the latter is doomed to a conservation of the status quo or to the strategic consolidation of the advantage on its own adversary by 'overcoming the enemy's capacity to resist' (Caygill 2013: 58). Hence, change and transformation can never occur on the basis of the action of power. If any transformation of its action occurs, it is given as a response to resistance or its possibility. A power relation that is not endangered by any virtual or actual resistance has no reason to modify its action. Only resistance triggers change by forcing power to reactively take action against its affirmation. 'Resistance in this sense is the provocation of a new action' (Proust 2000).

The primacy of resistance rests therefore upon its relation to the new, to creation, to a constitutive unpredictability that poses itself against the pretence of certainty that power attempts to affirm. Power relations are indeed only relatively stable and show a regularity that is constitutively made up by the unregulable. Against and beyond the illusion of power, resistance affirms its primacy through this appeal to the regularity of the irregular, the normality of the abnormal, the stability of the instable.

Resistance claims its appeal to the 'plenitude of the possible' (Foucault 1978: 145), the indefinite proliferation of possibilities that align practices to the ontological becoming of matter. Stasis is the accidental enemy that this creative eruption encounters. These crystallizations are nothing but temporary closures that reclaim an eternity that they will never be able to reach. We need to follow Negri's Spinoza in positively embracing the impossibility of an ultimate crystallization, an ultimate closure: 'Spinoza ... attacks and supersedes precisely these connections internal to the Hobbesian definition of Power; by analysing its own origins again, Spinozian thought demonstrates its inconclusiveness, recognizing the contradiction represented by an eventual closure of the system (effective in Hobbes) and, on the other hand, grasping the possibility of opening the constitutive rhythm toward a philosophy of the future' (Negri 1991: 70).

To each closure, there are an indefinite multiplicity of openings, creative trajectories oriented towards a future that is already present. But the present is already resistant matter. Power poses itself as the determination and constitution of the existent. The primacy of resistance denounces instead its obstinate obsolescence: the present of power is always already past as it is unable to account for movement towards the inexistent, towards what does not exist yet and yet exists. This is 'the real urgency of the inexistent' (Negri 1991: 160): the future is always already present. History and its becoming are therefore the continuous interplay of closures and new openings. The affirmation of resistance generates a trajectory on which power installs itself. Power usurps its energy, its élan and seals off its continuation. Resistance comes first because it always finds new routes, new paths, new trajectories, new openings. Will these contemporary openings be closed off by power? Most likely. But this is not a problem per se. The political principle that descends from the primacy of resistance is not the contraposition against closures in general. Rather, the primacy of resistance aims to constitute a mode of organization in which closures favour new openings, new creations, new becomings. Through the primacy of resistance, organizations are no longer measured according to their stability, but according to the degree in which they are able to favour and sustain their own overcoming, their own transformation.

Overview of chapters

The objective of this book is to transform the intuition of the primacy of resistance into a concept. This requires a radical rethinking of resistance that inverts its traditional subordination to power. The concept of resistance that emerges here moves away from traditional accounts of resistance as reactive by problematizing its oppositional stance. The latter is not understood as essential in the conceptual definition of resistance, but as accidental and contingent. We cannot simply ask against what a resistance is. This would imply a reduction that effaces the complexity and the materiality of the processes through which resistance emerges. Rather, we need to follow its affirmation in the multiplicity of its creative practices. The primacy of resistance rests upon this creative and transformational potential that appeals to becoming.

My personal engagement with resistance is situated at the crossroad between theory and historical practices. In the last decades, resistance has been exerted through a variety of dispersed and transversal struggles. This aspect finds a productive resonance in Foucault's concept of resistance. However, his idea ultimately lacks a robust and consistent conceptualization. The role of resistance in Foucault's model of power is still an open issue. In the reception of his work, resistance has been understood in the most diverse and conflicting ways, to the extent that some have come to the conclusion that no resistance can find room in his model (McNay 1994). This confusion is definitely the result of the lack of a unitary account, but it also amounts to the scarce attention given to other less known parts of Foucault's work. In particular, little effort has been made to take seriously Foucault's interview of 1982 in which he declares that 'resistance comes first' (Foucault 1997a: 167). I used this intuition as a guiding principle to research resistance in his work. To be sure, there is no intention of affirming that such a choice leads to the correct way of reading Foucault. It would be anti-Foucauldian to assume the possibility of an orthodox reading of his work. However, the primacy of resistance allows, on the one hand, an original rethinking of Foucault's resistance that accounts for the specific forms of struggle that have emerged in the last decades; on the other hand, it favours the prolongation of a conceptual trajectory from Foucault to a wider tradition based on the affinity of resistance and creativity.

This wider tradition has already been introduced earlier in this chapter. It is the tradition that connects La Boétie and Spinoza, Autonomist Marxism and poststructuralism. This constitutes the theoretical horizon of this book. Within this horizon, I looked for conceptual lines that could contribute to the conceptualization of the primacy of resistance. I propose four trajectories in which the conceptualization of the primacy of resistance has been problematized: human nature, labour, politics and ontology. These four trajectories represent affirmative openings of the primacy of resistance. Each trajectory has been observed in its historical and conceptual evolution, its multiple interactions and their relation with the present. In particular, I tried to observe whether these trajectories can still function today as conceptual lines of resistance. This led me to divide these four trajectories into two parts. The first part includes those problematizations that have historically encountered a closure to their affirmative conceptual path. For closure I mean an obstruction that inverts the conceptual lines at stake, using its potential to transform the concept in a way that neutralizes and annihilates that potential.

The challenge amounts to the fact of constructing a conceptual trajectory through conceptualizations that were originally oriented towards other problems. In none of the works analysed, the primacy of resistance emerges in a coherent and extensive way. There is a trajectory that binds various conceptual lines together, but none of these lines manages to create the concept of the primacy of resistance. This claim does not have to be understood in the negative, as lack. Rather, it is a matter of orientation: 'if earlier concepts were able to prepare a concept but not constitute it, it is because their problem was still trapped within other problems' (Deleuze and Guattari 1994: 27). What I have done in this research is to detect these 'earlier concepts', separate them for their specific problems and finally orientate them towards the problem of the primacy of resistance. But this requires a quite ambiguous enterprise: looking for something that is not (explicitly) there. For Bensaïd (2001), resistance has to do with moles: we need to acknowledge its presence even through its apparent absence. The bodies of thought discussed in the following chapters have been chosen keeping into account this fundamental principle. In these works, resistance is barely mentioned, but its presence can be grasped somehow through the lines of these discourses, it can be sensed in the omitted logical implications of a conceptual line, it can be imaginatively added to a theoretical framework that has obliviously built its own foundations on a terrain traversed by a multiplicity of mole tunnels.

Each conceptual line has been observed in its interaction with the primacy of resistance, although the latter has maintained a virtual status throughout this research as a conceptual line in becoming. The interaction between these conceptual lines and the primacy of resistance has been observed in both its presence and its virtual prolongation. In this sense, I followed the trajectories of these conceptual lines beyond their original content. When a line did not explicitly address the conceptualization of the primacy of resistance, I have tried to interrogate its potential prolongation, its unexplored connections or consequences. I often pushed the texts beyond the original intentions of their authors, trying to imagine possible continuations of their thinking. I read these sources in their openness, as living multiplicities.

The chapters that follow trace the trajectory of the primacy of resistance in the interplay of historical closures and contemporary openings. Chapter 1 serves as an entry point: it sets the theoretical framework and the terminology that support the overall project.[8] In this chapter, I attempt to build up a creative narrative that runs through Foucault's work driven by the problematization of the primacy of resistance. From this perspective, I first outline a definition of power relations in terms of circulation through multiple relays. Resistance does not find itself trapped as one of the relays in the relation. On the contrary, resistance remains outside power relations as an irreducible vis-à-vis, in a relation of co-existence but also of double conditioning. For the primacy of resistance though, this double conditioning needs to find its polarization. This task is facilitated by decentring the focus of the analysis on the dimension of the possible or the probable. Foucault presents resistance as doubled by its possibility, where power is redefined as the management of the field of possibility that is available to action.

The rest of the project is divided into two parts. Chapter 2 and 3 engage with the historical closures that have reactively usurped and obstructed the affirmation of the primacy of resistance. In Chapter 2, I focus on conceptual lines emerging between the sixteenth and seventeenth century in opposition to political authority articulated upon a certain appeal to nature. The latter is given as prior to power, as a state that precedes it. Power operates reactively upon a natural material that is recalcitrant to its action. The affirmation of the primacy of resistance consists of a radical rejection of the misfortune of power that implicitly opens to an art of not to be governed at all. In La Boétie's *Discourse on Voluntary Servitude*, there is an implicit call for reverting the misfortune. The affirmation of resistance against power draws a constitutive trajectory towards natural companionship and cooperation, in which forces are combined in their natural complementarity rather than restrained.

This trajectory though finds its closure with the liberal arts of not to be governed that way, where the state of nature needs to be escaped in favour of a civil power. The liberal discourse of the social contract from Hobbes to Rawls operates a closure by transforming the constitutive moment of the primacy of resistance into a matter of individual rights. The proliferation of rights seems to increase realms of social life liberated from power, but ultimately confirm and consolidate the necessity of its existence.

Following Deleuze's invitation to look for an echo of the primacy of resistance in Tronti's interpretation of Marxism, Chapter 3 focuses on the problem of labour. The primacy of labour might seem the economic equivalent of the primacy of resistance. Nevertheless, its creative potential allows labour to trespass this border and to affirm itself in the non-economic. This chapter is devoted to the analysis of this process of expansion or extensification, that is the inclusion of a range of activities traditionally not regarded as labour. This is at work in Arendt's idea of the modern victory of labour, where the primacy of labour is not structured upon its relation with capital, but with the other human faculties. An expansive conception of labour is presented also in the Autonomist tradition especially in the idea of self-valorization and refusal of work. Likewise, Gibson-Graham's insistence on the diversity of the economic landscape and the extension of labour to previously unrecognized forms of economic contribution participates to this conceptual body and to its enterprise.

On the other hand, there is a perversion of this process of extensification, a closure of this specific conceptual line that acts upon and against itself through neoliberal discourses. Here the process of extensification of labour aims at the effacement of antagonism in direct relation with the contemporary model of extraction and appropriation of value. The process of biofinancialization completes the transformation of labour into human capital initiated with the neoliberal discourse of Gary Becker. These two limbs of the bifurcation of the primacy of labour see their trajectories culminating in distinct but analogous scenarios where labour vanishes either in an apparent fusion with human action or in its becoming-capital under the drive of biofinancialization.

These trajectories are somehow obstructed and the affirmation of the primacy of resistance can hardly continue along these paths. However, its creative eruption constantly finds new openings. Chapter 4 and 5 explore these contemporary trajectories. Chapter 4 observes the avenues that politics offers today for (re-)thinking resistance. Although there is a series of manifest appearances of resistance in 2011 and its aftermath, it is necessary to refrain from celebrating these cycles of struggles as the hallmark of an age of resistance. This would only reproduce once again a reactive understanding of resistance. Through Rancière's coupling of politics and aesthetics and Negri's political ontology developed with and beyond Spinoza, the primacy of resistance becomes political creation, continuous and spontaneous affirmation. Political resistance makes history: no age can interrupt this eruptive flow. Once again, a Copernican revolution: an inversion that redirects the attention towards the constitutive and affirmative character of resistance, where the moment of opposition and negation becomes accidental and contingent.

Negri's political ontology defines also an additional trajectory that invites to an exploration of material becomings. Chapter 5 starts an experimental journey driven by the primacy of resistance that follows the evolution of Deleuze's ontology from his collaborative work with Guattari, *A thousand plateaus*, to his monograph on Foucault. The chapter attempts to reconstruct the trajectory through which Deleuze transforms his view on Foucault's resistance through the problematization of its primacy. This trajectory opens up to an ontology of matter that promises to be central in several debates that range from social science to political philosophy. This drives towards a conclusion that craves not to be a conclusion: an opening, a multiplicity of new creation, resistant re-existences.

1

'Resistance comes first': Metamorphoses, change, creation

The primacy of resistance is a Foucauldian concept: it borrows its wording and its defining conceptual coordinates from his work. Yet whether the primacy of resistance can be presented as a Foucault's concept remains debatable. The expression appears explicitly only in a 1982 interview later published under the title 'Sex, Power and the Politics of Identity'. Can we trust an interview? How can an intuition that appears in the context of an interview relate to the wider theoretical production of an author?[1] I propose to interpret this short appearance as 'a flash of lightning in the night which ... gives a dense and black intensity to the night it denies, ... and yet owes to the dark the stark clarity of its manifestation, its harrowing and poised singularity' (Foucault 1977: 35). These are the words Foucault uses to present the relationship between limit and transgression, probably the first embryonic version of resistance in his work. But, paradoxically, the same words seem to be able to describe also this irruption of the primacy of resistance in a late interview. On the one hand, it denies somehow the obscurity in which resistance has remained trapped both in Foucault's work and in its reception; on the other hand, the primacy of resistance owes to that obscurity and ambiguity the stark clarity of its irruptive manifestation. But despite its stark clarity, a flash of lightning vanishes so quickly that it goes largely unnoticed.

With few exceptions (Lazzarato 2002, Hardt and Negri 2004, Caygill 2013, Thompson 2015), several authors have ultimately paid scarce or no attention to this problematic appearance of the primacy of resistance in 'Sex, Power and the Politics of Identity'. This comes as no surprise given that Foucault's concept of resistance itself, let alone its primacy, has animated a long-standing debate with a large array of opposed interpretations. In particular, critics have either dismissed Foucault's understanding of resistance as futile, or, paradoxically, as naively charged with an unfounded normative character. On the one hand, the pervasiveness of power has been interpreted as a monolithic omnipresence that leaves no room for resistance (Callinicos 1982, Philp 1983, Dews 1987, McNay 1994). Power is therefore the primary pole of a relation in which resistance becomes little more than 'a gratuitous assertion' (Poulantzas 1978: 149). As such, Foucault's concept is held at best to be 'critical but not finally as contestatory, or as oppositional as on the surface it seems to be' (Said 1986: 152). This is at odds with another stream of critique that has detected in Foucault's work an unfounded and unjustified call for resistance (Fraser 1981, Taylor 1984), which amounts to an 'infantile leftism' (Walzer 1986: 51) or to a form of 'cryptonormativism' (Habermas 1987: 284). In this accusation of normative confusion against resistance, power is paradoxically exempted from this normative task. It is accounted for as a fact, a given that needs no normative justification. Again, the primacy is accorded to power, with resistance condemned to a secondary role and submitted to moral scrutiny. In short, both these two positions against Foucault's resistance converge towards the idea of the primacy of power and, accordingly, towards an account of resistance as exclusively oppositional.

This critical reception of the concept of resistance rests upon the fact that Foucault's account has remained largely undeveloped. But rather than a reason for its dismissal, this should be taken as a chance for expanding a concept that is by nature refractory to its own conceptualization (Caygill 2013: 6). It is not a matter of outlining what Foucault has meant for resistance, but of how Foucault can help us to draw the conceptual trajectory of the primacy of resistance. In this chapter, I will try to problematize some crucial excerpts of his work through this specific perspective. This allows to escape the critical concerns raised above. If resistance is postulated as first, the monolithic appearance of power becomes a caricature. Likewise, the primacy of resistance displaces the problem of normative confusion to the side of power relations: the onus of proof lies no longer with resistance, but with power insofar it is exerted in response to something primary that needs no justification (Kusch 1991). This highlights the affirmative and creative aspect of resistance and its affinity with becoming, in contrast with its traditional reduction to an exclusively oppositional stance. This creative character of Foucault's resistance becomes evident in his work on the aesthetic of the self. But although there is a shift in terminology marked by the relative disappearance of the concept of resistance in favour of 'critique' and 'freedom' (Butler 2001, Paras 2006), these arts of living can be more specifically articulated as 'arts of resistance' (McGushin 2010) in direct continuity with his previous work and his ongoing concerns on militancy and political practices (Hardt 2010, Hoffman 2014). As such, in this chapter I will try to demonstrate how this creative aspect is not only at play in Foucault's work on subjectivation, but it is already manifested in his microphysics of power. Resistance is creative to the extent that appeals to 'the plenitude of the possible' (Foucault 1978: 145), the insisting reality of its possibility that opens a breach in the present. It imposes change, mutation, an opening to becoming against the static and obstinate reproduction of the existent. And this creative character is what confers to resistance its primacy over power, in which we can appreciate 'the importance of resistance for its own sake, and not simply as a reaction against power' (Fassin 2014: 142).

Points, forces and relays: A microphysics of resistance

It is worth making clear at the outset that power relations are not to be held as a relation between power and resistance. 'Power is not exercised simply as an obligation or a prohibition on those who "do not have it"; it invests them, is transmitted by them and through them' (Foucault 1995: 27). Those who do not have power are nevertheless constitutive of the power relations ('it is transmitted by them and through them'). They are 'complicit' (Hoy 2004: 65), rather than just being the passive object of power. This is one of the crucial elements of Foucault's originality: there is no passive pole in power relations. There is an inequality, a dissymmetry, an imbalance, but both sides actively contribute to the mechanism of the power relation: 'power is not something that is divided between those who have it and hold it exclusively, and those who do not have it and are subject to it. Power must ... be analyzed as something that circulates' (Foucault 2004: 29). Power relations consist of this fluid and circulating effect that connects a multiplicity of elements, points or forces, rather than a struggle between power and non-power (Foucault 1996). Which of these elements, points or forces, refer then to resistance? None, insofar they function as relays of a power relation. If a power relation is defined as what circulates through a series of relays (no matter whether they are positioned at the top or at the bottom of the hierarchy that constitutes and is constituted by the power relation), resistance can occur either as an obstruction or a subtraction to this circulation. But insofar the circulation runs smoothly, the power relation at stake does not display any resistance.

We need to look at the first volume of the *History of Sexuality* in order to find a place and a definition of resistance. Although, the regularity of power relations displays a certain absence of resistance, there is still 'the distant roar of the battle' (Foucault 1995: 308) that reassures us that stability can be disrupted at any time. This distant roar is the evidence of an agitated and imbalanced substratum. Conflicts, struggles, confrontations ceaselessly redefine and modify power relations and their strategies. It is inevitably at this point that resistance begins to outline its contours within the picture. 'Where there is power, there is resistance' (Foucault 1978: 95) is Foucault's most well-known formulation of resistance. Refraining from reading this quotation as a dead and sterile litany, it is worth exploring the potential trajectories that explode out of it. What the quotation is affirming is the mere presence of resistance everywhere we find a power relation. The presence of power relations immediately implies the presence of resistance. It expresses their necessary co-presence, although the modality of this co-presence is not further specified.

Even the sentence that follows that statement ('resistance is never in a position of exteriority in relation to power') deserves a more critical attention. As it will thoroughly be discussed in the following section, this position of exteriority has nothing to do with a spatial determination. Not being in position of exteriority does not imply that resistance is internal or within power relations. Otherwise this will fall back on the problem raised above on a possible binary partition inside power relations between power and non-power/resistance. Following the model outlined so far, the fact of not being in a position of exteriority does not mean that resistances are within or inside power relations. We need therefore to shift the perspective from a spatial understanding to an ontological one. This task is anchored to a hint found in another quotation in the same text: 'Relations of power are not in a position of exteriority with respect to other types of relationships (economic processes, knowledge relationships, sexual relations), but are immanent in the latter; they are the immediate effects of the divisions, inequalities, and disequilibriums which occur in the latter, and conversely they are the internal conditions of these differentiations' (Foucault 1978: 94). Foucault uses the same expression ('not in a position of exteriority'), but in this case he adds a second clause: if something is not in a position of exteriority to its other, then it is immanent in the latter. If we consider this as a principle that poses exteriority and immanence as mutually exclusive, the previous quotation on resistance can be rewritten with the support of this principle: 'this resistance is never in a position of exteriority in relation to power (relations), but is immanent to it; resistances are the immediate effects of divisions, inequalities, disequilibriums which occur in power relations, and conversely they are the internal condition of these differentiations'. This ventriloquism already hints towards a certain idea of the primacy of resistance based on a sort of immanent causality. However, this would open to an ontological understanding of the primacy of resistance that is not tenable within a strictly Foucauldian context (Thompson 2015). Rather, this serves more specifically to displace the original excerpt: to say that resistance is not in a position of exteriority does not immediately refer to an indication of its spatial location. It does not imply that resistance is within power relation.

In fact, the way in which resistance manifests itself in the encounter with power relations is through a multiplicity of points: '[The] existence [of power relations] depends on a multiplicity of points of resistance. ... These points of resistance are present everywhere in the power network' (Foucault 1978: 95); 'the points, knots or focuses of resistance are spread over time and space at varying densities'; 'more often one is dealing with mobile and transitory points of resistance'; 'the swarm of points of resistance traverses social stratifications and individual unities' (Foucault 1978: 96). Points are the analytical manifestations of resistance. What is a point? It is the microphysical equivalent of the relays through which power relations circulate: a sort of elementary unit. Points of resistance are specifically those relays that do not operate within power relations. They are those where the circulation of power relations is somehow either obstructed or where it is attempted but with no success at all. To be sure, in relation to individuals, institutions or any global entity, points represent the explosion of these nominal units or integrated forms into their constitutive elements, which can be appreciated from Foucault's microphysical view of power relations. This microphysical gaze displays the complexity of the power network, the map of distribution of these points taken in power relations and those not taken, points of resistance. The latter determines the creation of regions where power relations cannot circulate: 'more often one is dealing with mobile and transitory points of resistance, producing cleavages in a society that shift about, fracturing unities and effecting regroupings, furrowing across individuals themselves, cutting them up and remolding them, marking off irreducible regions in them, in their bodies and minds' (Foucault 1978: 96). In the map of the complex strategical situation of a given society, these irreducible regions are the effect of the interaction between power relations and points of resistance. These are the zones that power relations are not able to cover. The idea of irreducibility gives the sense of a failed attempt or, anyway the evidence of the fundamental and constitutive impotency of power relations. And this seems one of the primary attributes that Foucault gives to these points of resistance: '[Resistances] are the odd term in relations of power; they are inscribed in the latter as an irreducible opposite' (Foucault 1978: 96). Although it might misleadingly seem to locate resistances within power relations, irreducibility necessarily implies a distance that is at once the effect of the constitutive excess of multiplicities. At best, points of the power relation and points of resistance might seem to touch each other, but they do not fully overlap. Insofar it is irreducible, a point of resistance is not a fully working relay for the power relation. This irreducibility manifests itself as the temporary effect of a contingent distribution of points in the network. Irreducible points of resistance can be appreciated through an 'instantaneous photography' (Foucault 1996: 260) of the network of power in a given society at a given time. Therefore, their irreducibility can be revoked at any time, as far as a certain modification of the power relations manages to include those specific points in the set of functioning relays through which power relations are transmitted. Likewise, irreducibility does not lean upon some natural feature or intrinsic property. Foucault firmly rejects this naturalistic account of points of resistance: '[Resistance] is not a substance. It does not predate the power which it opposes. It is coextensive with it and absolutely its contemporary' (Foucault 1988: 122). The distribution of points of resistance and points through which power relations circulate does not occur in two distinct temporalities but in a unique process of mutual determination. Therefore, there does not seem to be an intrinsic characteristic that differentiates between points of resistance and points of power relations.

From resistance to resistance-and-its-possibility

Power relations operate through a series of points that are actualized in a specific network at a given time. Resistance instead affirms its distinctive character by posing its presence even beyond the contingency of its actualization. There is a certain doubling of the concept of resistance, the integration of an additional (and perhaps more crucial!) dimension. What operates in the power network as the odd term of power relations is not simply resistance, but resistance and its possibility. The virtual threat of a potential resistance has a real effect on power relations. Resistance is considered not only in its concrete practices, but also in the absence of its actual exercise. Even the possibility of resistance disturbs or imposes a modification upon existing power relations. Therefore, it does have its own expression in the mapping of the power network. The importance of the possibility of resistance is decisive as it affirms its presence even when power relations operate smoothly and without a concrete attrition. Even where there is no resistance, there is its possibility. As such, it would be more exhaustive to refer to a different presentation of Foucault's relational model: 'as soon as there is a power relation, there is a possibility of resistance' (Foucault 1988: 123). This constitutes an insightful refinement of the more well-known quotation. For resistance, this adds a layer of complexity both to the actual dynamic and to its relevant analysis. 'Resistance is always possible. If it is always possible, it is unlimited' (Simons 2003: 82). The possibility of resistance exposes power relation to an indefinite range of risks, traps and sabotages that, although not present, constitute a real threat that power relations cannot avoid to face. Power relations respond or attempt to respond to this indefinite multiplicity of possible resistances or possible points of resistance.

The appeal of resistance to this virtual dimension is even more evident in his understanding of power as governmentality. In this sense, there is a clear continuity with his previous conceptualization of power and resistance analysed above. In 'Subject and power', Foucault defines a relationship of power as 'a mode of action that does not act directly and immediately on others. Instead, it acts upon their actions: an action upon an action, on possible or actual, future or present actions' (Foucault 2001: 340). There is a strong correlation or perhaps even a correspondence between points and actions. Their centrality in the model is due again to the microphysical approach adopted, where individuals (the 'others' in the quotation above) are more a compound of these micro-elements or an effect of their interactions (Foucault 1995), rather than a source of agency for those actions. Furthermore, there is again the temporal doubling that has been discussed in relation to resistance and its possibility. The actions that operate, interact or are taken into account within power relations are not only those which are concretely active (actual or present) at a given moment, but also those which are possible. There is a very tiny shift in the translation that partly obfuscates the inclusiveness of this aspect. Instead of 'an action upon an action', Foucault originally writes '[u]ne action sur l'action' (Foucault 1994: 236). Therefore, not upon an action, but upon 'l'action', upon action as such, action in general. This generalization is the perfect coupling of a concrete action and the indefinite multiplicity of possible actions that might or might not emerge in the context of a given power relation. But, indeed, 'l'action' seems somehow to privilege this dimension of the possible, its appeal to becoming. The multiplicity of the possible is the ultimate threat of the dreamed stability of power relations. Stability is crucially dependent upon the structuration of this multiplicity. A perfectly stable and repetitive mechanism ultimately neutralizes these multiple possibilities by determining always the same outcome. Therefore, the stability of power relation is measured upon the extent to which these possibilities are neutralized. Power relations produce their constitutive stability through the 'management of possibilities':

> [The exercise of power] operates on the field of possibilities in which the behavior of active subjects is able to inscribe itself. It is a set of actions on possible actions; it incites, it induces, it seduces, it makes easier or more difficult; it releases or contrives, makes more probable or less; in the extreme, it constrains or forbids absolutely, but it is always a way of acting upon one or more acting subjects by virtue of their acting or being capable of action.
> (Foucault 2001: 341)

Here the term 'power' functions in a slightly different sense, as the pole within power relations that through its actions aims to determine the future action of the other pole. This future action is the key element of this dynamic. The multiple possible actions that can be actualized in this future action constitute the terrain of power relations, in terms of their deployment, intentionality and development. First of all, if an action is required in order to induce a certain desired action by the other pole (i.e. the deployment of a relationship of power), it is because there is no guarantee that the desired action will be performed independently of the intervention of the first pole. The desired action is reckoned, by those who want it to be performed, as not likely to occur. It has scarce probabilities to be actualized. This is why an action is required. 'Power exists only where actions need to be constrained and, thus, only where there will be resistance' (May 1993: 115). In order to achieve a given outcome in which another subject performs a specific action that otherwise she/he would not perform, an action is necessary. What kind of action? Incitements, inductions, seductions, prohibitions, etc. Once the power relation is onset, the end of the exercise of power (its intentionality) is that the desired action will actually occur. The development of the power relations consists mainly of the set of actions required in order to make sure (or as sure as possible) that the desired action will be regularly and consistently performed. The depiction of this model highlights how crucial the management of the field of possibilities is for power relations. Furthermore, its centrality emerges even more cogently in the effort of distinguishing power relations from other forms or modalities of antagonism (violence, struggle, domination). The size of the field of possibilities functions as the very criterion for distinguishing power relations from relations of violence, confrontation or domination and to determine their respective relations with resistance, its possibilities or the forms that it might take.

Antagonistic metamorphoses

This moment of differentiating power relations from other kinds of relations is crucial to refine the model and highlight how this ultimately operates upon the structuration of probabilities. It is from this picture that this Foucauldian conceptual line of the primacy of resistance can clearly emerge. In 'Subject and power', Foucault offers a grid of intelligibility of the different forms or modalities determined by the metamorphoses of power relations and (possible) resistances: relations of violence (physical relations of constraint), strategies of struggle (relations of confrontation), dominations[2] (Foucault 2001). These different modalities are in a relation of mutual exclusion: at a given moment, each relation can display only one configuration that excludes all others. Nevertheless, these different and mutually exclusive relations constitute a continuum insofar each relation can turn either into the relation that precedes or follows it. What differentiates each segment is the specific modality in which antagonism is modulated (either as physical constrain, agonistic provocation or struggle) and the relevant features or elements that emerge in virtue of that specific modality or configuration. This grid of intelligibility serves to mark 'the limits of power' (Smart 1985: 133), the thresholds at which power relations mutate.

At one end of this scale of antagonism, there are relationships of violence or physical relationships of constraint. They are distinguished from power relations in virtue of their target. Relationships of violence consist of an action exerted not upon the possible or concrete actions of the other, but directly upon the body of the other: 'A relationship of violence acts upon a body or upon things; it forces, it bends, it breaks, it destroys, or it closes off all possibilities' (Foucault 2001: 340). The difference between the target of power relations (actions) and that of relationships of violence (bodies or things) determines a specific operational modality, which is unidirectional: from one pole to the other, but not the other way around. There is no circulation as in the case of power relation, but a continuous and reiterated transmission with a singular sense of direction, terminating in a pole that has no other possibility than suffering this action: 'its opposite pole can only be passivity' (Foucault 2001: 340). The passive pole of a relationship of violence is therefore characterized by the incapability of action due to the blockage of all its possibilities (or possible actions or responses). Without the possibility of acting, the passive pole remains incapable of affecting the relation, which in turn is completely determined by the action of the other. The relationship of violence reproduces itself as long as the one who exerts violence pleases.

What happens though when this capacity of action is restored? There is the possibility of resistance. In the range of possible actions that are available to the subject, a set of them consists of concrete or possible points of resistance. Only when both poles of the relations are active, then their combinatory interaction can generate a multiplicity of possible scenarios or interplays of actions. Relationships of violence produce a univocal scenario, which is entirely determined by the action of only one pole. But as soon as a possibility of resistance emerges, this relation of certitude between action and effect is immediately renegotiated. The man in chains is the liminal figure that occupies the point of transformation between power relations and relations of violence: 'slavery is not a power relationship when a man is in chains, only when he has some possible mobility, even a chance of escape' (Foucault 2001: 342). When the enchainment leaves no room for mobility or escape, the type of action performed generates a physical relation of constraint: a relation of violence upon a body deprived of its capacity of action. But as soon as this enchainment, for whatever reason, loosens and some mobility becomes possible, the inert body turns immediately into a subject capable of action. It is the sudden emergence of a minimum chance of escape that signals the passage from a physical relation of constraint to a power relation. The emergence of a power relation coincides with the emergence of a possibility of resistance. The future exploitability of the capacity of action of another is not decisive for the establishment of a power relation. The paradox of the man in chains is that even an accidental emergence of a chance of escape suffices to determine the shift from a relationship of constraint to a power relation. The primacy of resistance lies in the fact that power relations seem to emerge more in response to resistance and its possibilities, rather than in virtue of the outcomes and effects that one pole wants to achieve. The constitutive concern for power relations is the government of this capacity of resistance, the government of a capacity whose relevance is not primarily due to its action in general and the beneficial effects that can be achieved by manipulating it. The focus is on this capacity insofar it includes the possibility of resistance, source of instability and incertitude. The possibility of resistance is what generates a field of possibilities and necessitates the establishment of a power relation that structures that field.

The primacy of resistance manifests itself in this opening of possibilities that determine the instability that is constitutive of power relations. Now, this instability is modulated on a scale of probability. When the man in chains passes from a physical relation of constraint to a power relation in virtue of the emergence of a possibility of escape, the relation in which he finds himself approximates the top of this scale of probability: the possibility of resistance has a very scarce probability of being actualized. The relative field of possibility is therefore minimal. The points of possible resistance that swarms around the power relation define a scarce probability of actualization that is unable to disturb or affect the relationship of power. In this scenario, the action performed by the pole which exerts the power relation approximates the certitude of obtaining a desired outcome. The approximation of certitude constitutes the upper limit of power relations. Beyond that limit, power relation transforms into physical relations of constraint.

The lower limit on this scale of probability constitutes the other threshold of metamorphosis where power relations turn into a kind of relation whose circulation is continuously disrupted and the desired outcomes are more unlikely to be actualized. Relationships of power are constitutively instable, but they do display a certain stability. This is evident in the longevity of institutions, which code a multiplicity of power relations that, despite their relative opening to transformation, can be considered overall stable. Their continuous reproduction expresses the *scarcely instable stability* of power relations. When this stability fades off, power relations are disrupted. There is a level of instability that power relations cannot tolerate. When the regularity that the government of the field of possibility falls beyond a certain level, power relations transform into what Foucault calls relations of confrontation or strategies of struggle 'in which the two forces are not superimposed, do not lose their specific nature, or do not finally become confused' (Foucault 2001: 346). In the passage, the actions performed by the poles of the relation are clearly distinguished. They are no longer superimposed in the sense that one action is no longer upon the action of the other, but frontally against it. They do not become confused because the circulation is completely disrupted and the poles of the relation do not function any longer as relays, but confront each other as adversaries: 'Each constitutes for the other a kind of permanent limit, a point of possible reversal' (Foucault 2001: 346). We have seen above that the possibility of resistance immediately expresses a form of tension which confronts power relations. Here that tension intensifies up to the point in which it really becomes a struggle. The concept of struggle appears only at the precise moment in which power relations turn into relations of confrontations.

Struggle, as open and direct opposition, occurs only after the points of resistance and their possibilities that swarm around power relations are coded into an actual strategy. Struggle starts when relays turns into an adversary.

These relations of confrontation therefore display a specific dynamic. The interaction of adversaries takes the form of a 'free play of antagonistic reactions', where 'one must be content with reacting to [the actions of the other] after the event' (Foucault 2001: 347). Actions can no longer be anticipated and induced as in power relations. If the action of the other cannot be manipulated in advance, there is a wide set of possible action that has a similar chance to be actualized. As such, anticipation would be hazardous. Any action is no longer the reaction to an action and its relative field of possibilities, but only a reaction to the concrete move of the adversary. What would the course of action be then? It is the finality of the struggle that determines the evolution of the relation: '[a relationship of confrontation] is not a struggle to death' (Foucault 2001: 347). If the objective were the mere destruction of the other (as in relationships of violence), the relation would be a mere matter of strength: the weak would immediately succumb with the struggle vanishing on its ashes. Struggle is instead open, undecided. The poles of the relation share a substantial equality as their differential is insignificant.

Yet a struggle to death between two equal adversaries is more likely to become a quiet equilibrium: 'a face-to-face confrontation that paralyzes both sides' (Foucault 2001: 342). A mixture of Buridan's ass starving to death and Beckett's endless wait: each pole waits for the action of the other to plan its reaction – indefinite postponement and blockage of action. Nevertheless, the achievement of this static equilibrium is prevented by the attraction exerted by power relations over both the struggling poles: 'For a relationship of confrontation ... the fixing of a power relationship becomes a target at one and the same time its fulfilment and its suspension' (Foucault 2001: 347). The final objective of every relation of confrontation is the establishment of a power relation, where the action of the other is again governable. The defeated adversary needs to be transformed into a relay for a new power relation, while the coded resistances need to be redispersed and reduced to a sterile swarming or a 'distant roar of the battle'. Therefore, the actions that animate all the sides involved in relations of confrontation are moved paradoxically by the intention to exit such a relation. A relation of confrontation determines a necessary but unpleasant situation for all the parties at play. The participation to a relation of confrontation is merely instrumental in order to achieve a new and more stable configuration of the forces at stake in the network. As such, the way in which relations of confrontation deploy and develop displays somehow a tendency to its self-overcoming. The relation evolves up to the moment in which it finally turns into something other than itself. Its target is therefore at once its fulfilment and also its suspension. Its full evolution decrees its termination. Once the struggle reaches the moment in which the frontal confrontation achieves a new scarcely instable stability and the adversary turns into a relay, the struggle stops and a new power relation emerges. The struggle aspires to its own termination: 'every strategy of confrontation dreams of becoming a relationship of power' (Foucault 2001: 347). There is a clear aspirational tendency towards power relations. The latter seem to exert a certain attraction on the other relations. The fixing of a power relation is the final objective that makes the struggle worth to be fought. What wants to be achieved and what actually exerts an attraction are the establishment of stable mechanisms through which 'one can direct, in a fairly constant manner and with reasonable certainty, the conduct of others', where the actions of the other can be manipulated and induced 'in a calculated manner' (Foucault 2001: 347).[3]

In short, there are two main points that emerge out of the differentiation of this spectrum of antagonistic relations. Firstly, the spectrum is ultimately organized around power relations. They constitute somehow a pole of attraction for the other relations of the spectrum. The primacy of power relations over relationships of violence and relations of confrontations is built upon the specific course of action that each relation displays. The whole of the spectrum is articulated according to different combinations of certainty, stability and probabilities. Any differentiation corresponds to the modality in which these elements are reciprocally negotiated and determined. At the two extremes of this spectrum, we find the limits of power relations, the thresholds that mark the passage from one kind to the other. On the one hand, we have relationships of violence and physical relations of constraint, where action is upon a body whose capacity of action is suspended or annihilated: maximum certainty of the effect as this depends entirely upon the first action with no reaction from the other pole; maximum stability of the relation, as the suspension of the capacity of action blocks off all the possibilities of resistance as well; maximum probability of successful reproduction of the relation, as there is no field of possibilities to govern. At the other extreme of the spectrum, there are relations of confrontation. Relationships of violence virtually occupy a single point in the spectrum as the relation between an action and pure passivity does not allow to distinguish significant variations or different degrees within the same category. As soon as one pole changes from pure passivity to a chance of escape, the relation changes immediately. On the contrary, relations of confrontation occupy a larger segment of the spectrum. They cover a range of situations in which certainty, stability and probabilities are variable. There is very scarce or no certainty at all as the struggle determines a predicament of unpredictability; strong instability as there is a continuous possibility of reversal. The radical openness of the field of probabilities makes it ultimately ungovernable and actions take the form of reactions after the event, in the free interplay of antagonistic forces. Every relation that is in between these two limits can be considered a power relation: quite regular, fairly certain, scarcely instable stability, quite solid government of the field of possibilities.

Yet what is evident from this picture is the continuous appeal to the capacity of action of the other and the stability of its government. The way in which power relations are differentiated from the other relations of the spectrum has therefore an intrinsic reference to what determines the level of stability (and, accordingly, the levels of certainty and probability): resistance and its possibility. Furthermore, not only are resistance and its possibility to determine the internal differentiation of the various political relations, resistance determines also the hierarchization of these different forms of antagonism. Power relations are prior over relationships of violence and relations of confrontation. Their primacy is entirely dependent on the specific modality in which the capacity of action of the other is governed. The primacy of power relations is due to the successful usage of the capacity of action of the other. But the success or failure of this enterprise is not primarily measured upon the positive effects that the relation produces, but depends on the way in which this capacity is governed insofar it presents the possibility of resistance. The differential element is not the capacity of action of the other as such, but the capacity of action insofar it displays a capacity for resistance. The primacy of power relations rests upon the varying degrees of actualization of resistance and its possibility. Resistance becomes therefore the key element of the dynamic as it affects and influences the evolution of antagonistic relations in general. The attraction that power relations exert over the other kinds of relation in the spectrum is ultimately conditioned by resistance. A relation of confrontation wants to be overcome because resistance produces a level of antagonism that is unbearable for all sides involved. A relationship of violence is likely to be transformed because the incapacity of resistance of the other decrees the impossibility of its usage and of the futility of the relation, as no beneficial effect is produced through the relation. The only way in which a relationship of violence produces desirable outcomes is when it is functionally subordinated or it is instrumental to a power relation, which thereby asserts once again its primacy. Therefore, the primacy of power relations constitutes at the same time the result and the cause of the primacy of resistance and its possibility. The whole of the spectrum and the fluctuation between the multiple kinds of relations that it comprises are ultimately shaped upon resistance: this determines its primacy not only over power relations but, by extension, over any kind of antagonistic relationship. The primacy of resistance lies in the processes and the dynamics that resistance and its possibility activate, forcing power relations, but also other antagonistic relations, to a reactive modification. Resistance is ultimately what assures the dynamicity of the political, what compels antagonistic relation to a ceaseless metamorphosis, what maintains the flow of becoming against the dystopian dream of its ultimate crystallization.

Strategies of resistance

There is definitely an attraction exerted from power relations on relations of confrontation, but the path generated by this transition can be walked as well in the opposite sense. On the one hand, relations of confrontation are intrinsically oriented towards their own overcoming and transformation into power relations, for the sake of a less-instable stability. On the other hand, relations of confrontation do exert a similar attraction on power relations. Or better still, the possibility that an actual relation of power might be transformed into a relation of confrontation haunts its stability: 'Every power relationship implies, at least in *potentia*, a strategy of struggle' (Foucault 2001: 346). The problem is to decipher why a fairly stable mechanism virtually implies a moment of total incertitude. In the first case, there is a movement for which the whole of the relation displays an intrinsic tendency towards a less-instable stability. Despite the radical opposition that the confrontation implies, adversaries somehow share this dream of establishing a power relation (although the two dreams are likely to disagree on the specific mechanisms that this new power relation will adopt). In this case instead, the possible transformation into a struggle is not auspicated by all the parties in and around the power relation. The relative stability of power relations is beneficial for all the points in the relation, but its specific mechanism determines a differential redistribution of these benefits. A relation of power is more beneficial for who acts upon the action of the other, rather than for the one whose action is affected. As such, the smooth reproduction of the power relation at stake is primarily in the interest of the pole who acts upon the action of the other.

The other term of the relation instead is surrounded by the tempting multiplicity of possibilities of resistance. The more these possibilities are tempting, the more the relay progressively disturbs the actual circulation of the power relation. This determines a process in which the relay completely arrests the circulation (by stopping to act according to the partial determination of the action exerted upon it) and actualizes the possibilities that were previously swarming around it. The coding or actualization of these possible points of resistance turns the relay into an adversary with its own strategy of resistance, frontally opposed to the strategy of power (or of the pole that in the previous power relation exerted its action upon the action of the other). In comparison with the tendency of relations of confrontation to turn into power relations, here there is a one-sided appeal to transformation. It is resistance and its possibility, when properly coded and actualized, that provoke a change that is, at the same time, perceived as a radical danger from the standpoint of the power relation. The transformation of the power relation at stake into a relation of confrontation is a process that can be driven only by the side successively coded as a strategy of resistance.

This strategic deployment of possible resistances is somehow inscribed in Foucault's project, animated by what has been defined an 'ethic of permanent resistance' (Simons 2003: 87). There is a dimension of possible intentionality that aims to transform the possibility of resistances into a concrete struggle.

And this intentional formation of a strategy of resistance corresponds to an affirmative call for action or, as it will be seen later, for political creation. In the conclusion of the first volume of his *History of Sexuality*, Foucault addresses the problem of this power over life that emerges in the nineteenth century with its holds on sexuality and life: 'It is the agency of sex that we must break away from, if we aim … to deploy bodies, pleasures, and knowledges, in their multiplicity and their possibility of resistance in order to counter the grips of power' (my translation).[4] Against the holds of this specific power over life, it is necessary to affirm and deploy bodies, pleasures and knowledges (that are partly captured as relays in these power relations) through the multiplicity of points that actually constitute them. And these multiplicities are, by definition, not exhausted by power relations and contain possibilities of resistance. What we need to assert are exactly those possibilities of resistance that multiplicities display insofar they are not completely captured by power relations. This evokes a transformation, a passage from a virtual status of possibility to an actual and concrete exercise of resistance. This strategic deployment seems to consist of the actualization of singular possibilities and their grouping into a strategy of struggle that intentionally confronts the power relation: 'I want to show the reality of possible struggles' (Foucault 1996). Possible struggles are those projections of possible points of resistance against actual power relations. The reality of these possible struggles manifests itself on the one hand in the anticipation of the power relation that deploys itself in function of the multiplicity of points of resistance and of possible resistance. On the other hand, this reality represents a strategic promise: out of these possibilities, a real struggle can always emerge. The apparent stability of power relation is always confronted by a real danger that lies in the possibility of this reality. The thickness of the present radically coincides with the reality of possible struggles.

The primacy of resistance with and beyond Foucault

In the works analysed so far, the primacy of resistance emerges quite cryptically through the development and the prolongation of the conceptual lines actually drawn by Foucault. There is only one excerpt where he poses resistance as prior to power. Foucault hints to the primacy of resistance in an interview released in Toronto in 1982 and then published under the title 'Sex, Power and the Politics of Identity':

> if there was no resistance, there would be no power relations. Because it would simply be a matter of obedience. You have to use power relations to refer to the situation where you're not doing what you want. So resistance comes first, and resistance remains superior to the forces of the process; power relations are obliged change with the resistance. So I think that resistance is the main word, the key word, in this dynamic.
> (Foucault 1997a: 167)

The first sentence of the quotation should have become a sort of refrain by now. What follows might instead sound rather problematic. The reference to 'a situation where you're not doing what you want' seems in fact to reduce the complexity of power relations. When the discourse on power relations and resistance is articulated from a perspective focused on individuals and their wills, the outcome of the analysis might be confusing. There is a striking difficulty in responding to scenarios in which a relation of power is not felt as such by the pole of the relation that was supposed to exert resistance. For instance, the happy worker, oblivious of the exploitation that is inherent to the capitalist mode of production, is indeed doing what she/he wants. At the same time though, it might be argued that her/his misperception is the effect of another relation of power of which she/he is also not aware. As such, it would be naïve to reduce resistance to a problem of awareness and will, as the latter are the macro-effects of a whole microphysics of power. In addition, discourses of awareness and will imply a focus on human relations that reduces the potential that the microphysics of forces opens up. Perhaps, the sentence should be slightly tweaked in the lights of the specific mechanism of power relations presented above. Power relations consist of an action that induces or makes more probable a specific action of the other. The need for an initial action signals the expected improbability of the desired action. If one exerts an action upon the action of the other, it is because the latter is not likely to occur. So perhaps the sentence might be rewritten and a power relation becomes a situation where you are doing something that otherwise you would most probably not have done. Or, in order to release it from the hold of individuals and/or subjects, it might be rephrased as the situation where an action is performed even though it was not likely to have been performed. This definitely realigns this problematic sentence to the main narrative developed in this chapter. In fact, this tweak appears to even reinforce and strengthen the conceptual line and allows a solid continuation of the trajectory.

The rest of the quotation constitutes the core of the primacy of resistance. Foucault presents it in relation to force: 'So resistance comes first, and resistance remains superior to the forces of the process.' The concept of force immediately erases the fictional unity of an individual and her/his will. In the dynamic interplay of these forces, resistance affirms its primacy through a persistent superiority. It is not limited to the emergence of power relations, but also the development of power relations confirms the primacy of resistance. Resistance comes first because it constitutes the condition of existence for power relations. The 'so' that introduces the primacy of resistance refers back to the beginning of the quotation in which power relations owe their existence to resistance. As it has been discussed above, the peculiarity of power relations is that they constitutively necessitate resistance. Nevertheless, the primacy of resistance is not exhausted with the emergence of the power relation. The evolution of the process still displays its superiority[5] over the other forces.

The persistent superiority of resistance lies in the modality in which the interaction of power relations and resistance unfolds. 'Power relations are obliged to change with resistance'. The confrontation of forces constitutes a dynamic process that generates a continuous modification of the power relation. Nevertheless, these changes are held to be imposed by resistance. The way in which forces exert resistance provokes a modification of power relation. This modification cannot be a mere redefinition of the dissymmetry between power and resistance, a hint of reversal. The change obliged by resistance regards those forces that exert power. Any resistance provokes a reaction of power that adjusts itself in order to leave intact or reinforce the dissymmetry that constitutes the power relation. Its action is not an autonomous affirmation, but an imposed necessity. For the sake of their own reproduction, power relations need to be articulated in reaction to the autonomous affirmation of their counterpart. As discussed earlier, power relations are constitutively instable, but this instability needs to be continuously managed. There is always a range of actions that might increase this instability. These actions are always possible. What can be modified though is their probability. Power relations attempt to make resistances highly improbable. 'Revolts are irreducible because no power is capable of making them absolutely impossible' (Foucault 1981). The revolt can be defined as the moment in which resistances are coded into a strategy that confronts the relevant power relation, obliging the latter to enter a relation of confrontation. Power relations work on the probability of revolt as its possibility is irreducible by definition.

Nevertheless, it is crucial to bear in mind that power relations display a certain regularity and their stability is correlated by the rarity of revolts. As such, the moment of the revolt becomes a mysterious and enigmatic event: 'In the end, there is no explanation for the man who revolts. His action is necessarily a tearing that breaks the thread of history and its long chains of reasons so that a man can genuinely give preference to the risk of death over the certitude of having to obey' (Foucault 1981). What gives the enigmatic character to this event? Its actualization despite the highly unfavourable odds. Power relations ideally create the conditions for their smooth reproduction. They induce a certain course of action upon the other. Obedience guarantees the circulation of the relation and the secure regularity of beneficial outcomes for both parties. The final outcome expresses a dissymmetry in which the latter is somehow disadvantaged, but the cons are compensated and outbalanced by the regularity of the acceptable benefits. By submitting to a power relation, by functioning as the good relay, there is a small but guaranteed reward. Obedience gives the certainty of obtaining some beneficial effects. Revolt instead implies the renunciation to this certainty and the opening up of a risky situation. As it activates a relation of confrontation, the outcome is completely open to any scenario. This implies the risk of death or enslavement for instance. At the same time though, the struggle opens up the possibility of an actual reversal of the contested power relation and the creation of a new configuration. Such a result constitutes an effect that is by far more beneficial for the previously submitted pole in the relation. There are less chances of obtaining a beneficial effect, but this is compensated by the better reward that the new configuration might imply. Revolt is risky, but if successful, it promises to be more rewarding than the regular but scarce benefits that the power relation under attack could have offered.

Revolts constitute the limit of resistance, the moment in which the swarming of resistances and the possibility of resistance turns, through its coding, into a defined strategy of struggle. This binary opposition between the two series (obedience as security of scarce rewards vs. revolt as high risk but with possible high rewards) persists somehow even when resistance does not trespass into a proper revolt. This mechanism is at work even when the power network does not really display points of resistance but only their possibility. The choice between the two series above is reflected also at the level of the circulation of power relations. When one acts upon the action of the other, the latter has always the abstract possibility of choosing whether to obey or not. The action induced by the first pole occurs only if the other actually performs it. The other maintains the possibility to refuse it. It is like if the second relay has always the choice of allowing or blocking the circulation. Therefore, the complexity of the possible responses can be condensed into two modalities: obedience or resistance. Resistance constitutes the attempt of revoking the participation to the power relation. It is the attempt to stop functioning as a relay. But when the circulation is disturbed or interrupted, a certain modification is needed to restore it or to define a new one. There is no need for intervention when the circulation is smooth. If power relations constantly produce the desired result, their mechanism does not require any intervention. It is resistance 'what motivates all the new development of the network of power' (Foucault 1980). This constitutes the primacy of resistance. New possibilities of resistance impose a change or a modification of power relations. The latter need to respond to these new points and invent new mechanisms. These transformations are provoked by resistance and the proliferation of its possibilities. Resistance derives its primacy over power relation because it is what ultimately activates and modulates history and becoming.

Resistance, creation and becoming

If power seems to have an operational modality that is reactive, is the way in which forces exert resistance active? And what is an active force? To be sure, in this interview Foucault is not explicitly concerned with answering these questions, but again few elements can help us to start sketching the conceptual line of the primacy of resistance at the level of forces. In fact, when Foucault talks about the gay movement as an instance of ethical and political resistance, what strikingly emerges is the affinity of resistance with a series of concepts that undoubtedly converge towards the idea of active force. Practices of resistance are repeatedly associated with creation, invention, differentiation and becoming: 'We don't have to discover that we are homosexuals. ... we have to create a gay life. To become' (Foucault 1997a: 163); 'Not only do we have to defend ourselves, not only affirm ourselves, as an identity but as a creative force' (Foucault 1997a: 164); 'I think that S&M is much more than [the uncovering of tendencies deep within our consciousness]; it's the real creation of new possibilities of pleasure, which people had no idea about previously. ... it's a kind of creation, a creative enterprise' (Foucault 1997a: 165); 'the relationships we have to have with ourselves are not ones of identity, rather, they must be relationships of differentiation, of creation, of innovation' (Foucault 1997a: 166).

None of these manifestations of resistance are presented by Foucault as primarily oppositional, antagonistic or destructive. In all these quotations, resistance has to do with affirmative processes that are minimally concerned with the power they are confronting. Creation, becoming, invention, differentiation: autonomous impulses that determine the affirmation of forces that happen to stand only accidentally in opposition to power relations. Those affirmative practices that constitute the distinctiveness of resistance are far from evoking a relation of antagonistic confrontation, although embedded in such a relation. There seems to be a discrepancy between the propension of resistance towards becoming and its oppositional stance: opposition implies a relational process, but the resistance as becoming does not intrinsically demand the presence of a second element. Creative affirmation *can* be a relational process, but it does not have to be necessarily so. In the concept of resistance that emerges from these excerpts, there are moments of both creative affirmation and opposition, but their respective weights are differently distributed. This different distribution lies in the implicit rejection of the intuitive and linguistically sedimented understanding of resistance as a reactive and passive force. When Foucault says 'to say no is the minimum form of resistance' (Foucault 1997a: 168), he seems to allude to the explosive potential that remains unexpressed by the mere 'no'; a potential that lies in its affinity to creation, becoming, differentiation. When resistance is reduced to a mere refusal, it remains at its minimum. But the negative moment is always supplemented by this moment of positive affirmation and creation. This is what makes resistance the active element within power relations.

Furthermore, this coupling of resistance and creation hints towards an eminently constitutive moment. This emerges through an expression that Foucault probably does not use elsewhere: 'political creation'.

> Since the nineteenth century, great political institutions and great political parties have confiscated the process of political creation; that is, they have tried to give to political creation the form of a political program in order to take over power. ... [I]n the sixties and early seventies ... there has been political innovation, political creation, and political experimentation outside the great political parties, and outside the normal or ordinary program.
> (Foucault 1997a: 172)

Political creation stands on the side of resistance and is no longer tied to the objective of taking over power. What happens to political creation in the nineteenth century is that it takes up the form of a political program. This operation is performed by 'great political institutions and great political parties'. But this is an illegitimate appropriation ('confiscated'). In the 1960s and early 1970s[6] there is a partial reversal of this process: political creation passes in the hands of social movements. The peculiarity of the way in which political creation is deployed in this time is that it does not have a program and occurs outside the great political parties. On the one hand, the potential inherent to resistance is liberated by the rigidity of party politics and its domestication into a program. On the other hand, the objective of resistance passes from taking over power to social transformation. And Foucault sees that these processes have indeed provoked some sort of social transformation: 'These social movements have really changed our whole lives, our mentality, our attitudes, and the attitudes and mentality of other people – people who do not belong to these movements. And that is something very important and positive' (Foucault 1997a: 173). Here Foucault prefigures the constitutive moment of resistance that brings about political creation, change and transformation without the rigidity of power relations. The primacy of resistance as a constitutive principle stands for a process of organizing that remains absolutely open to its own transformation.

A process that seeks to reduce the level of dissymmetry that power relations necessarily imply. Lazzarato recognizes here an ethico-political stance that arises from the problem of rendering strategical relations symmetrical. And for this purpose, although soon interrupted, Foucault 'begins to tackle this thematic through the theme of friendship' (Lazzarato 2002: 109). This can partly suggest a path for the continuation of a conceptual line whose trajectory cannot be arrested at Foucault. 'Foucault's work ought to be continued upon this fractured line between resistance and creation' (Lazzarato 2002: 110). The primacy of resistance aims to deploy itself as a conceptual line that repairs that fracture and deploys itself towards further explorations.

2

Human nature and resistance. From La Boétie's companionship to the liberal closure

The philosophical discourse on nature is often embedded in the political debate. These political theories assume that nature has an intrinsic organization. The various discourses differ on what this organizational design looks like, which place the human occupies in this design, the composition and the internal dynamics of the human as species. There can be distinguished two approaches to this question. The first mainly consists of theories from the Aristotelian tradition and also from certain sections of Christian political thought. The conceptual line drawn by this group assumes that the order of nature (or God) prescribes a hierarchical organization of the political.

On the contrary, there are a series of discourses whose assumption is that even though a certain natural order exists, human nature is such that natural differences are not politically relevant. The immediate implication of this discourse is that no power can claim to be natural or conferred by nature. Nature prescribes absolute political equality and freedom for all human beings. Nature comes first. There is no power in nature, no natural restrain. Power intervenes upon something – nature – that is prior to it and that is also resistant. This conceptual line conflates nature and resistance and affirms their primacy over power. Its trajectory is traced by a common narrative that unites a series of highly differentiated discourses. They all share an understanding of nature not as an omni-comprehensive category that includes 'the totality of phenomena', but as a term of distinction (Strauss 1953). First, it refers to a state that precedes the emergence of civil power. The state of nature is chronologically prior to power, a pre-historical or hypothetical dimension where power is absent, although on the verge to be instituted (Ashcraft 1968, Simmons 1989). Nature represents a lost dimension whose abandonment marks the passage to civil government. But nature reappears also in the form of a nagging reminder against the abuses of power: a force of resistance. The recalcitrance of nature expresses itself as freedom against tyranny. Nature affirms itself as resistance against power.

However, this conceptual line problematizing the primacy of resistance in relation to nature is fractured by an internal bifurcation. There is a conceptual turn that marks the termination of a unitary trajectory of the naturalistic account of the primacy of resistance. In order to locate the conceptual coordinates of the bifurcation, it is necessary to focus on a variety of discourses between the sixteenth and seventeenth centuries that frequently mobilize this line. Foucault refers to this body of literature at a conference for la *Société Française de Philosophie* in May 1978. He frames this question as the historico-philosophical analysis of the art of government and of critique. Critique emerges in tension with discourses on power focused on the question of how to govern. What is critique then? It is 'the art of voluntary insubordination' (Foucault 1997b: 47), in French *'l'art de l'inservitude volontaire'*. This definition immediately evokes the title of La Boétie's *Discours de la servitude volontaire*. Foucault does not mention the author but the reference seems to be quite obvious.[1] La Boétie represents an emblematic author for this series of critical discourses to which Foucault refers in his presentation. These discourses challenge the arts of governing emerging at that time. Their critical attitude is translated into the will not to be governed *like that*, in that specific way, by that authority, by those laws. To different degrees, these discourses mobilize the problem of nature in relation to the question of government.

The problematic complexity of the discourses that politically mobilize nature is somehow intuited by Foucault himself. When asked whether next to the *art of not being governed like that* there is a more radical and absolute *art of not being governed at all*, Foucault remains cautiously ambivalent:

> As for the expression of not being governed at all, I believe it is the philosophical and theoretical paroxysm of something that would be this will not to be relatively governed. And when at the end I was saying 'decision-making will not to be governed', then there, an error on my part, it was not to be governed thusly, like that, in this way. I was not referring to something that would be a fundamental anarchism, that would be like an originary freedom,

absolutely and wholeheartedly resistant to any governmentalization. I did not say it, but this does not mean that I absolutely exclude it.

(Foucault 1997b: 75)

Foucault wants to focus on an art of inservitude that is always contextualized, referred to a specific government, but that, at the same time, accepts the rationale of government. It asks for a better government, for a legitimate one and anchors the criteria for legitimacy to a specific discourse on nature. Nevertheless, Foucault prudently admits that the specificity of his focus does not require the absolute exclusion of the possibility of articulating an art of not being governed at all.

These two approaches to the coupling of nature and resistance correspond to the two polarities that animate this chapter. La Boétie is the herald of 'originary freedom'.[2] His *Discourse* is a polemical observation of how power rests exclusively upon the scandalous consent of its subjects and the state of servitude it imposes. His attack against servitude moves from the natural affirmation of companionship and freedom, a condition where the absence of power fosters mutual solidarity and cooperation. Power is passive as it depends on the will of its subject to serve. But their voluntary servitude is nothing but the renunciation to resist. La Boétie poses power as an accident, a misfortune that denatures humans turning them away from their natural drive towards freedom and companionship. The call to revoke the consensus to one's own servitude is the beginning of the affirmation of an art of not to be governed at all, an art of absolute resistance. By withdrawing consent, power collapses and nature is restored: no opposition is needed. When power collapses, we (re-)discover a state of nature before the misfortune of power: natural companionship, mutual help and solidarity.

At the other extreme of the spectrum, there is the tradition of consent theory, those political discourses that create a genetic and moral account of power departing from the consent of those subjected to it. Social contract theories are most probably the most well-known expressions of this tradition. From its classic version – Hobbes, Locke, etc. – up to its contemporary revival – Rawls (1999, 2005), Nozick (1974) – there is the emergence of a moral and political conceptualization of nature intertwined with a strong appeal to the notion of rights. Humans are naturally free and power is absent in the state of nature. Therefore, freedom comes first and power can be criticized upon this assumption. Yet rather than an art of not to be governed at all like in La Boétie, social contract theories represent a *relative* art of not to be governed. The target is not power as such, but specific historical instances of power. The discourse of the contractarians is against a specific power that differs for any of these authors. The power fought by Hobbes through his contract is different from Nozick's polemical object. By criticizing a particular power only, they aliment and reinforce the demand for power as such. The natural unnecessity of power that aliments the initial emergence of this conceptual line is perversely used to secure the social necessity of power. The contract is the device that operates this transition. It marks the caesura between the state of nature and the civil state. In a way, the contract is the evil twin of La Boétie's misfortune, the accidental irruption of power through voluntary servitude. Instead of revealing its unnatural character, the contract sets the conditions for legitimate power by granting individuals the possibility to revert, only partly though, to that abandoned natural freedom. The discourse of rights is what allows this passage that ultimately marks the closure of the initial path of the conceptual line of the naturalistic account of the primacy of resistance.

This conceptual closure depends on the introduction of a series of elements that are not intrinsically germane to the discourse on nature. The individual subject replaces the indefinite multitude of human nature (which, as such, is potentially indifferent to any tension between the collective and the individual dimension). This individual is a subject of rights and enters in a relation with power that is presented as primarily moral. In principle, consent theory deploys a genetic account of power that is structured by a material process (both in the act of producing and subscribing the contract and in the reproduction of the machine of power). Nevertheless, through the idea of the subject of right, the moral relationship between subject and power takes over and ultimately rules out the material genetic account. This signals a major deviation from La Boétie's argument. Power is not depicted as materially constituted from below. Its constitution comes to rest exclusively upon the moral obligation of the rational subject of right. The decisive effect of this move is that while in La Boétie's account power would materially collapse and be eradicated once subjects withdraw their contribution to it, the discourse of moral obligation creates the ideal conditions to secure power as such by distinguishing those actual forms of power (liberal and democratic) that deserve obligation and those (despotic and absolutist) that do not and need to be replaced by a proper power. While in La Boétie we see the problematization of the material constitution of power and the possibility of its radical destruction, the liberal tradition points to the definition of the conditions that make subjects morally obliged to obey. In short, the perverse evolution of the naturalistic account of the primacy of resistance endorsed somehow by the liberal tradition culminates with the dismissal of its founding conceptual premise. It closes off the possible evolution of a cooperative model of organization based on companionship and mutualism and opts for an understanding of the political based on opposition that firmly requires the existence of power.

Towards an art of voluntary inservitude

In the previous chapter we have placed slavery at the extreme pole of the scale of antagonistic relations. Slavery was defined by a relation of physical constraint, where the capacity of action is annihilated (pure heteronomy). For La Boétie instead, servitude is a widespread condition. Yokes constrain entire masses. But these yokes are not constraints; they are rather the effect of a fascination. The servant voluntarily chooses to obey. If there is heteronomy, it paradoxically depends on the autonomous submission of the servant 'not constrained by a greater multitude' but simply 'delighted and charmed by the name of one man alone whose power they need not fear' (La Boétie 2008: 40). In La Boétie's terminology, the concept of servitude is detached from physical constraint and brute force. He does not provide a precise definition of the term, but it can be understood as the acceptance of a hierarchical distinction and the vow of obedience to those in power. The absence of physical constraint should in principle allow the possibility of inverting such a hierarchy. But the predicament of tyranny is such that people are incapable of perceiving this possibility. They act *as if* there were chains, *as if* this hierarchy could never be challenged, *as if* they were condemned to pure heteronomy. They act *as if* they were slaves. Indeed, this predicament is a matter of beliefs and perceptions whose exceptional strength is due to its commonness. Chains are immaterial, the force of the tyrant is much weaker than those of the servants and, above all, the possibility to invert that hierarchical relation exists. A tyrant can be resisted. Nevertheless, those who submit themselves to the tyrant's power deliberately renounce to the possibility to resist, they choose to serve while forgetting that such a possibility exists: voluntary servitude. The scandal of this condition resides not so much in the fact of the obedience of a multitude to a single impotent tyrant. Rather, what is scandalous about it is that, paradoxically, it is not perceived as scandalous.

As La Boétie never engages the classic debate in political philosophy on the good forms of government, the predicament of voluntary servitude can be escalated to any political regime that implies social division and a hierarchical distribution of power: 'it is a great misfortune to be at the beck and call of one master …. As for having several masters …, it amounts to being that many times unfortunate' (La Boétie 2008: 40). The tyrant represents power as such, while voluntary servitude appears not only as obedience to power but also as renunciation to resistance. The scandal is thus the normalization of hierarchy and power as accepted facts rather than as accidental anomalies.

The strength of La Boétie is to reveal the historical contingency of power. Power is an accidental misfortune, an unnecessity. Voluntary servitude has its own history, its specific point of emergence and its specific conditions that have determined its emergence. How has voluntary servitude become the norm? The understanding of voluntary servitude as a historical product is underdeveloped in La Boétie. The contingency of this predicament appears more through a process of logical exclusion. His argument is in fact mainly directed to rule out the hypothesis that such a political arrangement finds its rationale and its legitimacy immediately in human nature or, more in general, in the order that nature prescribes.

The contract's evil twin: The misfortune of servitude

As voluntary servitude finds no foundation in nature, its emergence has to be understood as a historical contingency. If human nature is supposed to be against this political state of affairs, as it will be evident when discussing companionship, there must be historical and therefore contingent factors that have determined the constitution of a hierarchic society. What determined the transition from that natural companionship of which we have apparently lost any memory to our civil societies rigidly structured on relations of power? Custom, discipline and civilization are enough to explain how this system of domination is constantly reproduced, but they say nothing of the specific moment of this transition. 'What misfortune has so denatured man that he, the only creature really born to be free, lacks the memory of his original condition and the desire to return to it?' (La Boétie 2008: 52). For this singular event that determines the passage from the harmonious natural community to the scandalous enigma of the voluntary servitude, there is just a mere label: misfortune – 'tragic accident, bad luck' (Clastres 1994: 172). A transition whose firm situatedness in history demonstrates its contingency and eliminates the very possibility of an intrinsic necessity. The word 'misfortune' expresses at the same time its fundamental relation with chance and the grievance for this unwanted and undesirable outcome. The predicament of voluntary servitude is even more tragic precisely in virtue of its contingency: it could have been otherwise and instead it happened to determine a scenario that is radically opposed to what nature had designed. The abandonment of the state of nature is not accompanied by a narrative of progress and evolution. For La Boétie, the misfortune brings about an absolute regression.

This infamous misfortune constitutes a temporal caesura between two distinct moments. Before the misfortune, there is a natural society, a community organized according to the prescriptions of nature. After the misfortune, there is a divided community where one governs and the others serve. This grid of intelligibility has the advantage of tracing an interesting comparison with other politico-philosophical traditions that chronologically follow La Boétie's work. To the eyes of the contemporary reader of La Boétie, the misfortune establishes a division between a society 'before the state' and a state-centred organization of the polity (Abensour and Gauchet 2002: 23). There is no doubt that even La Boétie is talking from a position that is eminently after the misfortune, especially in his role of civil servant. How can he possibly extend his gaze backward up to a moment that precedes the caesura? Several scholars have tried to individuate which historical event might have triggered La Boétie's *Discourse* (e.g. Barrère 1923, Keohane 1977, Rothbard 2008, Bentouhami 2009). Although the hypotheses differ, they all try to search for this event in the political history of France in the sixteenth century. In particular, there is a certain agreement on a precise event, namely the revolt of the municipality of Guyenne against the state taxation in 1548 (Abensour and Gauchet 2002: 31). There are no elements to support or discredit this thesis, but neither would it be vital to get a definitive answer on this issue. However, Pierre Clastres tries to reconstruct that historical context focusing on another event: the discovery of the New World (Clastres 1994: 186). It is commonly acknowledged that in the aftermath of this discovery there is a vast circulation of pamphlets and reports of the encounter with those indigenous populations. It is the encounter with these new people that animates the fantasy of La Boétie's contemporaries. This could explain his enigmatic reference to an imaginary new people never being accustomed to servitude and even ignoring the meaning of it: 'let us imagine some newborn individuals, neither acquainted with slavery nor desirous of liberty, ignorant indeed of the very words. If they were permitted to choose between being slaves and free men, to which would they give their preference?' (La Boétie 2008: 53).[3] It is a form of political imagination where the phantasies of the present allow the reimaging of a past in order to reinvent the future – societies that are coexistent with those of subjugation and that mark the accidentality of power, trapped between the past of the state of nature and a future return to it. The phantasies on indigenous population act as phantasies over another possible world, as traces of societies before the misfortune, before the state: a state of nature. This is where we can connect, although polemically, La Boétie with the tradition of the social contract. What he calls misfortune seems somehow to correspond to the contract that establishes the passage from the state of nature to the civil state. There are obviously substantial differences between them, but the misfortune and the contract arguably share this divisional position. They both serve the purpose of posing a caesura that distinguishes two qualitatively and temporally different social and political arrangements. La Boétie's misfortune stands to the contract as its evil twin. The contract marks the passage from the state of nature to the civil state, but for La Boétie there is no gain in that. The horrendous predicament of voluntary servitude reveals the regret for the lost dimension of the state of nature. In fact, while the contractarian tradition sees the state of nature as the unrestrained emergence of antagonisms, La Boétie hints to a state of nature affirming comradeship and freedom.

La Boétie's Leviathan

The transition from a state of nature to the civil state corresponds to a fall from grace. There is a process of voluntary alienation in which human beings lose their nature. The becoming-serf corresponds to the simultaneous abandonment both of the state of nature (social arrangement) and of human nature as such. It consists of a process of denaturation: the transformation of what human beings naturally are into a multitude that voluntarily submits itself to power. And this multitude is what materially constitutes the power of the tyrant. The body of the tyrant alone cannot determine any form of subordination of other bodies.

Yet paraphrasing Ernst Hartwig Kantorowicz (1997), the tyrant has got two bodies: one is the insignificant and impotent body whose force alone is not enough to demand obedience; the other is the one whose power is determined by the sum of the forces of those who serve. Is this second body the same 'body politic' that Kantorowicz traces back to a certain medieval political theology? Only in part. Because the account of La Boétie seems not to be merely symbolical. He understands that as a corporeal entity. In a series of rhetoric questions composing a description that strongly evokes the famous picture of the frontispiece of the original edition of Thomas Hobbes's *Leviathan*,[4] La Boétie wonders: 'Where has he acquired enough eyes to spy upon you, if you do not provide them yourselves? How can he have so many arms to beat you with, if he does not borrow them from you? The feet that trample down your cities, where does he get them if they are not your own?' (La Boétie 2008: 46).[5] This body is not only that which survives after the tyrant's death through the continuation of sovereignty – the king is dead, long live the king. This body has as many eyes, arms and feet as those of all the people that are under its domination. And this dimension can be understood as eminently material. Every state machine relies on the eyes, the hands and the feet of all those who concretely perform its functions. Power literally borrows the body of its tax collectors or its soldiers while they perform their task on its behalf: it acts upon their forces. The second body of the tyrant traced by La Boétie's refers, therefore, to the materiality of the operations that constitute any state apparatus. Being the sum of all the bodies of its subjected people, the second body of the tyrant necessarily displays a gigantic monstrosity. Its grandiosity reveals its fundamental impotency. Insofar the eyes of that body do not actually belong to the body, the arms and the feet of that body do not belong to that body either, to what extent is that body actually strong? Once the actual owners of all these eyes, arms and feet will resolve to serve no more, the monstrous body of this Leviathan will collapse immediately and break into pieces.

As servitude is voluntary, it implies an active participation to subjugation. But this participation can be withdrawn: subjection can be resisted. So (non-)resistance appears as constitutive of power. Power has no matter of its own. Its materiality consists of the accidental suspension of resistance. As such, power collapses as soon as resistance affirms itself: 'there is no need of fighting to overcome this single tyrant, for he is automatically defeated if the country refuses consent to its own enslavement' (La Boétie 2008: 44). Withdrawing consent is enough to dismantle power. What configures the primacy of resistance at this stage is that in La Boétie resistance appears, first, as decisive for the existence and therefore the end of power, and, second, as not essentially dependent on opposition and struggle. Opposition is superfluous as once resistance affirms itself by withdrawing its forces from the power relation (and possibly redirecting them towards a society based on comradeship and freedom), its opponent vanishes.

Spotting freedom among denatured beings

The denatured human being confuses its subjection with its natural status. Even at the very moment of birth, the human condition is already not natural. Human beings 'are born serfs and then' (only then!) 'reared as such' (La Boétie 2008: 61). The condition in which one is born differs already from the nature that is proper to human beings. Custom, discipline and civilization constantly assure the reproduction of the denatured being. But even before any process of disciplinarization, they have somehow already managed to fall from their natural condition. The only residue of nature in human beings seems to be some 'inborn tendencies' (La Boétie 2008: 51) towards freedom that La Boétie exhorts to follow and restore. These tendencies reveal the longing for freedom as essential element of human nature and, more in general, of what nature prescribes. Where does he find these tendencies? Among humans, there are and there have been few exceptions. Instead, among animals, the longing for freedom is widespread as servitude is for humans. Animals stick to their nature by manifesting a radical desire for freedom in their misfortunate encounter with humans and therefore with captivity. La Boétie bends this natural desire for freedom of animals to the point that he seems to turn it into a biological principle: 'just as the fish loses life as soon as he leaves the water' (La Boétie 2008: 51), many animals die as soon as captured as they do not want to survive the loss of their freedom. Animals commonly exert resistance against subjection. They reveal a natural desire towards freedom. And it is from this desire that denatured humans should rediscover their own natural propensity for freedom.

Among humans, there are only rare exceptions that object against their state of servitude. Freedom requires an imagination that goes beyond the existent to recover a lost condition. It is a backward look that enquiries the past not only to make sense of the present predicament, but also to turn it around. 'There are always a few ... who, possessed of clear minds and far-sighted spirit, are not satisfied, like the brutish mass, to see only what is at their feet' (La Boétie 2008: 59). This political imagination that resists servitude is an intellectual effort that few are able to pursue. This can be read as a self-reflective remark as La Boétie implicitly poses himself in that tradition of 'clear minds' and, through the quote above, he explains the method of his *Discourse*: to rediscover our true nature, we need to look beyond our denatured existent. This is the intellectual effort to conceive freedom and resist servitude. It is not a matter of practices as all it is needed for the collapse of power is a mere resolution to serve no more. As such, it requires a critical gesture that refuses subjection, but also the forms of subjectivation that have determined that state of subjection: customs, rearing, education. But at once it crafts an alternative subjectivity and an alternative path of subjectivation: critical observation of the present, study of past 'far-sighted spirits', imagination. It is the radical acknowledgement of the possibility of freedom and of its urgency: 'Even if liberty had entirely perished from the earth, such men would invent it' (La Boétie 2008: 59). Freedom can be invented. And La Boétie in a way invents his own.

His freedom is not just the opposite of servitude. It is not only freedom from power, a negative form of liberty. His freedom depends on comradeship and solidarity: 'we are all naturally free, inasmuch we are all comrades' (La Boétie 2008: 50).[6] The *Discourse* is ostensibly a pamphlet on freedom and there is no doubt that natural freedom plays an important role in La Boétie's argument (see for instance Margel 2009, Abensour 2011, García-Alonso 2013, Newman 2015). Yet the quote above suggests a slightly more specific reading. Unlike in the liberal tradition of the social contract, freedom on its own does not constitute the essence of nature: not just freedom, but comradeship and freedom. It is natural companionship that determines our freedom. The 'puis que' in the quotation is crucial to express this relation of dependence and subordination. If freedom were first, companionship would be just an independent and unnecessary accessory. The appeal to companionship shapes the kind of freedom that is proper to nature by sketching a state of cooperation and mutual support.

This radically distinguishes La Boétie from other versions of the state of nature in the contractarian tradition. In Hobbes for instance, absolute liberty inevitably results into the famous *bellum omnium contra omnes*: freedom is compatible with companionship, but also with antagonism and war. For La Boétie instead, freedom descends from natural companionship. The latter sets the conditions that make freedom possible. The primacy of companionship becomes utterly evident in the concept of voluntary servitude. For the servitude is voluntary, there must be a residual of that natural freedom even in the denatured human being. This remnant is at work both in the deliberate decision of submission and in the possibility to serve no more and restore freedom. Denaturation does not mean a complete loss of freedom. Rather, it consists in a misuse of that originary freedom. If denaturation in relation to freedom were due to force or constraint, the natural propensity towards freedom would have remained intact (as in the case of the animals fighting captivity). But insofar as servitude is not imposed but voluntarily chosen by those who serve, to what extent can be assumed that freedom completely disappears from this picture? Humans freely desire their own subjection: they use their natural freedom for neutralizing their freedom. In this process of denaturation, humans somehow conserve some of their nature by exerting their own freedom in the decision to renounce their freedom. They use their nature for denaturing themselves. This is probably one of the crucial passages in La Boétie's argument as it expresses the complexity and the paradoxical and enigmatic nature of voluntary servitude, of this 'Arcanum' (Abensour and Gauchet 2002). Human beings under the yoke of servitude become trapped within this logical paradox, where denaturation is at the same time in virtue of nature and against nature. 'Would the denatured man still be a man because he chose to no longer be a man, that is, a free being? Such is, nevertheless, the presentation of man: denatured, yet still free, since he chooses alienation. Strange synthesis, unthinkable conjunction, unnameable reality' (Clastres 1994: 178). But whereas freedom persists despite denaturation, companionship is the element of human nature that most strikingly disappears right after the misfortune.

'We are all comrades'

In La Boétie's argument, companionship and fraternal love are incompatible with domination and servitude. The elimination of companionship constitutes the ultimate product of the process of denaturation. The fall from the state of grace is primarily related to the loss of comradeship. The fall due to denaturation corresponds to the abandonment of the state of nature. Companionship is the constitutive principle upon which the state of nature is structured.

The discourse on the naturality of comradeship is articulated on the tension between resemblance and inequality. The resemblance of all human beings creates an obvious convergence towards the unity of the species. Other theoretical traditions have focused on the unequal distribution of virtues in order to legitimate and reinforce the existence and the reproduction of hierarchical division of society. The appeal to nature serves the purpose to crystallize existing relations of power. Whereas contingency displays the fragility and the potential reversibility of a given state of affairs, the naturalization of the existent aims to the eradication of the possibility of transformation or creative reinvention. Nature plays a strategical role. La Boétie's mobilization of a discourse on nature has also a strategical function. But his strategical approach consists of a critique of the existent. Natural inequalities form an invitation to comradeship, but the existent displays a predicament of subjection and servitude. As such, natural inequalities and their tension towards comradeship exert a critical function that resists the existent.

La Boétie radically reverses the coupling of inequality and hierarchization. He does not ignore the fact of natural inequality, but he rejects the hypothesis that such inequalities necessarily imply a specific hierarchical order. On the contrary, these differences among beings constitute the evidence of a natural cooperative structure.

> If in distributing her gifts nature has favoured some more than others ..., she has nevertheless not planned to place us within this world as if it were a field of battle ... [I]n distributing larger shares to some and smaller shares to others, nature has intended to give occasion for brotherly love to become manifest, some of us having the strength to give help to others who are in need of it.
>
> (La Boétie 2008: 50)

Inequality does not necessarily imply antagonism per se. There is no intrinsic connection between natural differences and the relations of force that may occur between the stronger and the weaker. Looking at nature, there is no hint that may suggest that antagonism is a necessary condition inscribed in nature. La Boétie operates a logical disjunction between the given of natural inequality and the possibility of the antagonistic formation of power relations. He opens up the field of possibilities inherent to natural inequalities to then pick up, strategically, a counter-intuitive possibility, a possibility lacking any evidence in the existent predicament of widespread servitude: comradeship, mutualism, solidarity. What nature prescribes is the opposite of the existing denatured mode of living. In the intentions of nature, differences function as a means to highlight the complementarity of beings. What the weaker is not able to do can be done by the stronger. Natural differences stimulate mutual cooperation. Rather than producing antagonism, inequality makes evident our fundamental incapacity of relying exclusively on our own singular forces. Inequality constitutes an invitation to collaborate and to provide mutual support and solidarity. Through the unequal distribution of resources, nature creates the conditions for the emergence of love among beings as the possibility to support each other occasions immediately the possibility to put this love into practice. This push towards mutualism and solidarity is a primary objective for nature. The way in which nature intends to achieve this goal is by introducing inequalities.

Language is the other evidence La Boétie presents to argue for the naturality of comradeship and mutualism. Even though he is never explicitly quoted, it is quite easy to detect throughout the text a continuous engagement with

Aristotle's *Politics* (Barrère 1923, Terrel 2009). For Aristotle, what makes human beings political animals is the possibility to utter moral judgements:

> Nature ... does nothing without some purpose; and she has endowed man alone among the animals with the power of speech. Speech is something different from voice, which is possessed by other animals also and used by them to express pain or pleasure .... Speech, on the other hand serves to indicate what is useful and what is harmful, and also what is just and what is unjust. For the real difference between man and other animals is that humans alone have perception of good and evil, just and unjust, etc.
> (Aristotle 1981: 60)

La Boétie uses the key elements at stake in this Aristotle's quote but putting forth a completely different theory. Firstly, whereas for Aristotle only human beings have some sort of moral sense, for La Boétie animals have an analogous sense as well. As discussed above, their resistance against captivity clearly manifests, in different forms, protests and complaints against the injustice they suffer. They do not simply, as Aristotle puts it, share their perception of pain and pleasure through their voice. The examples that La Boétie uses (especially captivity) might be interpreted as events that cover a proto-moral area, rather than being a mere matter of pain. What is somehow communicated by animals (either through voice or significant acts) is a rebellion for an action that is perceived as unjust. Aristotle argues that the moral sense that the gift of speech allows to human beings constitutes their defining feature as political animals. Language is what allows human beings to form communities on the basis of the fact that they can express and distinguish what is just from what is unjust. La Boétie slightly displaces this line of argumentation. The gift of speech is indeed proper to human beings. Communities do arise in virtue of this human capacity. Nevertheless, it is not primarily a matter of morality. As it seems to emerge from his discussion on animals, injustice can be perceived and communicated even through other means (e.g. physical resistance to capture, elephants' self-amputation of their tusks as attempt to get back their liberty). Instead, language eminently serves another social purpose: it operates in order to foster 'fraternal relationship, thus achieving by the common and mutual statement of our thoughts a communion of our wills' (La Boétie 2008: 50).

Whereas in Aristotle language is a device that introduces distinctions, in La Boétie it has an aggregative function by bringing people together as nature prescribes. Language is primarily a means for achieving unity within the social community. In La Boétie's natural design, voicing one's position does not mean to engage in an oppositional confrontation against other views. On the contrary, language becomes the locus where multiple voices recognize the fundamental natural unity that binds them together. Language articulates companionship by positively endorsing the tension between resemblance and inequalities. As Claude Lefort correctly observes, language is on the one hand the result of a mutual recognition – I speak with you insofar I assume you have my same capacity of understanding an oral communication. On the other hand, any linguistic act implies the presence of two distinct individuals that, as such, display their inequality implicit in their uniqueness. Therefore, language is constituted upon this tension, but at the same time it resolves it (Lefort 2002) determining an unlimited collectivity animated and bond together by natural companionship.

A cooperative state of nature

La Boétie's argument focuses on nature and the design that nature prescribes, particularly in relation to human nature. Nevertheless, the idea of the misfortune, which causes the fall from the state of grace that nature has designed and the transition to the predicament of the voluntary servitude, allows to slightly displace his argument. Nature is not only a design that the current reality fails to fulfil. Nature can also be said to inform a concrete society's mode of existence, both as logical possibility implied by the current state and as historical hypothesis of a society whose memory has been lost. Anticipating the contractarian tradition, this logical and hypothetical society takes up the form of a state of nature. Comradeship is arguably the cipher of this state of nature that precedes any kind of political structure or political organization of the social. This arrangement suggests the complete absence of power relations and the reproduction of an undivided society based on pure horizontality.

> The very possibility of formulating such a destructive question reflects, simply but heroically, a logic of opposites: if I can be surprised that voluntary servitude is a constant in all societies … it is … because I imagine the logical

possibility of a society that would not know voluntary servitude. La Boétie's heroism and freedom: precisely this smooth transition from History to logic ... The young La Boétie transcends all known history to say: something else is possible.

(Clastres 1994: 172)

By unravelling the logical structure that underlies La Boétie's argument, Clastres shows the two directions that the contingency of our divided society implies. On the one hand, the historical emergence, although located in a remote and unknown time, alludes to the existence of an alternative arrangement that is prior to the current one. On the other hand, everything that has a date of birth might at some point encounter its end. Voluntary servitude does not escape this rule. The logical possibility of its opposite constitutes at the same time the hope for the future occurrence of such an opposite. The forgotten existence of a cooperative and horizontal society is the proof of the possibility of its return. A return that will never be properly a return, insofar as the point to reach, even though similar to what preceded the misfortune, will necessarily contain the concrete memory of what followed the misfortune.

However, the fact that La Boétie's account of a society without power and inequality is only a logic implication of his discourse does not rule out the possible historical occurrence of such a society. This is, according to Clastres, one consistent difference with Jean-Jacques Rousseau (and perhaps also with the other theorists of the social contract). In his *Discourse on the Origin of Inequality*, he describes the fictional account of the misfortune that originated private property and inequality, but, at the same time, he makes clear that his description never actually took place. It is merely a fictional device. On the contrary, '[La Boétie] does not say that such a society could never have existed. ... [W]hat he knows is that before the misfortune, this was society's mode of existence' (Clastres 1994: 175). This difference could probably be elaborated further in relation to other social contract theories. What is the effect of determining whether a state of nature has actually occurred in history or is just a fictional device? Does the latter serve exclusively to justify the existence of power relations within society?

This parallel with social contract theories has a twofold effect, as it sheds light on both the poles of the comparison. By describing servitude as voluntary, La Boétie somehow prefigures the contractual origin of any society organized on antagonism and hierarchy. A contract that takes place as a tragic accident, a misfortune. This coupling of contract and misfortune evokes what Max Horkheimer and Theodor W. Adorno find sedimented in the archaic and enigmatic origin of languages. The contract immediately expresses '[d]eception as a mode of exchange' (Adorno and Horkheimer 1997: 60) as sanctioned by the similarity between *Tausch* and *Täuschen* in German and between *troque* and *truque* in French, respectively 'exchange' and 'deception'. By calling misfortune what for others is a contract, La Boétie unveils the deception implied by consenting to submit oneself to the rule of a master. No exchange is exempted from this unfair deception. Therefore, also the other contractarians are forced to admit the ineradicable presence of this infamous deception. Why is the exchange included in the social contract deceptive? Because there is an imbalanced distribution of what is given and what is received. What is exchanged is the possibility of resistance and therefore the possibility of living according to what nature prescribes (companionship and freedom). What is received is a civil state that constitutes the guarantee of the definitive abandonment of the state of nature. But in La Boétie the state of nature is far from being the undesirable locus of perennial war. The companionship of the state of nature is exchanged with the voluntary servitude of the civil state.

This genealogical approach that reads La Boétie via social contract theory and social contract theory via La Boétie allows the discovery of the political arcanum par excellence: the primacy of resistance. In La Boétie's scheme, the existence of power relies on the voluntary consent to servitude that is at the same time the voluntary renunciation to resistance. Power exists insofar resistance consents to it. The collapse of the Colossus of power could be brought about through the mere resolution to serve no more, namely through the resolution to resist. In this way, power reveals its reactive nature, its constitutive incapability of affirming itself. By the same token, resistance acquires its active dimension. Therefore, the resolution to serve no more that engenders the resolution to resist becomes the (re-)affirmation of natural companionship, rather than a reactive fight against power. The affirmation of resistance does not require a direct confrontation with power. Its affirmation merely provokes the reaction of power. This interplay of active resistance and reactive power can be detected also within social contract theory. By locating the legitimacy and authority of power on the contractual consensus of the subjects, the contract reveals once again the constitutive dependence and subordination of power to resistance. The state of nature represents the permanent threat to the civil state. The contract constitutes the transition from one to the other. At the same time, the contract itself is always under the threat of its annulment. If the majority of those who have subscribed the contract decide to recede from it, the contract becomes ineffective. And, accordingly, the civil state collapses. What does the contract prescribe? Nothing but the promise of renouncing to resist. The stability of the civil state rests upon this collective promise. This unveils the presence of an understanding of power as reactive at the foundations of social contract theory. If Hobbes's *Leviathan* were recorded on a vinyl, when played backwards it would have revealed the masked message: 'Resistance comes first'.

The liberal closure: Securing the necessity of power despite natural freedom

La Boétie can only occupy a quite peculiar position within the tradition of consent theory. As discussed above, he provides a genetic account of power based on the voluntary consent of its subjects. This consent is performed in the material participation to the functioning of the power apparatus: the material constitution of the Leviathan. La Boétie calls for withdrawing consent to power and provoking its collapse. Consent appears as the accidental misfortune that decrees the end of the state of nature. His position definitely shares some features with the hegemonic versions of consent theory, but it deviates on substantial elements. The key problem of consent theory is: '"Why ought I obey the government?" The theorist answers, "Because you have consented."' (Kann 1978: 386). The deviation from La Boétie's argument consists of having prioritized the moral question of political obligation towards authority over the genetic account of the constitution of that authority. The latter, that is pivotal in La Boétie, is obfuscated by the fact that the question of power and obedience is framed in moral terms. This moral turn creates the space for the successive introduction of the notion of rights. 'The Consent Theory merely claims that consent is a necessary condition for there being an authority relationship between a state and its members' (Beran 1977: 261). The authority established through consent is legitimate: as such it serves to explain not the existence of power tout court (as in La Boétie), but only the existence of *legitimate* power, power that deserves the political obligation of its subjects. Consent theory imposes a closure over the naturalistic conceptualization of the primacy of resistance by enforcing the apparently critical principle that only those powers which the people have consented to are legitimate. The inverse implication is that if power is genetically constituted through consent, it ought to be obeyed. Social contract theory is perhaps the form in which the idea of consent receives the greatest attention. Both in its classic version (Hobbes, Locke, Rousseau and Kant) and its contemporary revival (Rawls and Nozick), social contract theory presents an account of power as constituted from below – from its subjects – through a consent that is sanctioned with a contract (Barnett 1986, Lessnoff 1990).

Comradeship as self-betrayal

A comparison between La Boétie and the continuation of that conceptual line led by consent theory and social contract theory is crucial for determining which conceptual elements have provoked this bifurcation. The first step for this task is to define whether social contract theory postulates the existence of natural companionship as La Boétie does. There is a great variety of answers that animate this bifurcation of the conceptual line of the naturalistic account of the primacy of resistance. Nevertheless, the general answer is definitely negative. Companionship cannot be secured without a civil state. Human beings cannot be trusted to behave as comrades. In the state of nature, humans are most likely keen to enter into conflict and oppose each other. Hence the demand for power. A demand that is a sort of necessity but that, as in La Boétie's argument, has nothing to do with nature. Thus, power is interpreted as a remedy for the impossibility of companionship.

Nevertheless, companionship is not impossible but improbable, especially after Hobbes. Companionship requires a minimum of sociality that Hobbes denies completely in the state of nature. Any form of sociality can be instituted only after the exit from the state of nature. Hobbes fragments human nature into disconnected individuals. There is no innate tendency towards cooperation within this version of radical individualism: 'If we enter into cooperative interactions with other people, it is only because we perceive these interactions to be in our interest in some way' (Hampton 1988: 9). Any social interaction has an instrumental value for the Hobbesian egoist individual. It is worth noticing that here companionship has been transformed into a contractual cooperation, with all the limitations that this transformation implies. In the state of nature, these cooperative interactions are rare insofar as there is no authority that can guarantee a just exchange between individuals. Furthermore, in the rare occasions in which cooperation occurs, interaction relies on the irrationality of one of the covenants (individuals interact as covenants as every interaction can be subsumed into a contract).

> If a covenant be made wherein neither of the parties perform presently, but trust one another, in the condition of mere nature (which is a condition of war of every man against every man) upon any reasonable suspicion, it is void ... For he that performeth first has no assurance the other will perform after, because the bonds of words are too weak to bridle men's ambition, avarice, anger, and other passions, without the fear of some coercive power; which in the condition of mere nature, where all men are equal, and judges of the justness of their own fears, cannot possibly be supposed. And therefore he which performeth first does but betray himself to his enemy, contrary to the right he can never abandon of defending his life and means of living.
> (Hobbes 1998: 91)

As the first to perform has no assurance that the second will perform in accordance with the covenant, it would be a self-betrayal for the first part to perform at all. If the first part does perform anyway, it is acting against the demands of rational self-interest. In virtue of the absence of trust, any cooperative interaction depends on the irrationality of one of the parts. In the state of nature, any form of companionship is highly improbable as prudential calculation would recommend the abstention from performing. This amounts to what Susanne Sreedhar calls 'the reasonable expectation principle' (Sreedhar 2010: 42): assuming that all human beings cannot be reasonably expected to respect a covenant in the absence of an authority able to punish those who break it, the rational outcome is to renounce to behave cooperatively. Companionship is not just absent in nature; besides that, any interaction that would seem to display companionship relies on an irrational decision. The deliberative subject that arises from Hobbes's radical individualism ejects comradeship first from nature and then from rationality.

Rational self-interest prescribes to engage in cooperative interactions exclusively when there is a civil power that guarantees that law-breaking will be punished. Civil power is primarily the institution of legitimate and secure punishment. In the absence of a punishing authority, companionship is eliminated and replaced by an oppositional posture. Hobbes's state of nature is a state of war of everyone against everyone, but this war is a cold or even frozen war. Natural equality and natural freedom eventually determine the absolute paralysis of the social. In the state of nature, non-cooperative interactions are as much irrational as cooperative ones. As covenant can occur only occasionally in case one of the parties acts contrary to the demands of rational self-interest, the same holds for non-cooperative and antagonistic relations. If natural inequalities had been politically significant, no battle would have been fought as the outcome could have been anticipated in advance (Foucault 2004). In nature, differences among individuals are minor to the extent that there is a fundamental equality. If the outcome is not obvious before the confrontation takes place, everyone has virtually the possibility of waging war against the other. At the same time though, everyone is as well aware that this possibility is valid for any individual. The possibility of waging war is counterbalanced by the possibility of an infinite multiplicity of attacks. This compels each individual to a defensive posture against possible oppositions. The capacity of action and initiative is neutralized by the necessity of an oppositional posture: action is replaced by reaction. Instead of attacking and seizing the initiative, the Hobbesian warring subject deals exclusively with the indefinite fabrication of paper tigers, that is, declarations and gestures for intimidating the others (Hürlimann 2013). Action is castrated by fear. The creative potential inherent to natural freedom is reduced to the self-preservation of the subject of rights. Or better still, natural freedom is castrated by the fear of itself. Once atomized into individual freedoms or rights, each potential is afraid of the other potentials. Individuals are at once subjects of rights and deliberating subjects. But the deliberating subject among a multitude of subjects that detain their right of nature – Hobbes's name for natural freedom – is condemned to inaction exactly as Buridan's ass. Deliberating which option is better out of two identical ones is as much impossible as choosing among a multitude of indefinitely risky scenarios.

In short, the improbability of natural companionship creates a generalized diffidence among atomized individuals. Their freedom is potentially unrestrained and open to any course of action. But as each individual enjoys this unrestrained freedom, the subject is confronted by multiple potential oppositions, a state of war in which fear paralyses any action. Despite unrestrained, freedom becomes superfluous as opposition is its only result. How to restore freedom then? By managing fear. The contract does not eliminate this fear but administers it. The contract functions as an instrument of control of this fear – the management of risk that Foucault sees later on in the neoliberal governmentality (Foucault 2010). Through the contract, the deliberating subject can assume that covenants are likely to be respected as punishment is undesirable. The subject of rights liberates the paralysed deliberating subject by renouncing to the right of nature. This process determines the constitution of civil state. It is an ascending process that emanates from below, from the mutual fear of those who submit themselves to the civil state. In the management of fear, the renunciation of one's rights represents the price to be paid in order to enjoy what is left of natural freedom. It is a process of subtraction in which the creative potential for action inherent in natural freedom reappears in the civil state only at the expense of its own mutilation.

Where there is non-resistance, there is power

In Hobbes, natural freedom corresponds to the right of nature – the right to all things. The notion of right in Hobbes is subjective as it is owned by the individual and does not imply an obligation for others (Tuck 1981, Sreedhar 2010). A right is nothing but a moral permission to dispose of one's own force. It is moral as it determines what is just. In the state of nature, 'nothing can be unjust. The notions of right and wrong, justice and injustice, have there no place. Where there is no common power, there is no law; where no law, no injustice' (Hobbes 1998: 85). Any possible action is morally permitted.

What happens to the right of nature in this passage? It is transferred to the sovereign who remains external to the commonwealth and retains her/his own right of nature through which she/he can blamelessly perform the right to punish. Unjust behaviours are not eradicated. They are made less probable. Since the promise of punishment renders some actions less desirable, civil power reduces the range of probable actions and enhances predictability. Civil government is the management of fear: the solidity of the commonwealth is inversely proportional to the probability of forces of defiance against civil power. But the fact that an individual does not maintain the right of considering any of her/his possible actions just does not guarantee per se the solidity of civil power. For the solidity of civil power, each individual (or at least the vast majority of the subjects of the commonwealth) needs to promise, on the one hand, that will not consider just all possible actions (transferal of the right of nature), and, on the other hand, that one will not exert resistance against civil power. The distinction may be subtle but it is necessary in order to perceive how the discourse on rights alone is not sufficient to justify the existence of power. The moral promise implied by the renounce to the right of nature ('I will not judge just those actions that are against civil law') reduces the probability of the infringement of law but does not guarantee the eradication of its possibility. In the hypothesis that illegal actions occur with a high frequency, the civil state would immediately collapse as incapable of punishing. Although this scenario is improbable, its exclusion can never be secured. Power is constitutively impotent in these regards. Therefore, the solidity of civil power is founded not so much in the revocation of a blameless liberty, but in the promise of abstaining from that liberty: the promise of non-resistance.

This fundamental assumption is not just at the base of Hobbes's theoretical edifice but is common also to classic social contract theory in general (Baumgold 1993) and is arguably at work in any conceptualization of consent theory. The essence of this natural freedom and what is really at stake in its transferal to the sovereign are resistance. Power emerges through the partition of that fundamental freedom into resistance and (promise of) non-resistance operated by resistance itself. The constitution and the reproduction of power are the effect of a negotiation that is internal to resistance/natural freedom and in which defiance is outbalanced by non-resistance. Power is an effect of the internal differentiation of resistance. Resistance can be transferred as a right but not as a concrete possibility. In this sense, it retains its constitutive primacy over power, understood mainly in moral rather than material terms.

The primacy of resistance is here deployed at the moment of the constitution of power, although the moral dimension evoked by the discourse of rights limits this genetic account of power obfuscating the material dimension of its constitution.

Hobbes's Leviathan: A body without bodies?

The whole apparatus of civil power (in particular its punishing apparatus) eminently requires the active participation of a number of individuals. La Boétie's second body of power alludes to this material constitution and reproduction of power. The sovereign alone cannot impose its right to punish. She/he needs a number of individuals who can make her/his decision effective. By denouncing that the sovereign has as many eyes and hands as those of her/his subjects, La Boétie shows that once the provision of these services is discontinued, power collapses. The second body of power is constituted through the forces of its subjects. As such, they can materially withdraw the forces borrowed to this body causing its destruction. Through the discourse of rights, this material dynamic is obfuscated. Hobbes's Leviathan is a moral artificial body. It is not author of its actions as the (moral) authors of its actions remain its subjects (Orwin 1975, Copp 1980). As such, its artificial body does not represent so much the sum of all its material operations (as in La Boétie): the small individual bodies that compose the Leviathan are those who authorize it to act on their behalf. Its monstrous semblance represents the sum of the rights that these individuals agree to transfer. Power is *morally* constituted from below. The image of the Leviathan is misleading insofar it seems to evoke a *material* constitutive process from below, but the moral dimension takes over.

The privilege of the moral constitution of power attempts to neutralize the political effects of the primacy of resistance that still remain at the foundation of social contract theory. In fact, the introduction of the notion of rights marks an alternative continuation of the conceptual line of the naturalistic account of the primacy of resistance. This path inaugurates a perverted continuation of the line that folds upon itself de facto provoking a complete closure and inhibition of that same route. If power depends on the promise of non-resistance of its subjects, it cannot expect that these subjects will live nevertheless in a condition of complete vulnerability. Can the sovereign expect that an individual condemned to death will not resist punishment? In such an extreme scenario, the individual will most probably renegotiate the balance of resistance and non-resistance. Hobbes transforms the acknowledgement of this assumption into a right. The high probability of a subject resisting death penalty is transformed by Hobbes into a right of self-defence (Sreedhar 2010).[7] There is the reactivation of a portion, although very limited and confined to an extreme scenario, of that subjective right of nature. In that particular context, resistance is not unjust – the subject still enjoys a limited blameless liberty. This move properly inaugurates the tradition of the subject of rights.

The subject of rights expresses a topological tension between state of nature and civil state. The individual becomes a member of the civil commonwealth when voluntary abandons the state of nature. There is nonetheless a part of the subject that is recalcitrant to follow this passage. This part is constituted by her/his natural right(s). The subject of rights, even though member of the civil state, still enjoys an unrestrained potential for action under certain precise conditions. The Hobbesian subject of rights operates in a field of possible actions that is restrained by civil law. But when confronted with death penalty, that same subject can completely revoke the promise of non-resistance. This corresponds to a conditional and limited restoration of the series right of nature – natural liberty – resistance. In precise circumstances or contexts, the subject of rights enjoys blameless liberty.

The right to resist

The right of self-defence is the first to be formulated and is strictly connected to the more general right of resistance. How to negotiate the extent and the conditions of this right of resistance is one of the central debates of sixteenth- and seventeenth-century contract theory (Burgess 1994, Baumgold 2010). Grotius, Hobbes, Locke attempt to lay down the conditions in which individual or collective resistance against civil power can be morally acceptable. What is crucial for understanding how the creation of a right of resistance affects the naturalistic conceptualization of the primacy of resistance is not the different contents of this right, but its problematization. The centrality of the question has the effect of producing a tension between two antithetical polarities: on the one hand, it affirms the constitutive impotency of power – resistance can overthrow power (and in some circumstances, this is legitimate and morally permitted); on the other hand, it depicts power as necessary and omnipresent – only morally corrupted powers can be overthrown, but they need to be replaced by legitimate power. The first polarity engendered by the problem of the right of resistance ultimately represents the acknowledgement that any particular power is fragile and can be overthrown. When power is constituted by the voluntary participation of its subjects (either in the form of moral consent or material operations), it can be obviously expected that such a participation might be revoked. The problem of determining when resistance is morally allowed contains the intrinsic admission that power can never be completely secured and that resistance represents always a concrete possibility.

The second polarity – the affirmation of the necessity and omnipresence of power – reveals how the line of the natural conceptualization of nature folds upon itself and imposes a closure to that line. It starts off by framing the problem of the right of resistance specifically in terms of rebellion against the sovereign and disobedience. It has primarily to do with the problem of violence and the accountability of government (Baumgold 1993). The fact that power is accountable introduces an internal divide within the essence of power. There is in fact a distinction between good and bad modalities of exerting power. More in detail, this distinction produces a detachment of power as such and those who exert power. The modality of its exercise does not affect its essence. An instance of bad government says nothing on power as such; any critique is directed exclusively to those contingently in power.

This is a crucial difference with La Boétie, who radically refuses power as a hierarchical form of organization of the social, irrespective of its possible modalities of exercise. It is particularly interesting in this respect to refer to Locke's condemnation of absolutism: 'The moral condition of slavery ... is the condition of being rightless and under the dispotical power of another' (Simmons 1993: 49). Absolute government and despotic power engender a condition of slavery for the individual. This amounts to say that non-despotic power does not imply a relation of slavery between power and its subjects. Therefore, whereas La Boétie connects servitude and power tout court, Locke associates slavery exclusively to a condition in which power is exerted in a specific way (despotically). The problematization of power is transformed into the question of despotic power: from the art of not to be governed at all to an art of not to be governed by a despotic power.

Their dramatic divergence appears with even more clarity when examining what is the by-product of the latter paradigm. In fact, an art of not to be governed in that way, by a despotic power is immediately reversible into an art of government. Setting the conditions for a rightful resistance means at the same time providing a normative design for the morally irresistible sovereign. The subject can resist in certain given circumstances. But if the sovereign is able to escape all these circumstances, the possibility of being overthrown is ultimately erased from the range of rightful actions. The right of resistance functions also as a manual for the good sovereign. It prescribes how to avoid rebellions and turmoil. Therefore, the delimitation of despotic power rescues power as such from La Boétie's radical rejection. Non-despotic power needs to be secured. In this way, the line that initially departs from the primacy of resistance evolves into the affirmation of the necessity of power: 'any social contract argument works as a justification of the state' (Hampton 1988: 4). By anchoring its overthrowing to determinate conditions, the right of resistance implicitly demands that, once overthrown, power needs to be differently reconstituted.

However, when negotiating the conditions in which resistance can be exerted, there is not just the underlying affirmation of the necessity of power as discussed above, but also the logical implication that, before the right of resistance is installed, resistance can never be exerted and that power covers the whole range of possible actions. Asking *when* resistance is allowed implies that normally resistance is never allowed and power is omnipresent. Power pretends to come first. It is the same discourse that produces civil law that, at the same time, elaborates the conditions for the overthrowing of civil law. Power, which is indeed constituted by the couple nature-resistance, frames the question of resistance in terms of right. In so doing, it generates the illusion that it is power to decide where and when resistance can be exerted, where and when nature can be restored.

From the primacy of resistance to the necessity of power

To a certain extent, La Boétie's radical rejection of power can be said to survive in social contract theory under the guise of a certain antipathy for power. The right of resistance is an index of this mild repulsion. The individual receives (or maintains) a right to resist insofar certain ways of exerting power are intolerable. The necessity of power represents somehow a sacrifice for the individual. Of course, the passage to civil state is overall beneficial for the individual, but it implies a certain degree of renunciation to an original unrestrained liberty. Although power is rational, necessary and legitimate, it always remains suspicious. There is a persisting feeling that power is actually not the best option, but the least bad. Everything is better than the absence of power, but power is not good in itself. It obtains its positive evaluation through the fear that its absence provokes.

Likewise, natural liberty is good in itself, but if totally unrestrained engenders a state of war that is not desirable. This tension between love for natural freedom, necessity of power and antipathy for power structures the whole discourse of rights. Each right is the outcome of a process of negotiation on how to balance these elements. The right of resistance is appropriate for a civil state that continuously sees the proximity of its violent termination. Once power is secured enough against its violent overthrowing and can enjoy a substantial pacification of the commonwealth (a scenario that becomes typical in Europe after the seventeenth century), new rights can emerge. The history of the discourse of rights is the indefinite proliferation of rights, the continuous demand to power to let us act as in nature, while reproducing its necessity. The arts of not to be governed thusly alimented by the discourse of rights are indeed arts of getting rid of power but not completely. It progressively transforms itself into a quest for a power that is able to maintain its existence with the least of extension. The extreme development of this line does not end up in the eradication of power, but in its reduction ad infinitum that promises to never reach its completion.

This particular segment of the evolution of the conceptual line of the primacy of resistance deploys a narrative that inverts the initial assumption of the reactivity of power. Ignoring its material constitutive process, power is assumed to be a sheer fact that has successfully assaulted the natural individual. The hegemonic question that drives the continuation of this conceptual line becomes: in which circumstances, conditions or portions of human life, can the individual subtract her/his range of possible action from the constraints of power? Which segments of natural freedom can be restored? In which enclosures can the individual affirm herself/himself with blameless liberty? Human nature assaulted by power is progressively liberated right after right. Each right constitutes an enclosure from which power is excluded. Natural freedom is restored but only within the boundaries of the liberated areas. Within these enclosures, the restoration of nature corresponds to spontaneous and unrestrained affirmation. This mapping of the social through the creation of natural enclosures that apparently limit power's range of action is typical of the liberal art of government: 'liberal theorists preached and practiced an art of separation. They drew lines, marked off different realms .... Liberalism is a world of walls, and each one creates a new liberty' (Walzer 1984: 315). The fundamental question driven by the antipathy for power is how to expand these enclosures while escaping the dangers that these liberties may provoke. The problem is how much unrestrained natural freedom power can afford before degenerating into anarchy.

Traces of this liberal conceptual turn can be found already in Locke. Besides the right of resistance, the Lockean subject of right is endowed with a larger array of natural rights. It definitely corresponds to a different view on human nature than that of Hobbes. In the state of nature, individuals are keen to commerce and cooperate although there is no civil power. It is only in virtue of the possibility of irrational behaviours that civil power is constituted: 'civil government is the proper remedy for the inconveniencies of the state of nature, which must certainly be great, where men may be judges in their own case, since it is easy to be imagined, that he who was so unjust as to do his brother an injury, will scarce be so just as to condemn himself for it' (Locke 1980: 12). It is a necessary remedy to prevent the collapse of a system that nevertheless would generally function through 'natural law'. The state of nature is not immediately a state of war. The problem is that when an event provokes a state of war, this is irreversible. The only way to manage this potential risk is to escape the state of nature once and for all. Once civil power is constituted, the subject maintains a set of rights: life, liberty and property.

It is debatable whether those rights are inalienable or not (Dunn 1982, Simmons 1983), however the distinction is not crucial for this argument. What matters is that the subject consents to power but does not consent to its unlimited extension. When power becomes a necessity, there is little difference whether it is the subject to give everything but these rights to power or if it is power that allows the subject to maintain them. Although the former is definitely the fundamental principle of consent theory in general, by preserving the necessity of power, its liberal turn deflects the trajectory of consent theory and ends up picturing power as active in its controlled self-dismantling. Rights appear to be given to the subject as a concession. They appeal to the initial right of nature but they are materially promulgated and enforced by civil power. The discourse of rights is spoken directly by or via the civil state. Rights do not oppose power in an antagonistic confrontation but are actively produced and preserved by power itself. They are the effect of power self-dismantlement, a controlled process oriented towards the perennial reproduction of the power apparatus. Rights and civil state relate to each other in a similar fashion. They operate in a process of mutual reinforcement: the preservation of rights requires the necessary presence of the civil state, while the civil state guarantees its own reproduction by exchanging consent with rights. This is the liberal modulation of love for natural freedom, necessity of power and antipathy for power.

Towards the edge, never beyond the edge

Any liberal theory participates somehow to the evolution of this conceptual line. Laissez-faire is the imperative principle of organization that drives the proliferation of rights. It supports the idea that within certain boundaries, unrestrained forces can achieve more than when power intervenes upon them, although its intervention to set the boundaries is necessary. The object of negotiation is how and where to draw these boundaries, which enclosures need to be liberated. The attached problem to this question is to define at which point the stretching of these enclosures provokes the collapse of power and the consecutive eradication of the very possibility of setting boundaries. The liberal closure of the naturalistic account of the primacy of resistance occurs because the proliferation of rights represents an indefinite approximation to the extinction of power and the (re-)affirmation of nature and resistance, which is ultimately unwilling or incapable of reaching its final target. In fact, on the one hand, loyal to its pledge for freedom, it shows a destructive tendency against power implicit in the idea of consent: 'Carried to its extremes, consent theory must consider all political authority tyrannical and anarchism just'

(Kann 1978). It does consider political authority tyrannical, but the positive appreciation of anarchism is counterbalanced by the necessity of power. Indeed, the continuation of this process of expansion of natural freedom can be carried up for instance to the extreme of an ultra-minimum state as advocated by Robert Nozick (1974), arriving 'on the edge of anarchy' (Simmons 1993) without risking to go beyond that point.

It is in virtue of the notion of right that this approximation is prevented from ever culminating into an art of not to be governed at all. The modern notion of right (and this marks the difference between Hobbes and the liberal tradition from Locke onwards) – (Tuck 1981) establishes a correspondence between the individual liberty produced by rights and the duty of all the others to refrain from restraining that liberty. Nevertheless, the duty obviously imposes a certain restrain as well insofar it excludes a certain set of actions. The necessity of power is expressed once again in this tension between right and duty: 'the proliferation of rights is best understood as an expansion of, rather than a diminution of, [power]. The new rights are more about telling people what to do rather than telling them to do whatever they wish' (Burke 2000). The expansion of liberty is immediately the expansion of power. Not only this obfuscates the memory of power as accidental misfortune, but it also reduces freedom to an individualistic property unhinged from La Boétie's discourses on mutualism, comradeship and solidarity.

3

The primacy of labour: Processes of expansions and scenarios of extinction

In the previous chapter, the primacy of resistance has been followed along the trajectory traced after the conceptual and historical emergence of a discourse based on human nature. From La Boétie's natural companionship, the trajectory reaches a closure with the liberal discourse of human rights. But this closure cannot exhaust the eruptive potential of the primacy of resistance. The emergence of another set of conceptual lines animating the trajectory of the primacy of resistance amounts to the problematization of the relation between labour and capital. The indication comes directly from Deleuze. More than a proper suggestion, Deleuze's reference is little more than a hint, an intuition that is not strictly conceptual but more related to the history of ideas. When presenting Foucault's primacy of resistance, Deleuze in a note adds: 'In Foucault, there is an echo of Mario Tronti's interpretation of Marxism ... as a "workers" resistance existing *prior* to the strategies of capital' (Deleuze 2006a: 120).

An echo. There is a relation between Foucault's primacy of resistance and Tronti's primacy of labour according to Deleuze. But this relation is tenuous and left undefined. It is an echo to the extent that the noise of Tronti's idea can be heard in the background while reading Foucault's account of resistance. A distant rumour from another region that can be residually perceived but not fully acknowledged. Not even when Foucault himself speaks of the primacy of resistance, there is an explicit reference to Tronti. Yet the echo is somehow there. Deleuze does not build upon this thin relation and his hint remains at an embryonic stage. Nevertheless, in order to explore the conceptual affinity between Foucault and Tronti and whether there is actually any, defining the relation between the two as an echo interestingly serves the purpose. It does not solicit only the obvious question on why is there an echo. It also opens up a further scenario: why is there *just* an echo?

Tronti's conceptual line represents a Copernican revolution for Marxism (Toscano 2009). It turns upside down the relation between labour and capital both from a methodological perspective and at the level of struggle. Through workers' struggles, labour seizes the initiative in the confrontation, displaying a vital and affirmative independence. On the other hand, capital constantly needs to deal with its constituent subordination to labour that, even though becomes apparent through workers' struggle in a mature phase of capitalism – from the 1960s onwards (Cleaver 2000: 64), it can be retroactively extended to the very moment of its emergence:

> If the conditions of capital are in the hands of the workers', if there is no active life in capital without the living activity of labour power, if capital is already, at its birth, a consequence of productive labour, ... then one can conclude that the capitalist class, from its birth, is in fact subordinate to the working class. Hence the necessity of exploitation. ... Exploitation is born, historically, from the necessity for capital to escape from its de facto subordination to the class of worker-producers. It is in this very specific sense that capitalist exploitation, in turn, provokes workers' insubordination.
> (Tronti 1980: 31)

There is a historical and constitutive primacy of labour over capital that determines a factual subordination of the latter. The relation of power (what Tronti calls 'exploitation') at play between capital and workers emerges as a consequence of that subordination, in order to escape it. Given that capital is a product of labour, capital needs exploitation (a specific set of power relations – institutional, disciplinary, economic, social) in order to establish a vertical hierarchy. Rephrasing this argument, it might be said that the possibility of workers' resistance to the appropriation of their product engenders a series of measures that determine the emergence of a power relation (the capitalist mode of production).

From the conceptual line traced above, it becomes quite evident on which basis Deleuze can talk of an echo that from Tronti, and more in general from those who endorsed the basic tenets of *operaismo* (workerism), resonates in Foucault's idea of the primacy of resistance. There is a clear affinity in the dynamic of the models respectively emerging from these two conceptual lines. Although the forces at stake are different (power and resistance on the one hand, and capital and labour on the other), the way those forces interact is extremely similar. This becomes apparent by inverting the echo through a savage ventriloquism, by substituting the couple power-labour with power-resistance in Tronti's quote: 'if there is no active life in *power* without the living activity of *resistance*, if *power* is already, at its birth, a consequence of *resistance*, ... then one can conclude that *power*, from its birth, is in fact subordinate to *resistance*'. It is hard to tell whether this monstrous quotation could be virtually attributed to a Trontian Foucault or to a Foucauldian Tronti.[1] However, the affinity of the two models demonstrated through this experimental ventriloquism helps to hear the echo more clearly.

But an echo fades off at some point. There is a certain historical and conceptual overlapping, but this is not bound to last. The primacy of resistance presents necessarily an excess in relation to the primacy of labour over capital. The latter attaches itself on the suicidal trajectory that is constitutive of resistance: the ultimate dream of being superfluous, a becoming-superfluous. But while resistance survives even after its own suicide, emerging in new forms and creating new territories, when labour trespasses the borders historically confining it, it vanishes forever: an irrecoverable extinction. Once capital is defeated, capitalism collapses and labour is finally liberated: will it still be meaningful to speak of labour? Labour, orphan of its antagonistic other, becomes synonymous to (human) action, capacity of action, force. It loses its economic boundaries and flows indefinitely throughout all the spheres of human and non-human interactions. An expansion that overcomes all the thresholds ultimately constitutes an extinction. But before approaching this extinction, what is worthwhile rescuing is the process of expansion that the primacy of labour brings about.

Tronti and Autonomous Marxism in general represent the apex of this expansive trajectory. The concepts of the refusal of work and of self-valorization eminently target a reductive conception of labour. In political economy, already in the work of Smith and Ricardo, labour represents one factor of production that interacts with land and capital. It circumscribes labour to the amount of work invested in a specific production. It is considered labour, and therefore a source of value, only that specific amount that immediately participates to the labour process. 'In political economy labour appears only in the form of wage-earning activity' (Marx 1959: 30). In the capitalist mode of production, the wage has the additional function of defining what labour is: where there is wage, there is labour. It constitutes a limitation to the concept of labour insofar as the wage introduces a rigid delimitation of the range of human activities that concur to the economy. What is not rewarded with a wage is excluded from the economic realm.

The feminist tradition adds up an emphasis on housework, care, etc. as proper forms of labour that demand to be rewarded. This is a call for recognition, for recognizing that the immediate labour process is supported by a larger array of works that are not traditionally recognized as such. Gibson-Graham (2006) and their community economy perspective continue this tradition in a double fashion. On the one hand, an extensive account of labour emerges from a descriptive stance: capitalism is the top of the iceberg in the economic landscape and a great share of work occurs outside it. On the other hand, this stance turns normative: as the extended version of labour is fundamental for capitalism, it must be considered as an autonomous and independent resource that needs to be cultivated and enhanced. Nevertheless, in order to avoid any romantic appeal to a conception of labour somehow tainted by the remnants of a certain 'work ethic from below' (Weeks 2011: 59), it is necessary to start off with Arendt and with what she calls 'the modern victory of labour'. Here, labour is not analysed in its antagonism with capital, but as a circumscribed range of human life distinct from action and work. Rather than a desirable outcome to pursue, the expansive process that Arendt describes bears the marks of an already attained predicament: labour has already absorbed all the spheres of human life. The modern victory of labour constitutes a loss, a regression, something that gets really close to La Boétie's denaturation.

Arendt's diffidence towards labour is a warning against the possible deviations that this expansive tendency of the primacy of labour can take. But in a way, it constitutes somehow also a prefiguration of the way in which this expansive process turns into a movement of extensification that moves away from its initial emancipative character. The contemporary neoliberal phase of capitalism presents a radical transformation of the conditions in which the various conceptual lines of the primacy of labour have operated. The process of biofinancialization is the apex of a constant restructuration of capital and its discourses in response to the antagonism of the affirmative force of labour. While it criticizes both the reduction of labour to wage and the extraction of value from the labour process, it exploits this extension by extracting value from the totality of life. Whereas in the Autonomia's call, it is the capitalist regime that prevents the identification of labour with the fullness of life, biofinancialization realizes this identity exactly at the core of that regime. Labour is extensified in order to intensify its exploitation. The reactive character of capital is also displayed in the modality in which its own conceptual lines are deployed. Neoliberal discourse exploits the lines of the primacy of labour and imposes a closure on them. This leads to another scenario of extinction, although radically opposed to the one somehow implied by the Autonomist tradition and by the community economy perspective. Under biofinancialization, labour disappears through its transformation into human capital or, more precisely, into competing individual human capitals: the ultimate effacement of antagonism.

Arendt's (unwanted) primacy of labour

In *The Human Condition*, Arendt seems to announce that the primacy of labour is what characterizes modernity. In comparison with the other accounts that will be presented later on in the chapter, here the primacy of labour is already actualized. It does not function as a driving force towards a better future, but it is the hallmark of a dreadful present. For Arendt, the victory of labour means the regression of human being to a mere *animal laborans*. Nevertheless, this primacy of labour as the disgraceful product of modernity rests upon a completely different definition of labour elaborated through its relation to the human condition in general. In order to include Arendt's version into the development of the wider conceptual line of the primacy of labour, it is crucial to establish, whether possible, a certain commensurability with the other approaches. In the autonomist discourse, labour is understood as an antagonistic force both against capital in the labour process and against the capitalist in the class struggle (with an intimate relation between these two confrontations). Arendt treats labour from a radically different perspective, although it is hard defining this perspective with a simple label. Her definition of labour brings together etymological considerations on the word, the historical evolution of its meaning and the evolution of its value in relation to other human activities in the history of theology and philosophy.

The trajectory that constitutes the definition of labour is inextricably related to a series of activities that circumscribe its extent. The first distinction is that between *vita activa* and *vita contemplativa* (*bios theoretikos*). The latter consists of 'the experience of the eternal' (Arendt 1998: 20) and is regarded as the highest way of life throughout the ancient Greek discourse (as in Plato and Aristotle) and in early Christianity (as in Augustine). On the other hand, *vita activa* is defined as a way of life that is inferior and subordinated to contemplation:

> Traditionally and up to the beginning of the modern age, the term *vita activa* never lost its negative connotation of 'un-quiet,' *nec-otium, a-skholia*. ... The primacy of contemplation over activity rests on the conviction that no work of human hands can equal in beauty and truth the physical *kosmos*, which swings in itself in changeless eternity without any interference or assistance from outside, from man or god.
>
> (Arendt 1998: 15)

Labour obviously belongs to *vita activa* but it does not fully correspond with that. In fact, within *vita activa*, labour is distinguished both from work and from action. As labour and work emerge out of necessity, action remains the highest activity available within *vita activa* insofar as it bears the hallmark of freedom. Action coincides with political activity as performed in the Greek *polis* and in the Roman *res publica*. In short, there is a clearly defined range of human activities that is excluded from the realm of labour.

What deserves particular attention though is the distinction between labour and work. In the discourses explored in the rest of this chapter, there is ultimately no trace left of this distinction and the two terms are used interchangeably. Arendt is aware of the modern irrelevance of the distinction. Nevertheless, the existence of this distinction survives in the very fact that several modern European languages maintain two different words (work and labour, *Werk* and *Arbeit*, *oeuvre* and *travail*) for indicating approximately the same activity. Arendt recuperates the distinction between work and labour by looking at their respective etymologies. While work is related to fabrication, craftsmanship and artistic production, labour 'always had been connected with hardly bearable "toil and trouble," with effort and pain and, consequently, with a deformation of the human body, so that only extreme misery and poverty could be its source' (Arendt 1998: 48). From this distinction sedimented into various languages, Arendt explores their lost meaning and the history of the transformations that have somehow determined the overlapping of work and labour or, better still, the absorption of work into labour and the modern 'victory of the *animal laborans*' (Arendt 1998: 313). To an extent, this seems to represent an ambivalent form of the primacy of labour.

Labour has eminently to do with natural necessity understood in a strictly biological sense. It is what guarantees the reproduction of the human body and of the species. As such, it responds to a series of vital necessities that are imposed by the natural cycle of life that is common to any organic being. Any human life is conditioned by those necessities and labour is the activity that corresponds to them. The negative connotation that accompanies labour throughout ancient philosophy up to modern times is the absence of freedom that natural necessity determines. Labour is felt as a burden not primarily because of the effort and the fatigue of the activity as such. Rather, the toil and trouble lie in the fact that necessity deprives human beings qua species of the possibility of freely abstaining from labour. In the realm of necessity there is no freedom. The Greek *polis* fulfils this specific idea of freedom through slavery. Citizens are free and can participate to the political life of the *polis* only because they do not have to care for their own biological necessities. The labour of the slave creates the material conditions for the emancipation of the citizens from the toil and trouble imposed by natural necessity.

Does work arise out of necessity too? Partly yes, insofar it eases the labouring effort through the production of tools and instruments. But work occupies a higher rank in human activities because necessity does not constitute its primary concern. Labour already suffices to respond to vital and biological necessities. Work comes in support of labour in this enterprise by producing tools and instruments. But the products of work are not strictly necessary as the natural reproduction of human life can be guaranteed by mere labour. Work is primarily instrumental insofar as it serves purposes and ends that are external to nature and the necessities it imposes upon human beings. In the production of tools and instruments for instance, work serves the purpose of easing labour: it is not immediately concerned with the needs of biological life.

The discourse on the respective ends of labour and work is extended also to the qualities of their respective outputs. In particular, the discriminating quality is durability. Both labour and work produce objects, but their durability is radically different. On the one hand, labour produces objects for immediate consumption, where consumption equals the destruction of that same object. The products of labour do not last and are immediately metabolized by the body's life process. After the object is produced and consumed, the object disappears and leaves no trace behind it: 'It is indeed the mark of all laboring that it leaves nothing behind, that the result of its effort is almost as quickly consumed as the effort is spent. And yet this effort, despite its futility, is born of a great urgency and motivated by a more powerful drive than anything else, because life itself depends upon it' (Arendt 1998: 87). The objects produced by labour are necessary but futile because they lack durability. On the other hand, work produces durable objects because they are not destined to consumption but to use. This is already clear from the example of instruments and tools. These objects are used in other processes, but their use does not exhaust the possibility of reusing them. The objects of work are meant to last. In virtue of their durability, they are subtracted from the natural cycle of human bodies and they come to constitute what Arendt calls the world, that is, the human artefacts that transcend the futility of singular mortal lives and install permanence and durability in the midst of (and partly against) human natural processes. Work emanates somehow from a capacity that is eminently human, namely the 'capacity for their immortal deed' that is the 'ability to leave nonpersihable traces behind' (Arendt 1998: 19). This capacity intrinsic to work manifests itself most clearly in the work of art, the objects that transcends the mortal life of the artist and is not subjected to consumption and its inherent annihilation. In short, 'what consumer goods are for the life of man, use objects are for his world' (Arendt 1998: 94), where life is the overall biological process of nature as distinguished from the artificial and inorganic artefacts that are not subjected to this cycle.

Strictly connected with the different durability of the objects that work and labour produce, there is a further distinction that separates the two: their operative modalities. Work is performed in order to produce durable use objects. The object of work can be considered the immediate end of production in the sense that, even in the case of instruments or tools that are produced for an external end, the work itself achieves its completion when the product is finished and ready to be used. The durability of these use objects guarantees their relative permanence. This temporarily suspends the need for which the object was produced. Once a table has been produced, there is no immediate need for another one and work is over. On the other hand, what labour produces is destined to immediate consumption. This satisfies the immediate need, but it does not prevent its cyclical re-emergence: 'unlike working, whose end has come when the object is finished, ready to be added to the common world of things, laboring always moves in the same circle, which is prescribed by the biological process of the living organism and the end of its "toil and trouble" comes only with the death of this organism' (Arendt 1998: 98). Labour is trapped in endless repetition as the life of the species unceasingly requires the production of objects of consumption. The necessity of non-durable objects for the reproduction of life imposes the sheer necessity of labour. The labouring process never reaches its end: the termination of labour would interrupt once and for all the natural cycle of life. Therefore, the reproduction of life is guaranteed by labour only insofar as its activity is attuned to the circularity that nature imposes. This circularity is radically opposed to the linearity of work: its termination is the production of a durable object virtually subtracted to the natural cycle as its use does not imply its annihilation.

The modern victory of labour

According to Arendt, the pre-modern distinction of labour and work is primarily structured upon a series of dichotomies that regard necessity (biological process vs. world), durability (consumption vs. use) and mode of production (endless repetition vs. finite production). It is precisely in virtue of these distinctions that these two human faculties can be hierarchized. The underlying yardstick for their hierarchization is derived from an anthropological discourse that determines the conditions for the elevation of human beings out of the predicament of their animal status. What distinguishes human beings from animals is the capacity of producing deeds or objects that transcend the futility of its mortal existence. The pre-modern primacy of work over labour rests upon this distinction. Through work, human beings are properly human as they aspire to durability and permanence: *homo faber*. Labour instead is strictly related to the natural necessity of biological reproduction. This necessity is in common with all other animal species. Therefore, labour does not confer to the individual the possibility of elevating herself to the rank of *homo faber* or to the rank of human beings in general. The one who labours, unfree and under the yoke of natural necessity, cannot emancipate from her/his animality and remains an animal, an *animal laborans*. The subordination of labour to work corresponds to the primacy of the *homo faber* over the *animal laborans*.

This hierarchization holds true up to modern times. Arendt explores the historical and conceptual process of transformation that has led to the modern victory of labour and that finds its apex in the capitalist mode of production. To be sure, this modern transformation, which de facto is a reversal of the previous hierarchization of human activities, is presented by Arendt as a process of loss that in addition has sadly relegated action and speech to the lowest rank. Her polemical target is mass production and the consumers' society, whose effect is to establish a society of jobholders that

> demands of its members a sheer automatic functioning, as though individual life had actually been submerged in the over-all life process of the species and the only active decision still required of the individual were to let go, so to speak, to abandon his individuality, the still individually sensed pain and trouble of living, and acquiesce in a dazed, 'tranquilized,' functional type of behaviour.
>
> (Arendt 1998: 322)

In short, the modern predicament is the result of the reversal of the hierarchy of the three fundamental activities of *vita activa*. At a closer look though, what Arendt calls the modern victory of labour is even more radical than a mere inversion of the pre-modern hierarchy. Resting upon a series of conceptual lines intertwining theological, anthropological and philosophical discourses, capitalism determines a quasi-total absorption of the other activities into labour. The victory of labour leaves virtually no runner up.

The primacy of labour here equals to the transformative annihilation of all the other activities: work (and partly action as well) is subsumed into labour. The predicament of Arendt's primacy of labour lies in the fact 'that we have almost succeeded in leveling all human activities to the common denominator of securing the necessities of life and providing for their abundance. Whatever we do, we are supposed to do for the sake of "making a living"' (Arendt 1998: 126). This process of absorption occurs along the axes that have alimented the distinction between labour and work in pre-modern times: necessity, durability and operative modality. The *homo faber* has historically facilitated the task of the *animal laborans* by fabricating tools and instruments that could ease the toil and trouble of labour. Arendt's reaction to this function of support is ambivalent though. She focuses in fact on the danger that this process of facilitating labour implies, that is the risk of effacing necessity by removing the pain and effort from labour: 'The easier that life has become in a consumers' or laborers' society, the more difficult it will be to remain aware of the urges of necessity by which it is driven' (Arendt 1998: 135). If labour is performed without toil and trouble, its subordination to natural necessity apparently disappears. On the other hand, what truly disappears is the drive towards freedom that consists of the emancipation from necessity and the futility of a finite existence. The acknowledgement of human subjection to necessity is the fundamental condition for freedom.

The effacement of the urgent necessities that drive labour and the consequent reduction of work to labour occurs through the two pillars of capitalism: the division of labour and the accumulation of wealth. The former represents the quantitative decomposition of the productive process that annihilates any qualitative distinction. The latter instead follows the liberation of production from the urges of necessity: wealth is transformed into capital whose growth depends upon the cycle of production and consumption and therefore it requires an accelerated rate of consumption. The demands of these two elements (division of labour and indefinite accumulation of wealth) affect both the rhythm or the type of production and the durability of its products. On the one hand, the labouring process as mass production assumes an endless rhythm of circular repetition: there is no finished object that imposes an end to production as it was for the *homo faber*. On the other hand, the endless repetition of this process needs to be sustained by an ever-recurrent needs of consumption; the endlessness of production can be assured only if its products lose their use character and become more and more objects of consumption, or if, to put it in another way, the rate of use is so tremendously accelerated that the objective difference between use and consumption, between the relative durability of use objects and the swift coming and going of consumer goods, dwindles to insignificance.

(Arendt 1998: 125)

The primacy of labour results into an indefinite cycle of production and consumption, creation and destruction. Nothing is produced to last and to transcend single individual lives.[2]

Warning against extinction

There are a series of dynamics at play in Arendt's discourse that can be intertwined with the other conceptual lines of the primacy of labour. The difficulty of relating the primacy of labour as emerges in *The Human Condition* with the other approaches (the Autonomist and the community economy) lies in the fact that they all put forth a different definition of labour.[3] Arendt's perspective is peculiar because it challenges the contemporary understanding of labour and deconstructs the historical and conceptual circumstances that have led to it. She looks at the various conceptualizations of labour from ancient philosophy onwards while relating them to the material conditions and the mode of productions that have somehow facilitated the emergence of these different conceptualizations throughout history. She traces the history of what is meant by labour in pre-modern times and then inserts it into the modern scenario in which the primacy of labour is negatively depicted as loss and regression to animality, the victory of the *animal laborans*. This conceptual approach departs from the etymologies of the word 'labour' in several languages. Sedimented in the word there are already all the features that she will then develop throughout her discourse: pain, effort and even torture (from the French *tripalium* to *travailler*), poverty and necessity (Arendt 1998: 48–80). In short, labour is a necessary painful effort. Although Arendt quotes several other interpretations of labour, her basic definition remains ultimately unchanged. The historical variations of the conceptualization of labour do not affect this definition sedimented in this multilingual etymology. Rather, what changes are the axiological discourses that are attached to it. Her historical trajectory is focused on the history of the ranking of labour, its hike from the bottom to the top among the fundamental human activities that constitute *vita activa*. She acknowledges that the meaning of labour has changed too, but she measures this new meaning against her original definition: 'The modern age in general and Karl Marx in particular ... had an almost irresistible tendency to look upon all labor as work and to speak of the *animal laborans* in terms much more fitting for *homo faber*' (Arendt 1998: 87). From this quotation, it cannot pass unnoticed the negative judgement upon the modern redefinition of labour. Although the material conditions are changed (as she is utterly aware while discussing for instance the industrial revolution or the passage to mass production), she seems to claim that the meaning of labour should have remained the same. There is nostalgia in her discourse, the attempt of conserving an original meaning against the dynamism of a forgetful history.

There is also an underlying moral claim, namely that the original meaning should be restored in order to fully understand our modern condition. This move is definitely problematic as it somehow insulates her discourse from all the conceptual lines that endorse a different definition of labour. Arendt's approach seems to disqualify all non-etymology-based definitions of labour as missing the point. It closes off the possibility of renegotiating the meaning upon historical contingencies. In fact, her ultimate definition (necessary painful effort) implies a series of concepts that are subject to historical transformation. The reference to necessity, even when strictly narrowed down to biological needs, is more problematic that what it might sound. For necessity, Arendt's uses the example of the baker. It might be argued that the baker is inserted in the midst of an indefinite chain of interdependence where what is strictly necessary is hard to circumscribe. As for the painful effort, the easing of labour through the help of tools and instruments tends to strip off pain from labour. This should suffice to make the original definition anachronistic and scarcely relevant. This critique could be extended to the use of durability as index for distinguishing work and labour. In short, the same philosophical discourse she evokes in order to claim a stable meaning would actually be detrimental to that stability.

Nevertheless, there are some elements from Arendt's historical trajectory that respond directly to the issues raised in this chapter: the expansive tendency of labour and an alternative version of antagonism. In the other conceptual lines that compose the trajectory of the primacy of labour, the indefinite expansion of labour is a normative task driven by the recognition of the interdependence of economic subjects. Activities that are commonly excluded from the realm of the economy give a substantial contribution that guarantees the reproduction and potentially the transformation of the economic system. Their inclusion under the category of labour confers dignity to these formerly excluded subjects. In Arendt's discourse instead, this expansion of labour is the already actualized predicament of modern society. A series of factors, whose apex is capitalist mass production, determine the progressive subsumption of an ever-growing range of activities under the category of labour. This process sacrifices the freedom inherent to action and speech, and the world constituted through work. The primacy of labour marks therefore a recession to a state of animality. In short, in Autonomist Marxism and in the community economy there is an expansion to be fostered; in Arendt this expansion comes with a high price and has a strongly negative connotation.

The respective evaluations of the two approaches seem to depend on the difference in their, so to speak, political agendas. On the one hand, there is a project that tackles the exclusion and the inequalities that a reductive conception of labour produces. Arendt's concern is oriented towards human beings in their fundamental condition. What drives her project seems to be the fear of radical uniformity that denies individuals' uniqueness and their singular chance of leaving a trace that could survive their mortal existence. What Arendt rejects of the modern primacy of labour is not exploitation or inequality, rather 'the incapacity of the *animal laborans* for distinction' (Arendt 1998: 215). Her anthropological representation seems to have a sheer mono-dimensionality: a society of jobholders is a society of *animal laborans* and this excludes other modalities of life (work, action or contemplation). On the other hand, it might be argued that this individual tendency towards mono-dimensionality is contingent and depends on a series of historical circumstances. Rephrasing Marx in *The German Ideology* (2001), it might be said that a different configuration of relation of forces could in principle create the conditions for a multi-dimensional human being: an *animal laborans* for one hour, a *homo faber* for two hours, a philosopher contemplating the eternal for the rest of the day. In addition, a further critique to Arendt's emphasis on this capacity for distinction could be on the actual value of this capacity. It should remain open whether this capacity for distinction or the capacity of leaving a trace is actually desirable ends. It would be interesting to wonder whether this praise for distinction is nothing but another version of the effacement of interdependence that is functional to any exploitative economic system. For instance, the praise of the artist and her/his work of art is at the same time the implicit effacement of all those subjects that have somehow contributed to that specific product: her/his parents, friends, artistic predecessors, the producer of the canvas, etc.

Although Arendt's despise for the *animal laborans* remains problematic for a number of reasons, her approach helps circumscribing labour and subordinating it to other activities. Her interesting contribution to this conceptual line resides in this ambivalence that makes her discourse on the edge between the affirmation of the primacy of labour and its closure. Whereas all the other versions that present this process of expansion are oriented towards the future and advocate that very process as a remedy for the contemporary predicament, Arendt sees this process as already terminated and embodying a predicament itself. She perceives this expansion as problematic because indefinite. The extensification is at the same time an absorption, something that annihilates the peculiarity of what was distinguished from labour. This insight can be kept in mind when analysing the other versions of this conceptual line. Arendt's discourse functions as a warning for the other normative processes of expansion of the conception of labour. It is not a matter of endorsing her critique to the alleged victory of labour, but incorporating it as a remark for problematizing an indefinite expansion. In addition, she rightly recognizes that the predominance of labour over all the other human faculties is strictly related to capitalism and its core dynamics (division of labour and accumulation of wealth).

Nevertheless, her changing hierarchizations of human faculties introduce a certain antagonism between each of them. Action, work and labour seem to compete in a challenge for the predominance over the others. She fails to recognize the potential harmonization of these activities (as fantasized in the multi-dimensional human being presented above). Furthermore, this antagonism between labour, work and action seems sterile and more functional to hide other (more relevant?) antagonisms. The uniformity in which modern society is presented effaces its internal antagonism. From the standpoint of the human condition, '[t]he workers today are no longer outside of society; they are its members, and they are jobholders like everybody else' (Arendt 1998: 219) where for workers here she means the members of the labour movement. This somehow prefigures the scenario of extinction that is presented by the folding of this conceptual line. Thinking of the actual antagonism between labour and capital that is inherent in the capitalist mode of production, this equality under the label of jobholders hides the urgency of combatting an exploitative system where few illegitimately appropriate the surpluses produced by others. The idea of human capital and the biofinancialized existence mirrors the idea of a society of jobholders to the extent that they both represent scenarios where antagonism vanishes for the absorption of one pole into the other.

The trajectory of Italian autonomist Marxism

The theoretical trajectory of the primacy of labour in relation to capital emerges in direct continuity with the political and economic context of the post-war decades in Italy. In the 1950s, the resistances that had defeated Nazi-fascism have now exhausted their affirmative force. What is left of these resistances is the myth of Resistance with the capital 'R', the legacy of an experience of struggle crystallized into an icon of heroism. But its crystallization into the glorious event of a recent past severs the relation with its political potential for the present: 'The more [the Resistance] is beatified in the empyrean of political hagiography, the more it prevents its repetition in the terrene materiality' (Roggero 2019: 13).[4] For the working class, the first half of the 1950s represents a moment of crisis in which the movement, profoundly centralized by its traditional institutions (the socialist and the Communist party on the one hand, and the unions on the other hand), loses its political traction. In 1955, the elections of the internal commission at Fiat are emblematic in this sense. Fiat is the powerhouse of the growing Italian capitalism. The defeat of FIOM[5] at these elections is somehow the expression of a diffused passivity of workers and the signal of a successful capitalist offensive.

A rapid industrialization radically transforms the Italian economic and social landscape. The big factories of the North attract a continuous flux of workers uprooted from the agricultural context of the southern regions. Driven by the industrial sector, between 1954 and 1963 national economy is booming with wages growing rapidly and consequent positive effects on consumption. The industrial growth is sustained by a technical reconfiguration of the factory, its machines and the labour process. This transformation affects also the traditional role and professionality of the industrial worker in the face of the arrival of these unskilled young workers especially from the South. The new composition of the working class is expressed in this transition from the old workers' aristocracy to the new figure of the mass worker (as Romano Alquati would put it, in a definition that has been particularly successful in the first part of *operaismo*). Turin, the cold city of the North-West, headquarters of Fiat and its Mirafiori factory, is where this transition manifests more clearly its tensions. The arrival of the mass worker in Turin is met with immediate diffidence and hostility. He is a young man with no prior qualification or substantial education. He is a migrant with a different accent, peculiar habits and a distinct culture. He is not used to the factory and is not familiar with the liturgy of the unions. Thus, the more senior workers, especially those active in the party or in the union, hasten to dismiss the young migrant as passive, opportunistic and even hostile to the working-class movement: 'a reedition of the Paris lumpen proletariat depicted by Marx' (Roggero 2019: 48). The emergence of these 'new forces', as Alquati would call them, disrupts the old traditional schemes of workers' struggles. The novelty of this migrant youth represents the crisis of the labour movement. But it is precisely in that crisis that other new forces, that is new young Marxist intellectuals, foresee the opening of a novel revolutionary possibility.

The international political context sets the conditions for turning the crisis into a possibility or for exploring the materiality of this possibility. The Soviet intervention in response to the Hungarian insurgents in 1956 provides the occasion for manifesting the rupture that splits internally the working-class movement: on the one hand, the party and its orthodoxy; on the other hand, the class and its affirmative force. These young communist intellectuals choose to wager on the class: 'We could respond to 1956 without the constraint of the historic shackles that weighed upon the previous generation; we could seize the possibilities it opened up' (Tronti 2012: 132). At a distance from the party and its dogmas, the new intellectual forces meet those 'new forces' that have just reconfigured the large factories of the north.

The Copernican inversion of *operaismo*

This convergence produces the emergence of Italian *operaismo* (workerism). An important step towards that is the experience of the journal *Quaderni Rossi* (red notebooks). Among others, there are Alquati with his workers' enquiries and his co-research, Negri representing the experiences of workers' struggles in Veneto, the sociological perspective of Raniero Panzieri and the group around Tronti. The rupture between Panzieri and Tronti marks the end of that experience and the proper development of the *operaista* perspective. At this stage, Tronti begins to outline his theses on the primacy of workers' struggles over capital. Panzieri is sceptical of what it looks to him like 'a profoundly mistaken philosophy of history' (Panzieri 2008: 312).[6] From this rupture, Tronti's interpretation will play a crucial role in the trajectory of *operaismo*. According to Tronti, *operaismo* strictly speaking ends in 1967 and is largely represented by the publications of the journals *Gatto Selvaggio* (wildcat) first and then *Classe Operaia* (working class). Yet its conceptual and political legacy traces a trajectory that spans throughout the 1970s and 1980s with the variegated experiences of 'autonomist Marxism' (Cleaver 2000).

What persists throughout this entire trajectory of autonomist Marxism (or of *operaismo* and autonomia) is that axiom that famously turns classical Marxism upside down inverting the order of its main elements: workers' struggles precede and prefigure the successive re-configurations of capital. A century of Marxist orthodoxy had sedimented a messianic faith in an economically deterministic view of the revolution. With *operaismo*, the inexorable development of the productive forces as the motor of history towards communism is displaced from the economic to the political, while its scientific necessity is replaced by the need for the organization of the political will of the working class: 'We too have worked with a concept that puts capitalist development first, and workers second. This is a mistake. And now we have to turn the problem on its head, reverse the polarity, and start again from the beginning: and the beginning is the class struggle of the working class' (Tronti 2019: 87). Like every heresy, the axiom of the primacy of workers' struggle emerges through a return to the sacred authors of Marxism. It is a return to Lenin, to the need of the political organization of the working class – and Tronti makes it very clear by printing Lenin's name in large capital letters with the title of his article opening the first number of *Classe operaia*. And it is also a return to Marx. For Hardt and Negri (2002), the *operaista* axiom of the primacy of workers' struggle builds on Marx's intuitions in the first volume of Capital. In relation to machines and technological development, Marx writes: 'It would be possible to write a whole history of the inventions made since 1830 for the sole purpose of providing capital with weapons against working-class revolt.' (Capital, Vol. 1, Chapter 15, Section 5). Likewise, the introduction of legislation reducing the length of the working day is presented by Marx as 'the result of a long class struggle' (Capital, Vol. 1, Chapter 10, Section 6).

Yet, from Marx to Lenin, and then from Tronti to Hardt and Negri, the primacy of workers' struggle remains at the level of an untested axiom. It is not a single piece of legislation or an unwritten history of inventions that provide evidence for the primacy of workers' struggle. It is not either Tronti's analysis of the struggles in the 1960s or Hardt and Negri's reading of history from below in Empire and their successive works that function as a proof of the validity of the thesis. The primacy of workers' struggle is deliberately presented as a concept that is too busy with its urge to be politically effective to think about its own validity. As Hardt and Negri brilliantly put it: 'We have not offered an argument for it, really – precisely, we have treated it as an axiom. … What is more interesting, though, is the political effect of this axiom' (Hardt and Negri 2002: 13). The primacy of workers' struggle is just an axiom, but it is strategically effective precisely because it is just an axiom. It is a conceptual trajectory that emerges directly out of the antagonism it wants to represent and to which it wants to participate. It is a conceptual line shaped by and for struggle. From its early appearances, the primacy of workers' struggle has attracted criticism for the lack of empirical evidences in support. But this criticism is not addressed directly but it is used to rethink the role of thinking. Out of the early tensions between Panzieri and Tronti, the primacy of workers' struggle does not become more sociological: it does not go to look for the evidences that could justify its content. On the contrary, it chooses to become inactual: a concept that is never demonstrated as it is always busy in anticipating the future, in reading those tendencies within the present, in exploring the materiality of possibilities. This is the strength of the primacy of workers' struggle: an axiom, a method, a new mode of tracing conceptual trajectories.

A decisive step towards the primacy of workers' struggle is the analysis of the relations between capital and labour in the mutated context of Italian industrial capitalism of the early 1960s. Already in the first number of *Quaderni Rossi*, it emerges an attention to the political character of class struggle once capitalism reaches an advanced stage. On the one hand, the working class with its struggles that spill outside the boundaries dictated by the unions and by the party. On the other hand, the collective capitalist as a new figure that reunites the atomization and competition of the individual capitalist. The novelty of this new subjectivation of the collective capitalist as class lies in the fact that its ultimate goal is no longer the maximization of profit, but the reproduction of the contradictions that maintain its own existence. How does the collective capitalist achieve this goal? Through the unification of society, state and bourgeois ideology. And this implies a new relation between the factory and society. Tronti elaborates on this relation through an innovative reading of Marx's distinction between labour and labour-power. In 'The Factory and Society' (which appears on the second number of *Quaderni Rossi* in 1962), Tronti argues that the plan of capital progressively subordinates society to production:

> At the highest level of capitalist development ... the whole of society becomes an articulation of production., the whole of society lives in function of the factory and the factory extends its exclusive dominion over the whole of society. It is on this basis that the political state machine tends ever more to identify with the figure of the collective capitalist.
>
> (Tronti 2019: 26)

When the mode of production of the factory is extended as the only social relation, the worker appears merely as labour-power that can be exchanged in the sphere of circulation. The worker is integrated in society as the owner of a commodity, that is labour-power, that can be sold at the market. All of a sudden, the worker stands alone, atomized as individual, separated from the class. In this way the collective capitalist attempts to dismantle the figure of the collective worker. The collective capitalist aspires to resume those primitive conditions when the individual capitalist was free to contract workers on an individual basis. In short, the plan of capital attempts to naturalize the condition of the factory and its market ideology by counterposing the process of valorization to the labour process in order to internally divide the figure of the collective worker. The plan of capital wants the worker to see itself exclusively as labour-power integrated within the process of valorization of capital. Within the process of valorization, labour-power is productive labour as it produces the surplus. As surplus value is appropriated by the capitalist, labour is productive not for itself but for capital. In this way, labour-power effaces the ontological potentiality of labour as living labour. While this sets the conditions for the conservation and reproduction of the capitalist system, Tronti proposes to see, through the plan of the enemy, the material possibility of its defeat.

As much as the collective capitalist interprets and shapes this dynamic instrumentally for its own partial interest, Tronti engages with that from the partiality of the working-class point of view, adopting that fierce unilateralism that will be the cipher of the conceptual trajectory of *operaismo* and autonomia. A partiality that is immediately partisan as engaged in that antagonism that the counterposing of labour-power and labour attempted to eradicate. The working-class point of view follows the inverse path of the plan of capital. It follows the social relation of labour-power back to the factory where labour-power is no longer exchange-value but use-value. In the factory, the worker rediscovers the potentiality of living labour through the cooperative process of production, which at once is potential source of an alternative mode of production and of conflict. As the collective capitalist attempts to displace the encounter of labour and capital towards society, the collective worker brings it back to the factory, to the labour process and to its immanent antagonism. According to Tronti, only the struggle at the level of production can determine the implosion of the whole capitalist society. But this struggle is not between two elements (capital and labour) external to each other. The transition from the atomization of labour-power to labour as the working class or the collective worker passes through a process of counter-subjectivation: labour needs to understand how it stands in relation to capital, how it is constitutive of capital and how it can turn this relation into an antagonistic opposition.

> the working class should materially discover itself to be a part of capital if it wants to then counterpose the whole of capital to itself. It must recognise itself as a particular element of capital if it wants to present itself as its general antagonist. The collective worker stands counterposed to the machine, as constant capital, but to labour-power itself, as variable capital. It has to reach the point of having as its own enemy the whole of capital, including itself as a part of capital. Labour should see labour-power as a commodity as its enemy.
>
> (Tronti 2019: 31)

In the factory, the worker relates to capital primarily in the encounter with machines, that is constant capital. But the other figure of capital within the factory is the worker as labour-power that once sold becomes variable capital. Thus, the collective worker must recognize itself as constitutive of capital. The potential for antagonism emerges immediately out of this constitutive relation: as capital is materially constituted by labour-power, the reproduction of capital is constitutively dependent on whether the collective worker does not explore what else its labour can do. But before labour can explore its antagonistic potential, the collective worker needs to come to the realization that as much as capital is its enemy, its labour-power as variable capital is an enemy itself. Labour has to acknowledge to be *within* capital in order to then be *against* capital. This all passes through a process of counter-subjectivation, the projection of an extinction that will be evident later on: in order to liberate labour's potential, labour needs to eliminate labour-power, labour needs to be against (a part of) itself. This is the trajectory to retrieve the potential of living labour. In the *Grundrisse*, Marx says: 'Labour is the living, form-giving fire' to which Hard and Negri add: 'The affirmation of labor in this sense is the affirmation of life itself. … Dionysus is the god of living labor, creation on its own time' (Hardt and Negri 1994: xiii). This is labour beyond the imposition of the regime of work determined by the wage relation and the plan of capital. Once liberated, living labour refers to creation and its affirmation expands to the point in which labour coincides with the affirmation of life, namely the potentiality of all 'sensuous human activity' (Marx 1994: 99).

Yet, even under capitalist conditions, the excess of living labour acts already as the potential for subverting its process of reduction to labour-power. This enables a moment of affirmative resistance that reflects the primacy of labour over capital. How does this resistant potential of living labour operate within workers' struggle? There are still the traditional forms of struggle of the official institutions of the working class. But it is outside the unions and, at times, in direct opposition to them that alternative forms of struggle manifest conflict within the factory: wildcat strikes, direct action, sabotage. This creates a problematic tension within the working-class movement, a split between the spontaneity of the new young workers recently arrived in the large factories of the north and those workers who remain instead loyal to the organized struggle of the unions. At theoretical level, this split is mirrored by the problematization of antagonism between two polarities: spontaneity and organization. Panzieri highlights the risks of a thorough endorsement of spontaneity: 'We would end up mistaking sabotage for a vanguard form of political struggle, … while it is the permanent expression of its political defeat' (Panzieri 2008: 313). To an extent, spontaneity and organization are here presented as mutually exclusive and as an index to register the level of conflict that the working class is able to express. Sabotage is the sign that organized workers' struggle has failed and ultimately expresses passivity.

On the contrary, for Tronti and those who follow him after the rupture with Panzieri, even workers' passivity can be the expression of the resistant potential of living labour. *Operaismo* explores the materiality of this potential as a possibility which is present even in its absence. If the resistant potential of the working class is inherent to living labour in its encounter with capital, passivity can and should be read as a specific actualization of conflict. There is no longer diffidence against these 'new forces' represented by the passive migrant worker that does not want to join official union strikes. What does *operaismo* learn from their passivity, from their peculiar forms of struggle, from their modes of subjectivation, from their desires? They learn that these workers express both the inadequacy of the traditional institutions of the working class and the material conditions of its renovation. They express a force that still lacks an explicit political form but begins to trace a direct and autonomous working-class initiative that can decisively leave towards revolution. They are a sign that Marx's old mole is still burrowing its tunnels!

Tronti emphasizes the political character of Marx's thought: the idea of the ubiquity of revolutionary crisis, always latent, potential that can be actualized at any time. There is no inexorable development of productive forces, no economic determinism. The revolution can only be a matter of political subjectivity, of tapping into the resistant potential of living labour: 'revolution has been conceived of as [catastrophic] crash. But the exact opposite is the case – the necessary and automatic crash makes revolution superfluous' (Tronti 2008b: 118) [my translation]. If capitalism will necessarily collapse because of its contradictions, as economic determinism wanted, what is then the role of the working class? If capitalism collapses on its own, why would a revolution be needed in the first place? Tronti's autonomy of the political resumes the political significance of revolution. Instead of understanding revolution as an event, Tronti presents it as a process, the progressive movement of self-organization where the working class constitutes itself as the general antagonist of capital. And this is a process that occurs within and against the capitalist system. As such, it cannot be separated by an analysis of how the capitalist system itself develops.

Traditionally, capital has always been considered the highest point of development in capitalist societies. Tronti's Copernican revolution passes through the radical rejection of this point: 'Today we should indeed find the theoretical courage to say that within capitalist society the highest point of development is ... the working-class' (Tronti 2008c: 290).[7] It is a matter of courage as Tronti's primacy of labour serves to carry on a veritable epistemological rupture that has at once the tactical purpose of generating further mobilization. It is a theory born out of struggle that wants to contribute to that same struggle, a theory of struggle subordinated to the needs of struggle. What Tronti does here is to apply Marx's idea that reality can be understood only from the most developed forms it produces. Capital has to continuously produce and reproduce the working class. The development of capital constitutively depends on the development of the working class. In this sense, it is impossible to speak of capital without accounting immediately for the working class that reproduce that capital. Furthermore, capital on its own is not given immediately as a class. Individual capitalists are primarily related through the mediation of the market. Competition is the cipher of this relation. The becoming class of capital (the passage to the collective capitalist described above) is the political necessity that emerges as a reaction to class struggle. And this shapes its subsequent development: 'At the level of socially developed capital, capitalist development becomes subordinated to working-class struggles; it follows behind them, and they set the pace to which the political mechanisms of capital's own reproduction must be tuned' (Tronti 2019: 65). Capital becomes the reactive element in the relation, forced to respond to the affirmation of the working class through struggle. The bourgeois ideology that poses capital as the motor of progress and innovation is turned upside down through a simple and yet decisive theoretical inversion.

As we have seen in Panzieri's critique, Tronti is well aware that this theoretical inversion has quite an ambiguous relation with the materiality of the working class struggles of his times. Despite the novelty of the forms of struggle introduced to some extent by those new young workers, the early 1960s remain a moment of profound crisis for the working-class movement and the revolution seems everything but imminent. To an extent, Tronti's primacy of workers' struggle does not emerge organically from a cycle of successful struggle, but it emerges precisely despite the lack of a politically organized working-class movement. The primacy of workers' struggle wants to function as a catalyst for two goals: on the one hand, it has to introduce that working-class point of view that allows to see the effects of struggle even where there is passivity; on the other hand, it moves the focus on the political need of organization. The primacy of workers' struggles is the conceptual line that problematizes how the resistant potential of living labour can be aligned to a political form that organize those struggles: 'We may perhaps discover that "organizational miracles" have taken place already, indeed are always happening, within the miraculous struggles of the working class' (Tronti 2019: 71). There is organization within struggles even where there seems to be only spontaneity. And the more we adopt this working-class viewpoint, the lens of *operaismo*, the more we can observe the material power of the working class and its potential of conflict and alternative.

Working-class becomings

The working class appears to Tronti not as a sociological concept, but as the expression of a political will in becoming. Opposition is the hallmark of its relation to capital. Before the working class becomes organized as class, struggle and opposition emerge immediately as soon as the owner appears in front of workers: 'Workers didn't need the idea of socialism to organize themselves and fight against the owner. It was enough to have the owner standing in front of them. ... I don't need the "dream of something" to get the motivation to fight this barbaric form of civilization. It's enough to open your eyes and look at it straight' (Tronti 2009: 55) [my translation].

Yet this immediate antagonism exceeds its oppositional stance. The distinctiveness of the working class lies in its capacity of determining an undivided and autonomous force that implicitly prefigures an alternative civilization. It is not a struggle 'for' a specific society to come. The struggle is definitely given in its immediacy. But it is not even a struggle for the sake of struggle.[8] Tronti is definitely an author that puts struggle and opposition as the centre of his conceptual trajectory. His primacy of workers' struggle seems a matter of opposition. But in the plights of his theoretical elaboration, he seems to leave open a path to detach the primacy of workers' struggle from its oppositional stance. Beyond opposition, there is a moment of convergencies, of collective unification, of collaborative affirmation: solidarity. In contrast with the atomization and mutual competition that characterizes the capitalist class, we find 'a social mass that is not split by internal divisions ... and it organizes its own subjectivation through an instrument that in the tradition of the working-class movement is expressed through the word "solidarity"' (Tronti 2008c: 297). At the basis of its political potential, there is this unifying sociality that is the cipher of its distinctiveness in relation to capital and of its autonomy. In fact, while it is impossible to think capital without workers, working-class solidarity and the material possibility of its autonomous affirmation beyond capital are not just thinkable but also desirable. When we look at living labour as the source of an affirmative sociality potentially undivided and cooperative, the moment of opposition is decentred and somehow reduced to a historical and contingent necessity imposed by the misfortunate appearance of capital.

In fact, the discovery of the resistant political potential of living labour is matched by another discovery: 'We suggested workers, who lived daily their factory-ache ..., to fight. ... Later, we arrived to another discovery: workers didn't love struggles per se. They were forced [to struggle], they were thrown into [these struggles] by the interest of the owner for profit, always produced out of their exploitation' (Tronti 2008a: 45) [my translation]. There is no celebration of opposition, but only its misfortunate necessity. Workers do fight and their struggles force capital to respond. But they would have been better off if capital was already collapsed, if workers were already in control of their lives, their desires and their alternative ways of imagining a society liberated from capital: a society where living labour affirms itself autonomously. I think it is from this perspective that we should look at opposition through a successful expression that has characterized *operaismo*: the refusal of work.

It is a quite peculiar take for a workerist movement to arrive to the refusal of work! It is the ultimate heresy against that 'workerist ethics from below' (Weeks 2011: 59) that have characterized large sections of the institutional thought of the working-class movement. The success of the expression derives probably from the simplicity of its content. The refusal of work is the direct attack to the interests of the capitalist, to the capitalist process of valorization. But it is also the expression of a form of laziness and indiscipline. Why to put an effort into a product that will then determine my own exploitation? Why to produce faster? Capitalists need the worker to provide labour, but the worker has no interest in providing it at that pace, at those conditions, for that wage. The political organization of the plan of capital creates the conditions where the worker is obliged to exchange labour-power in return of a wage. But within the factory, the worker still retains the possibility of refusal. Faced by the request for collaboration in the labour process that comes from the capitalist, the worker can simply respond: no! The refusal of work is not, as it cannot be, against labour as such. Where labour is understood as living labour, namely as sensuous human activity, its rejection is deprived of any political significance. Rather, the refusal of work is against the concrete forms that (productive) labour assumes in specific labour processes. It is the refusal against the reduction of living labour to productive labour and its organization through a disciplinary regime of external constraints. These are external as they do not emerge out of labour itself and its affirmative force. On the contrary, these constrains are the effect of the organization of the labour process operated by the capitalist and prevent the affirmation of a creative process 'on its own time'. From this perspective, the problem with the work that is refused 'cannot be reduced to the extraction of surplus value or the degradation of skill, but extends to the ways that work dominates our lives' (Weeks 2011: 13) and the potential associated with our lives, that is, living labour. The refusal of work becomes an antagonistic moment of resistance and revolt against the capitalist system insofar as the latter bases the production of value and therefore its own reproduction exactly on labour under the regime of work. If work, as capitalistically organized and therefore restrained living labour, is the source of value and of the relation of exploitation between capital and labour, the refusal of work is immediately an attack to the capitalist mode of production.

The refusal of work is implicit in all struggles against capital since the beginning. What changes is the political character of the refusal and how it functions as an element of becoming in the formation of the working class: 'When it comes to the point of saying "No", the refusal must become political; therefore active; therefore subjective; therefore organized' (Tronti 2019: 260). What is then the highest point of development of this becoming political of the refusal of work? It is the moment where the coupling of refusal and demands is turned upside down. As capital has traditionally granted primacy over labour, workers' struggles have always been interpreted as demands: pay rise, shorter working days, better working conditions. They formulate a seemingly positive content through their demands, but this indeed reveals only a reactive posture and the hallmark of the subordination of the working class. The working class demands, the capitalist refuses: 'The subalternity of the working class within capital lies in the very fact that the working class is obliged to ask, to bring its demands to capital, while capital has the capacity and the possibility to refuse them' (Tronti 2008c: 295). Therefore, the ultimate objective encapsulated into the idea of the refusal of work is to invert that situation: capitalism will be forced to bring its demands to workers as it needs them for its own reproduction and subsistence. It is at that moment that the working class will have the capacity and the possibility to refuse them.

Expansion and extinction

According to Tronti, the experience of *operaismo* finishes in 1967 with the last publication of the journal *Classe operaia*. Yet its legacy traces a trajectory that finds a substantial development in the 1970s. Autonomia marks a direct continuity with *operaismo* by adopting the main axis of its conceptual trajectory: the primacy of workers' struggle. Living labour is the active and affirmative force that encounters the reactive closures of capital. Faced by this misfortunate encounter, living labour discovers its political and resistant potential that is affirmed simultaneously in the (unwanted) opposition against capital and in the process of creating alternative forms of co-operation based on solidarity. As such, the primacy of workers' struggle is immediately the primacy of living labour over capital. Its articulation is a matter of expansion and extinction.

Expansion operates through the active force of living labour and is expressed both as the refusal of work, namely liberating time from the task of producing value for capital, and as the affirmation of an alternative mode of valorization: 'the refusal of work and authority, or really the refusal of voluntary servitude, is the beginning of liberatory politics' (Hardt and Negri 2000: 204). In this reference to La Boétie, Hardt and Negri express the active character and therefore the primacy that is inherent to labour and locate the emergence of a becoming of liberation in the refusal of the constrains that prevent that free affirmation of the human creative potential: the refusal of work traces the beginning of the liberation *from* work (Virno and Hardt 1996: 264). Therefore, the refusal of work is also a process of extinction. It represents also the rejection of the mode of subjectivation that promotes the affirmation of a worker identity, which is nothing but the castration of the human potential that erupts out of the fire of living labour. The reference to this potential enables the refusal of work to introduce a positive process of affirmation that invents creation through the (voluntary) extinction of the worker: 'The refusal of work and ultimately the abolition of the worker does not mean the end of production and innovation but rather the invention, beyond capital, of as yet unimagined relations of production that allow and facilitate an expansion of our creative powers' (Hardt and Negri 2009: 333).

This process of imagining and inventing new relations of production or new actualizations of the potential of living labour constitutes a moment of creative expansion that finds its affirmative character in the idea of self-valorization. As the refusal of work liberates spaces and time from capitalist exploitation, it is in those liberated territories, that new relations of social production and reproduction occur (Cleaver 1992). It is a counter-process of expansion as it recuperates the spaces seized by capitalist exchange and enlarges the territories where the affirmation of living labour is unrestrained: 'Proletarian self-valorization is the strength [forza] to withdraw from exchange value and the capacity to base itself on use values' (Negri 2005: 241). Self-valorization consists of a constitutive and affirmative process of invention in which living labour is oriented towards the production of use-value. In processes of self-valorization, living labour is liberated insofar as its actualization does not respond to the constraints of an external force (capital) and its product remains within social wealth. As an expansive process, self-valorization tends towards the complete abolition of capitalism or of any other antagonistic and exploitative mode of production and towards 'the complete liberation of living labor within production and reproduction; it is the utilization of wealth in the service of collective freedom' (Negri 2005: 270). When living labour does not consent to its actualization into productive labour, it expresses its intrinsically social character.

In addition, the 1970s mark the passage from the mass worker within the factory to the figure of the social worker. This implies a new typology of struggle that trespasses the borders of the factory and traverses the whole of the social body: students, unemployed and the women's movement. Out of these struggles, there is a political recomposition of the working class, which is nothing but the extension of the working class to social categories that were previously thought not to belong to the struggle against capital: 'the "reserve army" was not really in reserve at all but actively put to work in the circulation and reproduction of capital (and thus part of the working class), [therefore] the rebellious self-activity of "unwaged" students and housewives convinced the Italian New Left that they were integral parts of the working class' (Cleaver 1992: 8).

The expansion of the political composition of the working class is intimately structured by the challenge to the reductive conception of labour that is built upon its relation with the wage. The 'reserve army' that is no longer (or has never been) a reserve army reclaims not just the political inclusion in the working class, but also, and perhaps more cogently, the recognition of their contribution for capital. Insofar the production of value is extended outside the walls of the factory, capital must account for that. As capital's 'recognition' of the contribution of labour is in the form of wages, the content of these struggles of/for expansion is the demand for wages. In particular, this is expressed by the feminist demand for wages for housework that characterizes feminist Marxism in the 1970s. Kathi Weeks (2011) refers to a handful of publications (Dalla Costa and James 1975, Malos 1980, Dalla Costa 1988) that contribute to lay out and articulate these demands. Their analysis is centred around the family and its effaced relation to the wage system: '[T]he family functions ... as a distributive mechanism through which wages can be imagined to extend to the nonwaged, underwaged, not-yet-waged, and no-longer-waged' (Weeks 2011: 121). The demand for wages for the housework seizes capitalism through a political re-negotiation of what deserves to be rewarded through the wage. And even if the wage is pivotal to the mode of exploitation of capitalism, the wage for women who perform housework constitutes at the same time a form of liberatory politics as it creates the conditions for a potential autonomy previously denied. Indeed, the debate on the recognition of domestic labour has been quite focused on this ambivalence, which is also projected onto the other discourses that present these expansive processes. The ambivalence lies in the tension between two polarizations: on the one hand, the wage is vital within the capitalist society and therefore the feminist struggle around housework needs to pass via the request of wages; on the other hand, the wage would not put an end to a system of exploitation and, as such, it can only ameliorate women's condition in the household, leaving fundamentally untouched the capitalist structure and its modality of illegitimate appropriation. In fact, as a general warning for any liberatory politics against capitalism, '[b]y attaining better work conditions, higher wages, enhanced social services, greater representations in government, and other reforms, workers can achieve recognition and perhaps even emancipation but only by preserving their identity as workers. Revolutionary class politics must destroy the structures and institutions of worker subordination and thus abolish the identity of worker itself' (Hardt and Negri 2009: 334). In short, the primacy of labour has to be articulated by a process of expansion, but it cannot do without a horizon of extinction, that is, the extinction of the worker as given under the capitalist mode of production which in turn will decree the extinction of the capitalist system.

In order to carefully seize this ambivalence between expansion and extinction, Weeks proposes to consider these demands as a political perspective that has however strategic effects in the overall extinction of capitalism: 'the demand for wages was conceived ... as an opportunity to make visible, and encourage critical reflection on, the position of women in the work society – both in the waged labor system and in its satellite, the family' (Weeks 2011: 129). The community economy approach developed by Gibson-

Graham and presented in the following section is deeply indebted to this tradition and as such it is challenged by similar theoretical concerns that at the same time help to disentangle the proximity and the distance from the conceptual lines that animate the other limb of the bifurcation.

The cooperativist principle of the sovereignty of labour

In the project of constructing a language against the hegemonic capitalocentric discourse, Gibson-Graham illustrate the multiform variety of economic activities that constitute the category of labour. Their focus is on mapping a series of practices, rather than providing a definition of what labour is. Nevertheless, there are hints that sketch a rough definition of labour. In line with the rest of the project, Gibson-Graham's objective is to revoke the identification of labour with wage labour and to expand its definition including practices normally excluded from the economic realm. Their section on labour opens with a generic indication of what they mean by it: 'The labor that supports material well-being is performed in many different contexts and is compensated in many different forms' (Gibson-Graham 2006: 62). This is not an exhaustive definition, but it indicates at least the trajectory of its process of expansion.

What kind of (human) actions constitute labour? There are three coordinates implicit in the above definition: the relation with material well-being; context; compensation. There are a variety of contexts in which labour is performed: warehouses, fields, shops, but also in the household, the family and the neighbourhood. The list can be imaginatively extended to any context. Labour can be performed anywhere. Therefore, the task of transforming contexts that are traditionally excluded from the economy by the capitalocentric discourse (e.g. the household) deprives the possibility of distinguishing what is labour from what is not labour by focusing on the context in which the action is performed.

Likewise, the form of compensation does not suffice for distinguishing labour from non-labour, that is, from the range of actions that cannot be subsumed under the category of labour. Compensation can take many forms beyond wages or monetary rewards in general. For instance, 'the rewards for [unpaid] labor may come in the form of love, emotional support, protection, companionship, and a sense of self-worth' (Gibson-Graham 2006: 62). Volunteering is an example of labour that is rewarded with social recognition and the psychological affects that it provokes. But following this line, any action may be said to provoke an effect or a psychological affect that can be considered as a reward or compensation (here this conceptual line interestingly overlaps with Max Stirner's (1995) anthropological discourse on egoism, where every action expresses an egoistic motive).

The relation with material well-being remains the only axis that promises to offer some solid ground for the continuation of the conceptual line of labour. Its appeal to materiality immediately evokes the dimension of production and accordingly anchors this specific understanding of labour to the more traditional discourses on labour. However, this does not prevent the emergence of a series of possible problematizations: what is material well-being? Does it include immaterial practices, affects, aesthetic pleasures, beliefs? Attempting to extract and develop scattered fragments from Gibson-Graham discourse in order to answer these questions, it might be said that the concept of material well-being at play here is in the process of becoming an all-inclusive dimension. There are substantial difficulties in defining the magnitude of material well-being and its difference with life in general. What is problematic in the positive effort of enlarging the discourse of what constitutes the economy is exactly setting up a limit to this expansion. On the one hand, it is extremely valuable and politically relevant to include activities normally ignored or underrated into an economic discourse and to disclose their contributions to material well-being (e.g. housework, care of the elderly, etc.); on the other hand, what requires attention is whether there are spaces of action, practices or possibilities that should be preserved from this expansive logic of inclusion. Once this discursive process of integration into the economic landscape is set, it is hard to imagine a possible way of negotiating what can or should be excluded from what supports material well-being. Exaggerating a radical development of this conceptual line, any action becomes labour and therefore it has an economic relevance. Although it remains open whether this is a desirable effect or not, this move risks to eradicate the positive possibility of excluding any range of actions from the category of labour. On the one hand, it accelerates the economification (the inclusion in the economic discourse) of practices, processes or actions that have no intrinsic economic dimension (though it is likewise problematic to label certain processes as intrinsically economic); examples of these practices might be hints of non-labour, for example, play, love, leisure, pleasure. On the other hand, more importantly, it risks remaining open also to practices and actions that have been historically interpreted as against labour. It might be argued that adopting an expansive practice for the definition of labour finds a conceptual threat in the risk of neglecting the relational and antagonistic character of labour. In autonomist Marxist discourse, labour is the antagonistic other of capital, it provokes capital's reaction, it aims at its own self-organization and the liberation from work. In Gibson-Graham's discourse, the oppositional stance is radically subordinated to the project of positively fostering alternative possibilities. Although this is an interesting strategy that is absolutely sympathetic with the idea of the primacy of resistance as affirmative and creative, within this conceptual line labour is still in need of a more nuanced and consistent definition if it does not want to be completely absorbed by the other conceptual line presented in the previous chapter, namely the discourse of the primacy of resistance based on human nature.

Another strategy to capture a definition of labour in the conceptual line developed by Gibson-Graham is to look at the rationale of their expansive and inclusive logic. Their project consists of displaying that the economy is more variegated and not limited to capitalism and that a large variety of activities contribute to the economic landscape. The ultimate aim of their project is to 'make the space for new economic becomings – ones that we will need to work at to produce' (Gibson-Graham 2006: 60). In particular the polemical object is the capitalocentric discourse to which they oppose a politics 'aimed at fostering conditions under which images and enactments of economic diversity (including noncapitalism) might stop circulating around capitalism, stop being evaluated with respect to capitalism, and stop being seen as deviant or exotic or eccentric – departures from the norm' (Gibson-Graham 2006: 56). Nevertheless, there are some underlying principles deployed in their discourse that seem to be firmly anchored in capitalism. In particular, in the process of liberating forms of work normally excluded from capitalism, what remains unchallenged is a certain ethic of work that is arguably one of the constitutive pillars of capitalism. The work ethic seems to be the rationale that drives this process of including a range of noncapitalistic economic activities under the banner of labour. Yet this critical scrutiny does not intend to reject Gibson-Graham's project. Rather, the intention is to tackle the potential pitfalls of a conceptual line that overall contributes consistently to the evolution of the primacy of resistance as labour.

It has been already highlighted the importance of including a variety of disqualified practices in the economic landscape in order to sabotage the discursive importance of capitalism. What still requires attention is to decipher whether this process is actually driven by the work ethic, whether this work ethic directly sustains capitalism and its reproduction and whether there might be alternative ways to foster alternative economies without recurring to this work ethic. The first step is to detect the ethic of work in the interstices of Gibson-Graham's discourse. Through the mapping of activities that are normally not recognized as labour, they aim to show and tackle the injustice and the psychological effect of this exclusion:

> To include all of this work in a conception of a diverse economy is to represent many people who see themselves (or are labelled) as 'unemployed' or 'economically inactive' as economic subjects, that is, as contributing to the vast skein of economic relations that make up our societies. It is also to recognize the multiple forms of work that most of us (and especially those, often women, who work the 'double day') engage in.
>
> (Gibson-Graham 2006: 63)

There is first of all the expression of a sense of injustice or unfairness against the denial of interdependence fostered by the radical individualism of the neoliberal discourse. Recognizing and fostering interdependence are one of the main conceptual lines that emerge out of their proposal of a community economy. Capitalism effaces the contribution of subjects to the economy outside the relation between capitalist and wage worker. Housework falls outside this category and its fundamental relevance disappears. By acknowledging the contribution of underrated forms of work, the discourse gives back a sense of dignity and self-worth to subjects that are otherwise trapped into a spiral of negativity. As one of their interviewees in an area with high rate of unemployment reports: 'What can I do? I can't do anything. People look at me 'cause I'm a dole bludger – a bum' (Gibson-Graham 2006: 141). What remains problematic though is the way in which the 'production of self-worthiness' is modulated.

On the one hand, it denounces that this negativity related to unemployment or economic inactivity is induced by the capitalocentric discourse and is functional to the perpetuation of a system of unequal distribution (the effacement of interdependence and the appropriation of surplus labour). On the other hand, it tackles the problem while accepting the same ethical dynamic it sustains. In fact, by transforming apparently inactive people into economic subjects, the underlying principle is that self-worthiness and dignity are exclusively connected to the economic contribution of the subject. What seems to pass unchallenged is the identification of inactivity and social blame, the overlapping of being inactive and being a bum. The effect of their conceptual move is only the mere rethinking of what economic inactivity is. Liberating some forms of work from the cast of inactivity does not imply that everyone is active. Rather, it is limited to attesting that the subjects that can be labelled as economically inactive are fewer than what appears through the capitalocentric discourse. There are fewer economically inactive subjects, therefore there are fewer bums. The effect is the mere reduction of the number of bums.

Gibson-Graham's discourse does not take issue with the ethic of work as such. It simply contests and renegotiates the parameters of the ethic of work. In this way it contributes to the idea of work as an end in itself. Work and economic activity in general are liberated from their subordination to consumption or to material reproduction. Through the ethic of work, economic activity is performed as an end in itself, instead of being considered as means for other purposes. Max Weber illustrates how the protestant ethic of work has contributed to the historical evolution of capitalism (Weber 2001). It is arguably functional for a system that is driven by indefinite accumulation. Nevertheless, there have been several discourses against capitalism that have nonetheless endorsed a series of revised forms of this ethic of work. Gibson-Graham's version can be said to collocate itself in this tradition that produces what Weeks calls an 'alternative work ethic from below' (Weeks 2011: 59). It combines a certain labourist work ethic, which celebrates the dignity of wage work, with the work ethic of feminist inspiration, which reclaims the recognition of the social importance of domestic work. This combination does not succeed in evading Weeks's doubts on the effectiveness of this approach for a post-capitalist scenario:

> There is no question that claiming equal rights and opportunities as productive citizens has proved enormously effective as a way to challenge class, race, gender, and sexual hierarchies. But all of these demands for inclusion serve at the same time to expand the scope of the work ethic to new groups and new forms of labor, and to reaffirm its power.
>
> (Weeks 2011: 68)

The problem lies in the suspicion that a mere revision of a fundamental pillar of capitalism, namely the ethic of work, might not be able to actually create the conditions for the collapse of capitalism. It solicits the question on whether there might be other viable ethics that can better serve the purpose of fostering alternative economic systems.

To be sure, Gibson-Graham themselves engage in this task emphasizing the importance for a community economy of an 'ethical praxis of being-in-common' (Gibson-Graham 2006: 88). This is the explicit ethical stance that they develop throughout their book. Nevertheless, it definitely creates some frictions with the ethic of work that lurks in the interstices of their sketched conception of labour. The alternative economic model they foster has its focus on 'the becoming of ethical communal subjects' (Gibson-Graham 2006: 125). What could be explored is whether this becoming intrinsically needs to pass through the monolithic dignity of the economic subject. Perhaps the becoming communal should deemphasize or even ignore the relevance of an individual's contribution to the community economy. The communal subject should probably move beyond the distinction between economically active and inactive subjects and the relative mechanisms of moral contempt that it inevitably provokes. The production of self-worthiness should probably be considered as a collective task and liberated by its reference to the economic contribution of a single individual.

The sovereignty of labour

The previous section constitutes an attempt to detect the conception of labour that functions in this conceptual line and the process of expansion and extensification that is attached to it. As no definition is preliminarily provided by Gibson-Graham, this task has been undertaken through the critical combination of dispersed fragments in the text. What is characteristic of this analysis is that all the references to labour have been so far mainly discursive. In particular, labour has been depicted as a category that contains an indefinite number of activities (or perhaps even the totality of potential and actualized activities) and the effects of social recognition that the discursive mechanisms of inclusion and exclusion provoke. Nevertheless, when presenting one of their case studies – the Mondrágon Cooperative Corporation (MCC), Gibson-Graham add another layer to the conceptualization of labour. And apparently this new layer has less to do with the discursive dimension in which it has been developed so far. In this case study, labour is presented from a relational and eminently antagonistic perspective that echoes more intensively the traditional Marxist mobilization of the term.

The MCC is an intentional economy installed in the Basque region of Spain. It represents a well-functioning example of what Gibson-Graham call community economy, an actually existing utopia that involves over one hundred cooperatives oriented to the formation of new cooperatives fostering the development and well-being of the whole community of the region. For the present research, the focus will be restricted to the analysis of two of the guiding principles of the cooperative that have a manifest affinity with the conceptual line that has been explored so far in the chapter: the sovereignty of labour and the instrumental and subordinate character of capital (Gibson-Graham 2006: 104). This affinity though deserves a careful scrutiny in order to avoid the risk of a pre-emptive identification with the other declinations of the primacy of labour presented in the chapter.

> Sovereignty of labor. Control of the cooperatives is in the hands of the worker owners, and they have a primary role in the distribution of surpluses. There is no distinction made between so-called 'productive' workers (direct producers of surplus) and 'unproductive' workers (office and sales personnel, who do not produce surplus, but enable its realization and are paid out of distributed surplus). All are assured of the right to determine how surplus will be distributed within and without the cooperative enterprise.
>
> (Gibson-Graham 2006: 104)

There is a clear shift in the use of the word 'labour' respect to the precedent discursive analysis. In the previous section, labour functions as a label for a dignified activity, a mark that produces self-worthiness. In the quotation above instead, labour refers to a group of people (rather than to a set of activities) and is firmly situated in a capitalistic scenario. Here labour consists of the workers of the MCC, those engaged in both productive and unproductive activities. Although it refers to a cooperative whose constitutive principle is the participation of workers to the ownership of the business, there is a residual reference to the capitalist system. The identity of workers and owners is what confers sovereignty to labour, but in a scenario in which sovereignty usually stands to the side of capital. The sovereignty of labour represents a principle that stands in opposition to the usual arrangement of capitalist enterprises where workers are rewarded exclusively through their wages and where owners control and appropriate the surpluses produced by workers. The sovereignty of labour has here a double function: on the one hand, it serves the purpose of claiming that the right of controlling and distributing surpluses should remain in the hands of those who participate (directly or indirectly) to the working activity (i.e. the production of surpluses); on the other hand, it implicitly expresses a critical deviation from the capitalist norm that subordinates labour through a predatory mechanism of exploitative appropriation. In short, the relational and antagonistic character of labour, which is scarcely relevant or even absent in the task of defining the discursive expansion of labour to an indefinite range of activities analysed in the previous part, strongly re-emerges when labour is understood in this modality. It re-emerges when labour is understood as sovereign, necessarily implying the existence of something different from labour (possibly not only capital, but any form of exploitative appropriation) over which this sovereignty is exerted. The sovereignty of labour is the sovereignty over other economic forces, agents and/or models. Narrowing it down to capitalism, the guiding principle of the MCC proclaims the sovereignty of labour over capital understood as a virtual group of economic agents that would unfairly appropriate the surpluses of others' labour – a group that does not actually exist in the MCC as the workers themselves control their own surpluses. The sovereignty of labour is intrinsically relational as it makes sense only in a scenario that includes model in which labour is instead subordinated to another economic subject (the landowner, the slaveholder, the capitalist, etc.).

Thus, there are two different understandings of labour depending on the layer that is analysed: on the one hand, the discursive definition articulates labour as an affirmative process of indefinite inclusion that is not developed through its confrontation with another force or agent; on the other hand, the affirmation of sovereignty depicts labour exactly through its antagonism with other forces. It remains ambivalent whether these two understandings require either their combination or a decision on which path to take. There is in fact a tension between these two conceptions that undermines their mutual compatibility. In the sovereignty of labour, the extent of the category is strictly circumscribed and has an expansive orientation only quantitative but not qualitative as in the discursive articulation of labour. In the case study, labour consists of all the 'official' worker owners of the MCC, all those who perform a specific task that is traditionally recognized as 'real work' and are rewarded in monetary form. Despite its strong commitment to the community of the region, the sovereignty of labour does not include subjects who are external to the MCC. For instance, all the housework that is necessary for the well-being of MCC's worker owners is not considered as labour for the MCC. Using the argument developed in the discursive analysis, it might be said that MCC effaces the interdependence and the contribution of economic subjects that perform their labours around the boundaries of the MCC as their form of labour is excluded from sovereignty. Although they might also be the recipients of part of the surpluses under the form of social investments for the community, these forms of work external to MCC are excluded from the sovereignty of labour by having no access to the control of the cooperative's surpluses. If there is a process of expansive inclusion, this is purely quantitative. As a substantial part of the MCC's surpluses are reinvested for cultivating new cooperatives, there is a process of numeric expansion of labour insofar as a growing number of subjects will become worker owners of the MCC. But in qualitative terms, there is no process of inclusion of 'informal' activities under the banner of labour.

Neoliberal closures

The processes of expansion described above exert a critical function that affirms the primacy of labour over capital. But this opening arrives to a halt when an analogous process of expansion is driven by a radically different objective. The closure of the primacy of labour occurs when the process of expansion of labour comes to coincide with a process of extensification in the extraction of value. This closure consists of exploiting this extension by extracting value from the totality of life: biofinancialization. If we maintain that labour is the source of all value and that value in biofinancial times can be extracted by any segment of the life spectrum, we can conclude that labour comes to coincide with our own existence, with our life. Whereas in the autonomist Marxist call it is the capital regime that prevents the identification of labour with the fullness of life, biofinancialization realizes this identity exactly at the core of the capitalist regime. Biofinance occurs through a culture of valuation based on the principle of investment and returns. At the level of culture or intelligibility, labour is captured within this fishnet and suffers a radical transformation: labour becomes human capital.

Extending labour to the whole of life: Human capital

The contemporary neoliberal phase of capitalism presents a radical transformation of the conditions in which the various conceptual lines of the primacy of labour have operated. The process of biofinancialization is the apex of a constant restructuration of capital and its discourses in response to the antagonism of the affirmative force of labour. The reactive character of capital is clearly displayed in the modality in which its own conceptual lines are deployed. In a similar fashion with the liberal discourses of power based on the idea of social contract that closes the line of the primacy of resistance founded upon human nature and natural companionship, the neoliberal discourse of capitalism exploits the discourses of the primacy of labour and closes them upon and against themselves.

The closure first emerges with the theory of human capital, the conceptual line that participates to the trajectory of American neoliberalism from the 1950s onwards. The Department of Economics at the University of Chicago is the birthplace of this new economic attention to human capacities in terms of investment and returns. At the core of this research programme, there is the work of Theodor W. Schultz (1971) and of Jacob Mincer (1991, 1993). But with the publication of his *Human Capital* in 1964, it is definitely Gary Becker the leading proponent of this idea. This research group sets up a process of expansion that tries to progressively understand all aspects of social and personal life through economics: 'human capital was an illustration of what distinguished economics from other social sciences was not so much the object as the approach' (Teixeira 2014: 15).

Foucault's lectures at the Collége de France in 1978–9 *The Birth of Biopolitics* (2010) offer a very interesting overview of this conceptual line of human capital. In a close similarity with what highlighted in the other conceptual lines of the primacy of labour, Foucault sees expansive tendencies at work in the neoliberal discourse:

> the theory of human capital [...] represents two processes, one that we could call the extension of economic analysis into a previously unexplored domain, and second, on the basis of this, the possibility of giving a strictly economic interpretation of a whole domain previously thought to be non-economic.
> (Foucault 2010: 219)

What is the primary object that sets in motion these processes of extension? Labour. The neoliberal discourse closes the conceptual line of the primacy of labour at this very point. It moves from a critique of classical economics and its reduction of labour to productive labour, which appears only as an abstraction through the factor of time.

> Now, say the neo-liberals – and this is precisely where their criticism departs from the criticism made by Marx – what is responsible for this 'abstraction'. For Marx, capitalism itself is responsible; it is the fault of the logic of capital and of its historical reality. Whereas the neo-liberals say: The abstraction of labor, which actually only appears through the variable of time, is not the product of real capitalism, [but] of the economic theory that has been constructed of capitalist production.
> (Foucault 2010: 221)

The strategic inversion of the critique of abstraction (that Foucault refers to Marx but that can be extended in the conceptual lines presented in the previous sections) occurs through a double process. On the one hand, the primacy of labour is obstructed by negating the contingency of capitalism – when the problem of the abstraction of labour is no longer related to the contingent mode of production in which it occurs, capitalism becomes naturalized and effaces its contingency. On the other hand, the naturalization of the contingency immediately implies the constitution of an 'accepted' reality that can become an object of analysis and measurement. What can be critiqued for the abstraction of labour is not reality, the no-longer-contingent reality of capitalism, but the modality in which this objectified reality is observed. The critical object is displaced from the contingency of the object to its grid of intelligibility.

Therefore, the problem with the reductivist conception of labour is no longer related to the castration of the immense creative potential of living labour. Rather, it has to do with the economics and its narrow focus. The neoliberal discourse claims that economic analysis cannot have as its object only the processes of production, exchange and consumption. It needs to expand its focus on the internal rationality that guides individuals' activity. Economic analysis enters in the mechanics of individual behaviours, absorbing what was previously excluded by the narrow focus of classic economics: '[Economic] [a]nalysis must try to bring to light the calculation – which, moreover, may be unreasonable, blind, or inadequate – through which one or more individuals decided to allot given scarce resources to this end rather than another' (Foucault 2010: 223). This is an embryonic 'culture of valuation' insofar the analysis itself assumes that individuals act according to economic calculation and that individual activity can be measured through economic parameters. It is this extensification of the economic analysis that sets in motion that tackles the problem of the abstraction of labour in the neoliberal sense. Labour, under the lens of this extended economic analysis, is released by the constraints of its reduction and becomes gradually extended to the whole of human activity and human rationality. This process starts off with the analysis of labour from the worker's point of view. For classic economics, productive labour is wage labour and the wage is the price at which the worker sells her/his labour-power. For the worker, when accepts the reality of the wage system and of capitalist exploitation, the wage is simply an income and is, as such, a desirable end.

> How can we define an income? An income is quite simply the product or return on a capital. Conversely, we will call 'capital' everything that in one way or another can be a source of future income. Consequently, if we accept

on this basis that the wage is an income, then the wage is therefore the income of a capital. Now what is the capital of which the wage is the income? Well, it is the set of all those physical and psychological factors which make someone able to earn this or that wage, so that, seen from the side of the worker, labor is not a commodity reduced by abstraction to labor power and the time [during] which it is used. Broken down in economic terms, from the worker's point of view labor comprises a capital, that is to say, it as an ability, a skill; as they say: it is a 'machine'. And on the other side it is an income, a wage, or rather, a set of wages; as they say: an earnings stream.

(Foucault 2010: 224)

Here the liberation of living labour from its commodity form is not a desirable future to come but a measurable reality. Labour is no longer limited to the labour-power exchanged for a wage, but the full potential of a human machine that produces earnings streams. As a machine, it is taken into account in the economic analysis not only during its labour time or the immediate labour process. The economic relevance of the machine corresponds to its full existence. Labour qua neoliberal machine covers the whole spectrum of life. Each aspect of the machine can be broken down into its components, which can be in turn valued, measured and inserted into strategic calculations for future desired ends.

It could be ironic to ask what the 'price' is for this process of expansion and extensification, but it might also be illuminating. When labour enters in the economic analysis from this liberated perspective, it turns into a source of returns, a capacity of making investments and producing an earnings stream. The already-liberated living labour that is presented in this neoliberal discourse transforms itself into human capital. Labour vanishes. The primacy of labour is closed off by this anomalous drive towards its identification with the full human potential under the pretentiously neutral guise of (human) capital. Here Foucault refers to a body of literature that includes a series of works by Becker (1976), Schultz (1971) and Michelle Ribaud and Feliciano Hernandez Iglesias (1977). It is definitely impressive to juxtapose the definition of human capital that Foucault extracts from this body of literature ('the set of all those physical and psychological factors which make someone able to earn this or that wage') with the definition of living labour as the capacity of human being, given by Marx in the first volume of *Capital*: 'the aggregate of those mental and physical capabilities existing in the physical form, the living personality, of a human being, capabilities which he sets in motion whenever he produces a use-value of any kind' (Marx 1977: 270). Beyond the striking affinity, there is a discrepancy when comes to their respective ends: a wage or an earnings stream on the one hand, and a use-value on the other hand. When the machine is constantly active as in the neoliberal economic approach, the production of value and the construction of an earnings stream are no longer limited to the immediate labour process. Each activity of the neoliberal machine of human life is somehow functional to the production of an earnings stream. Likewise, every sensuous human activity has a certain use-value. The closure occurs in the moment in which use-value is translated within a logic of investments and returns with pretentiously nothing that exceeds this translation.

With this move, the neoliberal discourse operates the ultimate effacement of the antagonistic relation that constitutes the substance of capital and of its own reproduction. It imposes the conversion of human sensuous potential into human capital and transforms the economic landscape into a competition between human beings qua earnings producing machines, where 'the worker himself appears as a sort of enterprise for himself' (Foucault 2010: 225). Labour and its antagonistic relation with the exploitative processes of capital are completely effaced from the economic landscape. Therefore, economic analysis can be smoothly extended to all the various components of human existence: genetics, education, environment, health care, public hygiene, migrations, etc. This generalization of the enterprise form to the whole spectrum of human existence 'involves extending the economic model of supply and demand and of investment-costs-profit so as to make it a model of social relations and of existence itself, a form of relationship of the individual to himself, time, those around him, the group, and the family' (Foucault 2010: 242). The economic rationality of capitalism loses its contingent character and becomes the principle of intelligibility of social relations and individual behaviour. The non-economic of human life is absorbed and accounted for by economic analysis.

However, even if the neoliberal discourse is able to exclude the antagonism between labour and capital from the scenario that its conceptual line produces, it still needs to account for the possibility of antagonism as such. In the world of enterprises there is still room for deviant or anti-social behaviours: political criticism and economic analysis need to account for and even articulate these instances. There is for instance an economic analysis of the drug market and of criminality in general. But, drawing a connection with the discourse of rights and the social contract of the previous chapter, the political critique of governmental action here becomes channelled, both at the level of analysis and at the level of practice, through the logic of the market and the relations between enterprises:

> [the economic grid] involves scrutinizing every action of the public authorities in terms of the game of supply and demand, in terms of efficiency with regard to the particular elements of this game, and in terms of the cost of intervention by the public authorities in the field of the market. In short, it involves criticism of the governmentality actually exercised which is not just a political or juridical criticism; it is a market criticism.
>
> (Foucault 2010: 246)

This anticipates the idea that, the more these mechanisms reproduce themselves and get crystallized, the more they force social conflict to be modulated and articulated through the principle of (capitalist) economic rationality. The development of these lines and mechanisms condense in the process that currently shapes the social and economic scenario: biofinancialization. 'Financialisation turns "bio" not only because it is actively embedded in people's lives, bodies and their environments but precisely because this embeddedness, this becoming fleshly of financialisation, came to constitute anew how social conflict unfolds and social struggles are performed' (Lilley and Papadopoulos 2014: 6). Activating and developing a series of lines already at work in the closure operated by the neoliberal discourse, biofinancialization constitutes the current form of reaction of capital against the constitutive primacy of labour or of whatever can replace labour out of the range of the primacy of resistance in this biofinancial phase of capitalism.

Biofinancialization

From the 1970s onwards, there have been a series of trends that have determined the rise of the share of capital invested in the financial system. The financialization of capitalism is the result of profound changes in the sphere of production (not only in terms of technological innovation, but also in the cost of labour as a result of workers' struggles), in the international monetary framework (collapse of the Bretton-Wood agreement, progressive deregulation) and in the functioning of the banking system (orientation towards financial trading over traditional outright borrowing and lending) (Lapavitsas 2013). '[F]inance, long an intermediary in the process of capital accumulation, became an autonomous and privileged site of accumulation' (Labban 2014). Nevertheless, the autonomy of the realm of finance is an illusion created through the complexity of its mechanisms and its capacity of virtually generating no resistance. In fact, following the Foucauldian method of using resistance as chemical catalyst for spotting power relations (Foucault 2001), finance would seem to enjoy its autonomy without engaging in any antagonistic confrontation. On the contrary, finance must be understood as the strategic response of capital in its neoliberal phase (Harvey 2005). Finance is not autonomous with respect to the rest of the economy. Even though financial profit seems to be independent from the capitalist process of accumulation, its substance comes directly from a 'common pool of idle money generated in the course of capitalist accumulation but also more broadly across society' (Lapavitsas 2013: 135).

However, this process of financialization does not limit itself to the immediate system of value production and turns bio: it becomes culture pervading 'everyday life, subjectivity, ecology and materiality' (Lilley and Papadopoulos 2014: 1). In particular, it imposes a specific 'financialised ethics' (Beverungen, Dunne et al. 2013: 104) that consistently appeals to investment and human capital. The culture of valuation, already at work in the neoliberal discourse, is developed and articulated through 'the primacy of investment value over other values (aesthetic, use, moral, ecological, material, cultural) that predominantly assess the future monetary profit to be gained from potentially any field of life or the environment. The principle of investment value hinges on the belief that the future is exploitable' (Lilley and Papadopoulos 2014: 3). The mode of accumulation becomes extensified even beyond the exploitation of the singular existence of the worker: 'value production becomes embodied. ... The situated and embodied quality of work includes all things and artefacts that constitute the worlds in which we exist, our social relations as well as the broader networks of the commons that we rely on to maintain everyday life'

(Lilley and Papadopoulos 2014: 5). In the biofinancial phase of capitalism, the productive source of value, that is labour, expands even beyond the borders of human sensuous activity and involves a multiplicity of hybrid compounds and interactions.

This process tackles directly the primacy of labour as understood in the autonomist Marxist approach and the refusal of work. The process of extensification brought about by biofinancialization responsively obstructs the continuation of the primacy of labour in its previous forms. 'One cannot say as an expression of autonomy today "I don't want to go to work because I prefer to sleep". The refusal of work is impossible not only de facto – that is because work is indissoluble from the body of working people, animals and things – but also because it is not desired' (Lilley and Papadopoulos 2014: 7). As production in the Global North has changed profoundly, visionary entrepreneurs can play on this impossibility and on the desire that forms the obstruction by liberating an unwanted space of freedom: 'It is left to the employee alone to decide if and when he or she feels like taking a few hours, a day, a week or a month off' (Branson 2014). Employees at Virgin *can* say 'I don't want to go to work because I prefer to sleep', but they, most probably, will not. There are obviously a number of lines that intersect this wave of 'friendly' capitalism (you might think of Netflix, Slim's three-day work week, Google's 20 per cent free time): installing a system of self-surveillance and self-responsibility that complements an enhanced network of peer-surveillance, the concession of a space of freedom that is way more binding that any disciplinary constrain (Rose 1990), the reliance on a culture and a distinctive ethics that are so deeply rooted in everyday life that even its proclaimed contestation leaves it intact (Beverungen, Dunne et al. 2013).

But the most distinctive character of this organizational strategy is the removal of the classic dimension of extraction of surplus value: time. In the case of Virgin, the working time disappears or becomes undifferentiated from the non-work sphere. Here the extensification corresponds immediately to the process of intensification. The employer requires not just the production of value during a set working time (as classic Marxist theory of value would want), not even the mere appropriation of knowledges, skills and activities that are not immediately relevant for the labour process itself. Here what is at stake is complete devotion, full commitment: not just the primacy of the labourer over the multiplicities that traverse the body, but a body that is nothing beyond work. The liberation from the constrains of a fixed working time contains a clause that would be clearly implicit even if not stated at all: 'they are only going to [take some time off] when they feel a hundred per cent comfortable that they and their team are up to date on every project and that their absence will not in any way damage the business – or, for that matter, their careers!' (Branson 2014). The worker is potentially exposed to a recurrent question that comes in every day before the start of her working day: 'Shall I sleep today? Do I feel a hundred per cent comfortable that my absence will not damage the business, my colleagues and my career?' where the 100 per cent is the figure that any system of valuation will accurately exclude. When work is imposed, there is margin to refuse it. When work is necessary only upon a certain condition – that the calculation has not produced a 100 per cent as a result – then the measurement or the valuation of the feeling of comfort with renouncing to work becomes the only available option. The autonomist Marxist refusal of work emerges in a regime of production in which the individual is an agent endowed with the possibility of determining politically whether to work or not. In this biofinancialized context of which Virgin may be a sort of prototype, the refusal of work is outside the political and outside any antagonistic dimension. The refusal of work becomes a calculable outcome. To work or not to work can be decided after a rational valuation and measurement: it is the resulting number that decides over the political agent.

This is the biofinancialized culture of valuation at its purest. Work and leisure (the day off or the preference for sleeping) become commensurable and find their commensurability in their being both investments. An investment in leisure might determine a series of outputs that affect both the sphere supposedly beyond work (personal relations, family, etc.) and the business, the colleagues and the career. Those outputs need to be valued and then measured comparing the possible returns with the returns that an investment in work might produce. The imperative to work becomes therefore the result of a financial evaluation. Once submitted to financial evaluation though, future gains can come only from a full commitment to work, where work becomes an ever-present dimension even beyond the workplace, when life becomes the workplace. A fusion that promises to be more productive than an old-fashioned extraction of surplus value through the intensification of either the duration of the working time or of the labour process. The complete absorption of life under work is the ultimate intensification, an exhausted intensification that is indistinguishable from the process of extensification.

Scenarios of extinction

In all these lines that engage in processes of expansion, there is a series of elements that alter not just the definition of labour but also of its primacy. These processes of extensification culminate in diverging scenarios of extinction.

For what concerns the trajectories of the critical understandings of the primacy of labour, the scenario of extinction is articulated upon the successive disappearance of capital and labour. When discussing the principle of the sovereignty of labour in the cooperative economy, it has been mentioned that the sovereignty was in that case over the virtual threat of capital. Capital becomes virtual as an external appropriating agency in virtue of its absence from the cooperative itself. This helps deciphering the contingency of capitalism and the radical possibility of its overcoming, but also it hints towards the suicidal tendency that the primacy of labour partly shares with the primacy of resistance. The sovereignty of labour is attached to the direct control and distribution of the surpluses that labour produces. The cooperatives affirm this principle because consider illegitimate the appropriation of surpluses by a single agent (the capitalist, the shareholders, the landowner, the state, etc.) at the expense of others. Labour is confronted with a variety of reactive forces (or economic agents) that attempt to illegitimately appropriate its surpluses. The relations that emerge out of these confrontations are necessarily antagonistic. Accordingly, these relations are contingent, historically situated and open to possible modifications. The sovereignty of labour of the cooperative model is ultimately a sovereignty over nobody, over no other actual force. The illegitimate appropriator of surpluses is nothing more than a virtuality. The magnitude of its virtual threat is inversely proportional to the proliferation of models in which labour is sovereign over nobody. In a utopic scenario where no labour is illegitimately appropriated, the sovereignty of labour is ultimately deprived of any significance. When there is nothing left to be sovereign over, the sovereignty of labour triumphantly vanishes. This is its ultimate suicidal aspiration: the most profound dream of this conceptual line is its becoming-superfluous.

Likewise, the primacy of labour or the primacy of workers' struggle is situated in a historically contingent relation of forces that is oriented towards the utopic absolute and unlimited sovereignty of labour that would decree its self-annihilation. Because the sovereignty of labour that emerges in the cooperative model is nothing but a partial actualization of the primacy of labour. It is partial because the rest of the economic landscape remains substantially constituted by multiple models of illegitimate appropriation of surpluses. Once labour becomes finally the only actor in the economic landscape, that is when there is no actor that expropriate the surplus of others (as the sovereignty of labour in Mondragon cooperative), labour becomes a lonely affirmative force. Labour alone becomes human action and loses its antagonistic character that has made it so prominent in history. A labour that does not have to struggle is eventually no worth of celebration. It vanishes in the joyous aftermath of a battle that proclaimed its ultimate victory. The ultimate victory is again a decree of superfluity.

On the other hand, the neoliberal discourse of human capital brings about a similar scenario of extinction, where labour turns into human capital. The difference though is that this extinction presents itself as a fulfilled here and now, rather than a promising future utopia. The primacy of labour and workers' struggle finds itself blocked by the closure that this biofinancialized present imposes. But the obstruction of this trajectory is not the final word on resistance and its primacy. Its creative eruption explodes into new contemporary openings that power has not managed to close off yet.

4

Power as interruption and the affirmation of potentia: Politics and resistance between Rancière and Negri

Some resistances are sexier than others. While many remain largely ignored and fail to leave a mark in history, there are some resistances that manage to pass the threshold of interest for global public opinion. When images of squares backed by chanting protesters circulate all over the media, we have the impression that these resistances have achieved something so important that they finally deserve to be televised. We tend not to focus on the vested interests that determine whether an event constitutes a news or not. If media talk about resistance, it must be because these resistances have been successful. And this generates a form of enthusiasm that does leave a mark.

> Mass resistance ... marks the politics of the twenty-first century. A series of protests, spontaneous insurrections and occupations and the desire for radical change broke out everywhere. They include the Paris *banlieues* riots in 2005, the Athens December 2008 uprising, the Arab spring, the Spanish *indignados* and the Greek *aganaktismenoi* occupations, Occupy Wall Street, Occupy London and similar occupations around the world. ... Ours is an age of resistance.
>
> (Douzinas 2013: 8–9)

These events have created an impact in our collective political imagination. The way in which these various events of revolt or resistance resonate with each other creates a red line that connects them all and presents them as something new that interrupts the monotony of the neoliberal regime of democracy. Yet what the primacy of resistance expresses in politics surprisingly shatters this commonplace assumption: *pace* Douzinas, this is *not* an age of resistance.

The logical implication of the tempting proclamation of ours as an age of resistance is that the age preceding this one was not an age of resistance. What was it then? An age of power and domination? An age with no resistance? This would betray not only the primacy of resistance, but even the relational character that binds resistance and power in an indissoluble co-presence. The objective of this chapter is to rescue Douzinas's enthusiasm for those political events (and for all those that have alimented a wave of resistance for the whole decade) from a reactive understanding of resistance. Through Rancière's coupling of politics and aesthetics and Negri's coupling of politics and ontology developed with and beyond Spinoza, the primacy of resistance becomes political creation, continuous and spontaneous affirmation. Political resistance makes history: no age can interrupt this eruptive flow.

As a methodological precaution, although political resistances make history, history cannot be the starting point of this conceptual exploration unless history dismisses its events. The problem with the historical or sociological analysis of events such as those presented by Douzinas is that they are over-exposed: full squares and barricades are diluted into an incessant flow of images. This gaze sees facts, rather than products. The occupation of public squares is the fact of resistance against globalization, austerity or whatever is the contingent target.[1] The 'against' is so manifest in the event/fact that resistance remains stuck to a reactive role, a response. But when we look at political resistances as instantaneous photography of a continuous and dynamic flow, the event is finally perceived as product. In order to detect the affirmation of the primacy of resistance, it is necessary to switch from a historical and sociological attention for these macro-emergencies of resistance to a (micro- and meta-) physical analysis of the field of forces in which these emergencies occur. Foucault's microphysics of power contaminates both Rancière's aesthetics and Spinoza's metaphysics: the conceptual line that emerges from this contamination turns history upside down and substitutes these macro-events with the mapping of its dynamics and the constitutive process that the primacy of resistance drives. Once again, a Copernican revolution: an inversion that redirects the attention towards the constitutive and affirmative character of resistance, where the moment of opposition and negation, although necessary, becomes accidental and contingent.

Openness and creation

Rancière and Negri are robust allies for taking up this line in Douzinas and projecting it towards a trajectory that fully reveals and liberates the constitutive and affirmative potential of resistance in the political.

The political trajectory of the primacy of resistance is first of all a profound rupture with any form of dialectics. Resistance does not represent the negation waiting for its supersession into a pacified and conclusive synthesis. For Rancière, the anarchic foundation of the political implies the sheer contingency of any social order and the impossibility of a final closure. A radical openness which for Negri corresponds to the non-conclusiveness of being of Spinoza's ontology. Any idea of synthesis or final organization of the existent is a strategic mystification of the reality of the creative impulse that resistance continuously actualizes. The pacification of synthesis is nothing but an attempt to restrain this affirmative flow, an attempt to conserve and reproduce the existent. Synthesis is ontological negation, a poorly concealed opposition. Resistance affirms itself transforming the existent, pursuing the tracks of the intrinsic dynamism of being. How can this process of transformation and creation be reduced to a mere negation? A moment of opposition and negation is definitely manifest when resistance is exerted. Yet the relational character of struggle must not divert our attention from the constitutive moment from which resistance derives its primacy. In fact, the opposition is accidental and not intrinsic to the development of affirmation. The encounter of confrontational conditions that obstruct the affirmation of the ontological flow of resistance is the undesired moment in which the potential towards transformation and emancipation is dispersed. Resistance aims to affirm itself: any force exerted against another is a force subtracted to the enhancement of being. As such, resistance can often not avoid engaging in struggles and dispersing its force, but this oppositional moment cannot be its primary objective. Even when Rancière defines the logic of politics as a moment of interruption that disrupts the police regime, he hints to a negative dimension, but this is immediately subordinated to a properly affirmative moment: the creation of new worlds through the emergence of new regimes of perception. Resistance affirms itself in this creation whose political character is indissolubly intertwined with aesthetics.

In Spinoza, Negri retrieves this moment of political creation at the level of material collective praxis that forms being. Politics merges not only with ontology and metaphysics, but also with ethics, as an attitude for pursuing these ontological tracks of creation. *Potentia* qua resistance produces being, it is the dynamic element that sets becoming in motion, it is constitution and creation. No traces of negation or opposition can deprive resistance of its creative and affirmative potential. The political primacy of resistance therefore intercepts those conceptual lines that pose labour as a unique source of potentiality that affirms itself against and beyond the parasitical attempts of capital. The primacy of labour and workers' struggle partly overlaps with the political understanding of the primacy of resistance that Rancière and Negri frame in relation respectively to aesthetics and to ontology.

Incessant creation, primacy of resistance qua production: we are deeply in a materialist ground. Yet it is a Spinozian materialism. Imagination reclaims its material dignity and effective reality. It is exactly with the materiality of imagination that resistance projects the existent towards the future. Once again, we are dealing with resistance and its possibility, or better still, resistance and the reality of its possibility. With Rancière, the creation of new worlds passes through the affirmation of non-existences that cannot be heard and cannot be seen but do exist and demand to be heard and seen. With Negri's Spinoza, these non-existences impose their ontological necessity: the inexistent presses on the existent manifesting the reality of its urgency – the present is already pregnant of the future.[2] It is resistance and its eruptive potential that anticipate the dynamic transition. An unstoppable moment of transformation that is radically oriented towards emancipation while being radically open and anti-teleological.

The primacy of politics in Rancière

Rancière's concept of the political is developed around the conflict between two opposite logics: politics and police. He calls them two 'modes of human being-together' (Rancière 1999: 28), but indeed, as it will be shown later on, these two logics seem to define a quite circumscribed sphere that, despite its openness, does not encompass the entirety of possible human (and non-human) interactions. These two logics are conceived of as antagonistic to each other and their interaction determines the organization of a community. In particular, the police determines a system of allocation that politics interrupts and contests.

> [The police is] the set of procedures whereby the aggregation and consent of collectivities is achieved, the organization of powers, the distribution of places and roles, and the systems for legitimizing this distribution. ... The police is thus first an order of bodies that defines the allocation of ways of doing, ways of being, and ways of saying, and sees that those bodies are assigned by name to a particular place and task; it is an order of the visible and the sayable that sees that a particular activity is visible and another is not, that this speech is understood as discourse and another as noise.
> (Rancière 1999: 28)

> [Politics is] an extremely determined activity antagonistic to policing: whatever breaks with the tangible configuration whereby parties and parts or lack of them are defined by a presupposition that, by definition, has no place in that configuration – that of the part of those who have no part. ... Political activity is whatever shifts a body from the place assigned to it or changes a place's destination. It makes visible what had no business being seen, and makes heard a discourse where once there was only place for noise; it makes understood as discourse what was once only heard as noise.
> (Rancière 1999: 30)

The logic of police ultimately prescribes the hierarchical organization of a given community. This defines a certain order of domination. Such an order is nevertheless doomed to be constitutively illegitimate. Any domination reveals its absolute contingency in the impossibility of an *arkhé* that might prescribe a universal natural order. The equality of all speaking beings, 'the equality of anyone at all with anyone else' (Rancière 1999: 15) is enacted by the logic of politics directly in opposition to the existing police order. In particular, the staging of equality aims to disrupt and revoke 'the purported naturalness of the existing order of domination' (Bosteels 2010: 80). This is the disruptive logic of politics that interrupts the order of domination and puts forth an alternative order that includes, counts and accounts for those who have no part in the current order. The encounter of these two logics determines a moment of struggle that does not result in a dialectical synthesis (Deranty 2003), but in the constitution of a new order with a new system of distribution of the sensible that will inevitably turn into a new system of domination and social hierarchy.

Politics does not tend towards the eradication of domination as such, but towards the transformation of a given and historically contingent social hierarchy. In fact, '[a] police order, some police order, is inevitable' (Chambers 2010: 62). And this is mirrored by the assumption that 'Politics will always fail to deliver on promises to implement freedom and equality integrally' (Rancière 2010: 80). Nevertheless, the role that politics plays within the whole of the dynamic appears to be crucial under two aspects. Firstly, if the logic of police enacts an existing and functioning order, the disruption of this order cannot stem from the same logic. It is politics that forces the order of domination to arrest its ordinary circulation. The antagonistic encounter of the two logics occurs exclusively through the interruption that politics brings about through its enactment. The effect of this interruption is the transformation of the present police order into a new one.

Yet this transformation is necessary but undesirable for the logic of police. The transformation is imposed, solicited or provoked by the other pole of the relation, that is politics. The logic of the police order indefinitely perpetrates the divisions and the distribution that the order prescribes at a given moment. The drive towards transformation is not inherent to its logic. Rather, there is a drive towards stasis and conservation, the securing of the current order of domination. If a police order changes (or is replaced by a new order), it is not because it wants to, but because it has to. And politics is exactly what imposes this transformative moment, the dynamism that contrasts the conservative drive of the police order. To be sure, this does not mean that the police order does not have its own drive for transformation. Rather, this drive is activated only in virtue of the sudden interruption that politics brings about. Politics functions as the factor in the relation that imposes a transformation over the other.

Therefore, Rancière's logic of politics functions as the pole that forces the other to change. This designs a certain imbalance in the relation between the logic of the police order and the logic of politics. This does not attempt to undo the constitutive relational bond of the two logics but determines a certain polarization of the antagonistic dynamic around the logic of politics. Can we say that Rancière thinks of politics as prior to police? Is there a primacy of politics over police? The primacy of resistance definitely seems to intercept and perhaps even overlap with the conceptual line that emerges out of Rancière's definition of politics. In this section, I will try to unravel how the conceptual lines of Rancière's politics connect with the wider trajectories of the primacy of resistance; whether they can reciprocally affect their respective paths or whether their lines can symbiotically converge.

From equality to obedience

In order to test the possible interactions between the primacy of resistance and the eventual primacy of politics, it is necessary to look at the specific operational modality that politics displays in its encounter with the logic of police. Rancière's dynamic seems to start with the fact of domination. Either based on arithmetic or geometric equality, there is a natural system of distribution. This is interrupted by the institution of the people, of those who had no part and have no specific value except than freedom, which is the empty property of those who have no value. But paradoxically, this freedom is as much proper to the people as it is improper to them. Freedom is an empty property, which designs the whole of the community while at the same time being proper of that part who has no part. The interruption of the natural order that freedom brings about reveals a fundamental presupposition: that of the equality of anyone at all with anyone else, which is immediately the sheer contingency of any social hierarchy and the impossibility of *arkhé*: 'the anarchic foundation of the political' (Rancière 2010: 54). This equality of all speaking beings constitutes a presupposition both for the egalitarian logic and for the logic of police.

Although no common stage is existing in the world that police defines, an ultimate equality is revealed from the commonality of an 'initial logos that orders and bestows the right to order' (Rancière 1999: 16). This equality is postulated not on logos tout court, but merely on the capacity, inherent to this initial logos, that allows someone to understand the order and understand that she/he must obey to it. On the one hand, equality is the condition of possibility of politics; on the other hand, it also constitutes the condition of possibility of any police order and the inequality that the latter produces.

> There is order in society because some people command and others obey, but in order to obey an order at least two things are required: you must understand the order and you must understand that you must obey it. And to do that, you must already be the equal of the person who is ordering you.
> (Rancière 1999: 16)

The inequality of a hierarchical order rests upon two prerequisites (the understanding of the order and the understanding that the order needs to be obeyed) that in turn reveal a pre-existing fundamental equality ('you must *already* be the equal of the person who is ordering you'). The equality of all speaking beings is totally foreign to the mechanisms that establish a hierarchical order and its relative inequality. Yet, without this equality, 'none of [these mechanisms] could ultimately function' (Rancière 1999: 17). This is what Rancière defines both as the 'primary contradiction' that taints the initial logos and as 'the ultimate secret of politics': 'the presupposition of the equality of anyone and everyone, or the paradoxical effectiveness of the sheer contingency of any order' (Rancière 1999: 17). Inequality occurs both *despite* the equality of all speaking beings and *in virtue* of this same equality.

Rancière seemingly anchors this dynamic between equality and inequality to a dimension focused primarily on logos. Yet there is a supplementary implicit dimension that can be extracted from his conceptual line. The equality of all speaking beings in relation to the dynamic that bonds order and obedience needs to be problematized from the perspective of the practices that support it. Although equality functions to explain this dynamic of order and obedience, is this equality at the level of logos enough to account for the establishment or the emergence of the dynamic itself? The primary contradiction inherent to the initial logos might seem to subordinate the primacy of equality to the inevitability of inequality. But to what extent can inequality be presented as a necessity? If inequality is based on this mutual capacity of ordering and obeying in virtue of the equality of all speaking beings, do we need to conclude that obedience is a practice that is necessarily inscribed in logos? The hypothesis is that the two prerequisites (understanding the order and, more specifically, understanding that an order needs to be obeyed) seem to be historical products, rather than being installed within logos as its necessary and primary contradiction. Accidental and contingent products of history, of processes, of the sedimentation of habits or of the crystallization of relations of force: misfortune.

The first requirement ('you must understand the order') rests already upon a triple ambivalence that presupposes a whole series of practices. It requires in fact that: first, the order is understood as a meaningful linguistic unit and not as a noise; second, the order needs to be understood qua order, a distinctive linguistic unit and not as a whatever kind of communication (this constitutes the core of the second requirement 'you must understand that you must obey it'); third, the order needs to be understood in its content (which particular actions are required). These three levels of deciphering the first requirement all converge towards the necessity of an already existing order. The possibility of understanding that a series of noises is meaningful rests by definition upon a prior distribution of the perceptible. A dog barking does not express a meaningful linguistic unit and let alone an order. This is not because barking does not belong to logos, but because the contingency of the existent regime of the perceptible does not allow us to understand that noise as something meaningful. But imagining that these noises were perceptible as something meaningful that constitutes a command, will the dog's order be obeyed?

Obedience as accidental misfortune

The second requirement ('you must understand that you must obey [the order]') can be explained only through a performative dynamic. The order commands an action to be performed by the recipient. But if this action needs to be the object of an order, it means that the recipient of the order is unlikely to perform it spontaneously. The order is based on the expectation that the other will possibly perform an action that would not have been performed otherwise. If this action is performed, the order is obeyed. Yet if the order is disobeyed, the order does not cease to be an order. A disobeyed order remains nevertheless an order. Rancière's second requirement rests exclusively on the fact that orders demand obedience. It is indifferent whether they are obeyed or not.

However, the coupling of order and obedience needs necessarily to rest upon a specific regime of the perceptible. And this regime cannot be otherwise than contingent and accidental. The order remains an order even though is disobeyed only in the specific and contingent regime of the perceptible where orders are understood as demanding obedience. But the emergence of such a regime can only occur on the threshold when a noise recognized as a meaningful language unit is also recognized as an order. This passage occurs only through the first obedience, the performance of an otherwise-not-likely-to-be-performed action. Reiterations of obedience constitute the emergence of Rancière's second requirement.

Rancière recognizes the accidental character of philosophy, but it is at the same time extended to art and to politics itself. Through this equation, politics urges to be understood as 'an accidental activity. Not as a necessary activity, inscribed in the order of things, … or borne along by an historical destiny, but as a chance, supplementary activity which … could just as well not have existed' (Rancière 2010: 217). Developing this conceptual line perhaps beyond Rancière, the emergence of the two requirements (the understanding of the order and the understanding that the order needs to be obeyed) needs to be explained in its exceptionality, in its contingency as accidental misfortune that could have not occurred.

With La Boétie, the act of obeying is a counter-natural habit induced by the sedimentation of costumes after a tragic misfortune. Understanding that an order is due to be obeyed is the essence of this misfortune, it is what possibly triggers and perpetrates the betrayal of natural companionship and the establishment of a reactive order of domination. With a ventriloquism that reads Rancière through Rousseau's *Discourse on the Origin of Inequality*, we might say that a noise is transformed into an order only once the first idiot voluntary submits her/his action to the will of another.

The very possibility of giving an order (that is also the very possibility of understanding that a noise is an order and needs to be obeyed) would have not existed if nobody had ever obeyed (or if nobody had ever performed an action unwillingly). It is the very first obedience to a noise, on the threshold of becoming an order or a command, which institutes simultaneously a new regime of the perceptible and an unequal hierarchical distribution of police. Therefore, a police order does not need to be presupposed till the moment that no order has ever been obeyed. With the first obedience begins the dynamic that Rancière illustrates, where equality and inequality are intertwined in a circular mutual presupposition. In fact, the circle of equality and inequality is based in turn on the presupposition that orders can be obeyed. No equality on the basis of a common capability of understanding an order as such and that the order needs to be obeyed (Rancière's two requirements) could have ever been found before the accident of the first obedience that transforms a noise into an order. It is after the first obedience that orders can be issued as noises that deserve obedience. It is only this constitutive interaction where a noise is transformed into an order by being obeyed that produces a world in which issuing orders or establishing a social hierarchy becomes a possible logic of human being together.

Equality and inequality form an indissoluble bond that implies mutual presupposition and circularity. Their dynamic interplay results from the moment in which an accidental obedience transforms for the first time a noise into an order. Rancière's concern is legitimately centred exclusively on this particular stage in the history of human interaction, in which orders can be understood as such and as imposing obedience. But if the analysis of the principle of equality needs to be understood in purely logical terms, a fictional moment[3] that precedes the perceptibility of orders needs necessarily to be taken into account. This moment that precedes the bond of equality and inequality does not need to be understood as a historical moment lost at the beginning of time. Rather, it is a radical logical possibility that disrupts the ineluctable character of hierarchy. The conceptual line that derives from this move relegates the principle of equality and its bond with inequality to a historical contingency that emerges out of precise circumstances as a product, the accidental result of a process.

This process seems to remain only implicit in Rancière as his focus is only on the world created by this process. New worlds are continuously created once the dynamic is set up, but they will all fatally share this trait where orders can be understood as worth obedience. Rancière's conceptual line serves to explain the dynamic once has been set up. But the setting up remains excluded from his analysis. Prolonging this conceptual line though, the primacy of resistance accounts also for that very moment insofar it explains also the moment in which noises/not-yet-orders are issued and the moment in which they are obeyed. Equality/inequality does not explain this. Resistance does: the noise is produced as a strategic attempt to impose an action over the action of another. It is only the accidental suspension of resistance that generates the transformation of the noise into an order, the institution of a hierarchical distribution and the possibility of resistance. It is an accidental misfortune that inserts a caesura within history, a radical partition between a world before the coming into being of orders and a world after that.

Interruption comes first

Reading Rancière through the hypothesis of the accidentality of obedience opens up new conceptual trajectories to establish a relation between his account of politics and the primacy of resistance. Rancière defines politics as a logic that has a specific modality of operation whose principle is that of equality. Therefore, they are conceptually distinct and not intrinsically intertwined. '[The] sole principle [of politics], equality, is not peculiar to it and is in no way itself political. All equality does is lend politics reality in the form of specific cases to inscribe, in the form of litigation, confirmation of the equality at the hearth of the police order' (Rancière 1999: 31). The way in which this principle acts within the logic of politics is somehow by activating a specific part (those who have no part in a specific order) that is non-existent in a given order. The universality of the principle appears only through specific processes of political subjectivation and interruption of the relevant police order, that are local and contingent to specific circumstances or social arrangements: 'people sitting at lunch counters did not display the general idea that all people are equal. ... Their actions were more local in character. Their message was, more specifically: we are equal to others who sit here' (May 2010: 76).

Through the process of political subjectivation, in which subjects who had no part behave as though they were equal, namely they enact a capacity for enunciation not previously perceptible in a given field of experience, there is a reconfiguration of the field of experience that creates a world of the wrong (in which those who have no part exist) opposed to the world of police where they do not exist. Politics as the encounter of the heterogeneous, of the egalitarian logic and its opposite, is also the encounter of two worlds within a single world: 'there is not only what there is. There is more' (May 2009: 267). This exposure and processing of the wrong, of the fundamental miscount that institutes community as divided, coincide with the interruption of a given police order by politics and its reconfiguration, its forced transformation.

The interruption operated by politics is always oppositional, but its action is by no means limited to it. In comparison with vitalistic conceptions of the political where action is purely affirmative, Rancière definitely maintains a clear moment of negation (May 2009). Nevertheless, the specificity of political action poses this oppositional aspect as somehow subordinated to creation. Rancière states clearly that politics is primarily about the alteration of the field of experience and the creation of new worlds, 'positing existences that are at the same time nonexistences – or nonexistences that are at the same time existences' (Rancière 1999: 41). Politics operates through the creation of a new world, that is, a new regime of the perceptible with and against the world where the part who has no part is non-existent. 'To have no place within the police order means to be unintelligible and not just marginalized within the system, but made invisible by the system' (Chambers 2010: 63). This part cannot be seen, let alone be seen as equal. It cannot be seen because the regime of the perceptible, or the world of that specific order, excludes that part of those who have no part. It is political subjectivation – the very institution of a part of those who have no part – that determines the encounter of the two antagonistic worlds. The world of politics and its specific subjects are non-existent before this institution. The creation of a new world occurs through the transgression of these subjects, which alters the existent world by counting and accounting for themselves. Before this moment where politics occurs, there is the order of domination on its own. The creation of a new world interrupts the normal course of the police order, the ordinariness of the order.

Rancière finds the concept of interruption in one of Plato's invented etymologies of *blaberon*: 'that which stops the current' – 'the original twist that short-circuits the natural logic of properties' (Rancière 1999: 13). This reconstruction accounts for the historical process that Rancière places at the beginning of politics. The natural order of arithmetic and geometric equality is interrupted by the appearance of the demos with its empty freedom. This founding event has its own precise historical coordinates. But this has a further effect: the terminology and the conceptual representation of the dynamic are tailored precisely upon the contingency of that event. The historical event is projected on the logical dynamic. The natural logic of properties or the natural order of domination is beyond the distinction between nature and history (or nature and custom). In this case, the adjective natural designs the contingent police order that politics encounters at its first historical emergence. It is nothing but the existing order of domination. The order flows indefinitely as a current till the moment when politics pops up and interrupts it. The sequence nature-interruption is anchored upon the historical beginning of politics. The conceptual representation that derives from this move is affected by the fact that seems to introduce a succession of two elements, where the current exists prior to the interruption of politics.

The problematization of the sequence becomes evident in the reiteration of the dynamic. The current is interrupted, but then a new current starts flowing till a new interruption will occur. After the very beginning of politics, the reiteration of the series current-interruption-current-interruption-current ... makes the temporal ordering of both terms ultimately meaningless. Outside of its historical reference, this same series could as well be deployed as a pure logical dynamic or mechanism where the current *follows* an interruption: interruption-current-interruption-current-interruption. Interruption comes first. This series is meaningless as much as the other, but it serves the purpose to highlight even more clearly the primacy of politics that Rancière's model implicitly contains. Presented as interruption, the attention on politics seems to remain polarized on its oppositional character. When politics is presented as a break between two police orders, this creative aspect seems to be doomed to a brief existence. But this contrasts with the key role it plays in the dynamic.

When the order of domination is understood as accidental and historically contingent, politics can fully express its creative role and its necessary primacy. The order of domination is not the current: it is what interrupts the flow of creative becoming.[4] Politics is what restores this creative current by reshuffling the perceptible through the creation of a new world, a new distribution of the perceptible in which those who had no part can be heard and seen. Politics is the current that makes worlds. Domination is what interrupts the current of creation through the perpetuation of the existent. This radical inversion emphasizes how the primacy of resistance and the primacy of politics extracted by Rancière can overlap upon an operational modality that privileges creation over opposition.

Political resistance creates worlds

The inverted drama of interruption and restoration reveals the accidental and historically contingent character of any police order. What still requires attention is the process that leads to the emergence of politics (as restoration of the creative flow and as interruption of a given police order). The order of domination corresponds to a world in which the political-subjects-to-be do not exist yet. They are not counted or accounted for by that police order. Yet their non-existence must still consist of something that will then constitute political subjects. What is the substance or the material that is transformed into political subjects? Why does this transformation occur?

> A mode of subjectivation does not create subjects ex nihilo; it creates them by transforming identities defined in the natural order of the allocation of functions and places into instances of experience of a dispute. ... Any subjectivation is a disidentification, removal from the naturalness of a place.
>
> (Rancière 1999: 36)

The identities given by the police order are the substance that is transformed through political subjectivation. These identities correspond to roles or positions in the distribution of the order of the perceptible. The process of subjectivation starts when these identities remove themselves from their allocated places and define new patterns, new connections, new combinations. 'A political subject is not a group that "becomes aware" of itself. ... It is an operator that connects and disconnects different areas, regions, identities, functions, and capacities existing in the configuration of a given experience' (Rancière 1999: 40). There is a creative reshuffling of these identities that confronts the given police order. At the core of this process there is the refusal of the allocated place, its transgression. It is the proletarian poet, who transgresses her prescribed mode of being, of acting and speaking by behaving as though she/he were a bourgeois. Or the plebs who retreat on Aventine Hill, where they give themselves names as though they were patricians. This process of political subjectivation, that is, the transformation of given identities, aims to expose the contradiction of two worlds in a single world:

the world where they are and the world where they are not, the world where there is something (a common stage) 'between' them and those who do not acknowledge them as speaking beings who count and the world where there is nothing.

(Rancière 1999: 27)

This common stage is existent and non-existent at the same time. This double status has primarily to do with the opposition between the police and the egalitarian logic. It might be argued that there is another level at which this existence/non-existence can be deployed. Although the common stage is not perceptible for the police order, the fact that politics can happen to perceive it and to enact it is due to the fact that a relation between those who have a part and those who have no part exists before identities are reshuffled and transformed into political subjects. This relation is the effect of the given police order. Before the plebs gather on Aventine Hill, it does not exist as a political subject but exists nonetheless in the face of the police order of the patricians. What is already in common between them is the relation of power that determines a distribution where the patricians act somehow upon the action of the plebs. This is a common stage that is not political though. This common stage exists at once as relation of power and does not exist (yet) in the political. The plebs are not invisible or silent for the patrician but can be seen or heard only as non-political subjects whose actions can be governed. The logic of politics instead introduces a dispute over the existence of a political common stage. This distinction is crucial for understanding the specificity of politics and of the political in Rancière. Relationships of power are not automatically inscribed within the political. Their distinct operational modalities might as well overlap but do not form a necessary correspondence.

> [N]othing is political in itself merely because power relationships are at work in it. For a thing to be political, it must give rise to a meeting of police logic and egalitarian logic that is never set up in advance. ... But anything may become political if it gives rise to a meeting of these two logics.
> (Rancière 1999: 32)

This can be elaborated beyond Rancière, through an operation that is opposite to the process of extensification encountered in the previous chapter. By setting up the specific conditions and the specific dynamic of the political, Rancière isolates a precise sphere of human interaction. Not all resistances that confront power relations display the antagonistic encounter of the logic of the police and the logic of politics. But some do. Resistances may become political when they enact this encounter, when they operate in a specific modality. In particular, the hallmark of politics is bestowed upon resistances that create a world in contradiction with the existent and force the given order to change. Political resistances make worlds.

This shift, that partly drives the current conceptual line beyond Rancière, serves two additional purposes. On the one hand, it helps defining a continuous process throughout the hiatuses of the circle of interruption and restoration. On the other hand, it defines the specificity of a modality by excluding a range of resistances from the political sphere. These two questions are necessarily related. It might be argued that a police order is somehow supported by a complex series of interrelated power relations. In altering the existent order of the perceptible, political subjectivation does not necessarily determine a total resistance to the entire network of power relationship. Rather, politics occurs through specific and local resistances to a precise set of power relations. The political is narrowed down to this localized area of conflict. But these resistances need to display a specific modality of action. In order to be political, the practices of resistance need to be 'driven by the assumption of equality between any and every speaking being and by the concern to test this equality' (Rancière 1999: 30). This means that practices of resistance that are not driven (or not driven yet) by the principle of equality are not political.

What is the relation between political resistances and non-political resistances? There are some traces that suggest a continuity between the two, in particular when Rancière discusses the revolt of the Scythian slaves. They enact equality by arming themselves and confronting directly their masters, who are warriors returning from an expedition. The specific hierarchy that the Scythian slaves attempt to interrupt defines a partition between those who have a part because in arms (the warriors) and those who have no part because unarmed (the slaves). By arming themselves, that partition is ultimately revoked: the two opposing armies are not hierarchically divided but they oppose each other on a common stage that displays their fundamental equality. But for Rancière, this is only 'a purely war-generated achievement of equality between the dominated and the dominator. … What they cannot do is transform equality in war into political freedom' (Rancière 1999: 13). Rancière maintains the possibility that a purely war-generated equality can be transformed into political freedom. The resistance of the Scythian was close to become a political resistance, although it fatally misses that chance. Nevertheless, despite the outcome, the Scythian resistance sets up the condition of possibility for the emergence of politics.

It might be argued that there is a potential continuity between dispersed and wild resistances and resistances driven by the assumption of politics and by the concern to test this equality. Through this continuity, politics can be said to rest on a process of coding of resistances. This ongoing process runs ceaselessly both through the order of domination and in the interruption of this order by politics. But its proper emergence is exclusively located in the transition between one order and another, that is, in the antagonistic encounter of the logic of police and that of politics. In the long segment of the order of domination, politics is eclipsed in the sense that the resistances at play are not coded (yet) into a strategy that can interrupt the flow of domination and/or the coded strategy does not turn out on equality as its principle. This understanding reconnects the otherwise problematic divergence between politics as rare and sporadic on the one hand, and the monolithic presence of the order of domination on the other hand. The rarity of politics seems initially to crystallize the solidity of the police order. The idea of non-political resistances introduces some fractures that can potentially drive towards that process of disidentifications and recombinations of identities that is at the core of political subjectivation.

A physics of resistance: Potentia and being in Negri's Spinoza

With Rancière, politics vindicates its own specific operational modality and founds its dynamic upon aesthetics and through conflicting regimes of perception. Negri instead looks at Spinoza in order to construct a conception of the political that is immediately related to ontology, metaphysics and ethics. The immediateness of this relation is radicalized by the continuous insistence on the concept of *potentia*, which represents the *conatus* of singular existences, their productive force, their constitutive and collective coming together, up to the totality of being and divine power. *Potentia* is at once labour, life and being in its fullness. This inextricable intertwinement of these different realms or planes is the expression of the excessive character of this eruptive and creative force. *Potentia* expresses not only the specificity of each realm but also the logical impossibility of comprehending one of the planes without alluding to the others, without marking the trajectories that trespass into allegedly foreign territories. With Negri's Spinoza, politics presents an excess that ties together life and labour (*potentia* as collective productive forces) while collocating itself at the hearth of ontology.

In Spinoza, the role of politics is fundamental. 'Politics comes first' (Negri 1991: 126). The centrality of politics derives from its constitutive role insofar it defines an active process of constitution and creation. Politics is appreciated in its materialistic horizon of interacting forces: 'Politics is not the realm of what "ought" to be done; rather, it is the theoretical practice of human nature seen in its effectual capacity' (Negri 1991: 186). The effectual capacity of human nature is given in the materiality of the existent as product of this capacity, but also in its potentialities shaped through (accidentally antagonistic) collective interactions.

In this materialistic horizon, where passions, affects, imagination concretely participate to the field of forces, where the metaphysical framework is immediately 'deployed on the terrain of practical being: experentia sive praxis' (Negri 2004: 12), politics (as much as ontology) becomes a matter of physics: 'a question of lines, planes, and bodies' (Spinoza, Ethics, III, preface, quoted in Negri 1991: 33). If this is not yet a micro-physics of power *a la* Foucault, it certainly shows its conceptual proximity. Bodies are in fact immersed into a dense net of interactions or affect insomuch each body is capable of affecting and being affected in different degrees. Through the affects, individual bodies are deconstructed and aggregated according to their multiple interactions. We have abandoned the terrain of the individual and her rights. In the materialistic terrain of praxis, that individual is traversed by lines and planes that are dynamically recombined. Therefore, the only adequate method that is able to decipher the complexity of the ontological and political fabric of being is a 'political physics' (Negri 1991: 194): A physics that deals with singularities in their continuous motion and recombination of multiplicities.

The constitutive dynamic character of being emerges through the interplay of affirmative (re-)openings and contingent closures. *Potentia* is the motor of being, but its spontaneous affirmation encounters *potestas* as attempt of organizing the spontaneity of this flux. Potestas, historical constituted power, is never able to fully control the expansivity of being that *potentia* expresses by setting in motion the supersession of the existent. *Potentia* is the agent of the expansion of being, of its development and, as such, continuously destroys the contingent power (*potestas*) that encounters while engaging in an affirmative and constitutive process. But, as it will be fully presented in the following sections, *potentia* achieves the supersession of the existent only insofar it is actualized into resistance. It is *potentia* qua resistance that guarantees the openness of being. Therefore for Negri, Spinoza's political philosophy can be nothing but 'a physics of resistance' (Negri 1991: 226).

The dangerous process of the construction of being

The problem of Spinoza's political project is the foundation of the state and the articulation of natural and civil right. It is the problem of modernity, of the contractarian tradition. But Spinoza enters within this discourse and engages with it only to discover the fragility of its foundation and the necessity of a different politics adequate to being and its infinite activity. For Negri, Spinoza's anomaly consists of posing the positivity of the scandal of the impossibility of an ultimate pacification: 'Spinoza ... attacks and supersedes precisely these connections internal to the Hobbesian definition of Power; by analysing its own origins again, Spinozian thought demonstrates its inconclusiveness, recognising the contradiction represented by an eventual closure of the system (effective in Hobbes) and, on the other hand, grasping the possibility of opening the constitutive rhythm toward a philosophy of the future' (Negri 1991: 70). The line that from Hobbes goes up to Rousseau and Hegel poses the state as the rational pacification of antagonism. Spinoza's politics, in line with his metaphysics, cannot conceive a final closure of being that blocks and regulates once and for all its spontaneous flux. His thought recognizes in the infinite activity of being (*potentia*) that dynamic element that affirms itself in an open horizon naturally projected towards the future. We are not far from Rancière's idea of the fundamental wrong of politics and the contingency of any organization or closure. Even La Boétie's refusal of servitude might depict a similar scenario in which no order can find its ultimate rational foundation.

Yet Negri's interpretation of Spinoza's politics shows its own specificity in leaning remarkably on ontology and metaphysics. Political physics is immediately the physics of being as being is given in its interconnectedness, constitutive infinity and active totality. Natural right shifts into the right of being, of each being, that is, *potentia* in its materiality. The discourse of rights dissolves into the realm of physics.

> For since God has right to everything, and God's right is nothing else but God's power conceived as absolutely free, it follows that every natural thing has by nature as much right as it has power to exist and act; since the power of every natural thing, whereby it exists and acts, is nothing else but the power of God, which is absolutely free.
> (Spinoza, Political Treatise (II:3) quoted in Negri 1991: 192)

An ascending flux that affirms the continuity and fullness of being. God (the totality of being) is constructed as the aggregate of every natural thing in a continuity that dissolves right into *potentia*. Being, as much, as politics, is a matter of *potentia* or, better still, of *potentiae*. In fact, the unity of being does not deny multiplicity. On the contrary, multiplicity becomes immediately constitutive of this unity, without being finally resolved into it. The multiplicity is given in its expansive and spontaneous flux, where 'every natural thing has by nature as much right as it has power to exist and act'. But this autonomy and freedom of each *potentia* necessarily generate the possibility of conflict. *Potentiae* can and do struggle among each other: the political scenario is given as antagonistic. Yet this antagonism pushes towards liberation and the refusal of servitude. Spinoza presents this positive horizon of war as primarily a horizon of liberation.

This antagonistic scenario seems to merely replicate the idea of the state of nature proposed by the 'orthodox' contractarians. But here the state of nature is not something to be superseded once and for all with the contract and the transferal of rights. In Spinoza, *potentiae* can be managed, coerced, combined, destroyed but cannot be transferred. The state of nature and its antagonism of *potentiae* need to be superseded, but not in the form of a passage to a civil state. When politics is understood in its materiality, the passage cannot be given as nothing changes at the level of *potentiae*. For political physics, each scenario of multiple *potentiae* is and remains always a natural state, making the distinction with the civic state redundant. The political horizon is constituted and traversed by conflicting autonomies and opposing *cupididates*:

> Antagonism is a second frame, a necessary one, in relation to the first frame, that of power [*potentia*]: It integrates the first, opposing power [*potentia*] to the negative determination of the order of being, to its limit-which is established within being itself. Therefore, the problem we are left with does not deal with impossible processes of pacification but instead opens up to a dangerous process of the construction of being. Of politics.
>
> (Negri 1991: 194)

The antagonistic state that opposing *potentiae* determine is the very condition of being in its fullness. Antagonism is not given as a predicament to be replaced by (civil) order. The spontaneity of being and its creative flux do not accept any order and trespass its boundaries. Antagonism, insofar it expresses the eruptive character of *potentia*, is necessarily the effect of this spontaneity and overabundance. Antagonism is integrated in the positivity and fullness of being. This maintains the horizon necessarily open. *Potentia* and its spontaneous and antagonistic flux determine the non-conclusiveness of being. Politics is a dangerous process because of its openness: not its disgrace, but the perfection of its condition – risky, experimental and beautifully inconclusive.

In virtue of its integration in the positivity of being, antagonism is itself constitutive. The encounter of conflicting *potentiae*, as much as it determines an antagonistic state, creates as well the condition for the convergence and aggregation of these singularities. Different *potentiae* can be combined and concur in a singular effort:

> The autonomy of the subject is tempered, must be tempered, in the interhuman relationship. But 'if two come together and unite their strength, they have jointly more power, and consequently more right over nature, than either of them alone; and the more there be that join in alliance, the more right they will collectively possess' (II: 13). ... The collective dimension dislocates the antagonistic process of being. The multitudo is no longer a negative condition but the positive premise of the self-constitution of right.

> ... The greater number of people, starting precisely from the natural enmity that forms their behavior, begin to constitute a political and juridical body.
>
> (Negri 1991: 194)

In this shift there is the fundamental inversion that radically breaks with the contractarian legitimation of constituted power or *potestas*. In Spinoza, antagonism does not function as the spectral threat that justifies the existence of order and power. Here, antagonism is immediately source of sociability, condition for collective processes where multiple *potentiae* converge forming new more powerful singularities. An upward process of constitution: multiplicities that converge into singular aggregates, a unity that nevertheless maintains and exalts the autonomies that compose it.

Corrupt imagination creates worlds too

No constitution can actually completely satisfy the urgency of affirmation that the *potentia* which the multitude expresses. No matter how strong the unity produced by the multitude as constituent subject, its *potentia* makes it necessarily elusive.

> This is the crucial paradox -the one formed between the physical, multiple, elusive nature of the multitudo and its subjective, juridical nature that creates right and constitution. ... No, the relationship between the absolute and the multitudo, between the two versions of power [*potestas* and *potentia*] is not closed: the one concentrates toward the unity of the political, and the other spreads out toward the multiplicity of subjects.
>
> (Negri 2004: 40)

This clearly expresses a double movement. On the one hand, the savage multiplicity of the multitude expresses constitutive power (*potentia*): the affirmation of this *potentia* generates a combination of collective convergence that founds and reproduces a constituted power (*potestas*). On the other hand, the nature of *potentia* is such that the unity of this constituted power, even though it represents nothing but the crystallization of previously aggregated *potentiae*, is in turn always confronted with a movement of *potentia* that urges to supersede the existent. *Potentia* installs *potestas* but then immediately sets the condition for its supersession. The problem with *potestas* is that is static: its unitary tendency represents a contingent closure of the horizon of cupiditates. Against any contingent closure, *potentia* antagonistically affirms its material eruption.

There is necessarily a struggle between *potentia* and *potestas*. But as the latter is nothing but a product of *potentia*, this antagonism needs to be understood within the continuity and fullness of being. Any contingent *potestas*, any temporary crystallization of the spontaneous flux of *potentia* needs to be understood as a dislocation of being, a dislocation of *potentia*: 'The State ... is ... a natural determination, a second nature, constituted by the concurrent dynamics of individual passions .... It is a dislocation of power [*potentia*]' (Negri 1991: 110). *Potentia* is dislocated to the extent that its flux is partially driven towards unity. Nevertheless, the contingency of each dislocation is once again antagonistically confronted and taken as its physical limit by the elusive excess of *potentia*. Therefore the development of being is a matter of ceaseless dislocations of *potentia*: 'The nexus of composition, complexity, conflictiveness, and dynamism is a continual nexus of successive dislocations that are neither dialectical nor linear but, rather, discontinuous' (Negri 1991: 151). There is a discontinuous sequence of dislocations of power that define the dynamism of being. There is no dialectical final pacification and no form of teleology whatsoever. The non-conclusiveness of being guarantees that the sequence of dislocation is endless and no closure can be achieved.

Negri finds once again Spinoza's polemical target in the line Hobbes-Rousseau-Hegel. The theory of the state that emerges out of this hegemonic modern thought produces a path of legitimation of the existent through a juridical discourse on human rights that resolves the crisis inducted by the fear of the masses and their productive forces. As such, Negri highlights how this project concurs in serving the bourgeois ideology of the market and the necessity of the relations of production:

> The ideologically hegemonic vein of thought is that which functions toward the development of the bourgeoisie. This vein yields to the ideology of the market, in the determinate form imposed by the new mode of production. The problem ... is the hypostasis of the dualism of the market within the

metaphysical system: from Hobbes to Rousseau, from Kant to Hegel. This is, then, the central vein of modern philosophy: The mystification of the market becomes a utopia of development.

(Negri 1991: 219)

This thought is given as mystification as it does not adequate itself to being and to its constitutive character. What modernity produces is nothing but a juridical account of legitimacy that fictitiously subsumes the material concreteness of being that only political physics can bring to light. Through the mediation of the market, antagonism is apparently resolved in the pacification of civil society and civil law. This process of mystification leads to 'the primacy of Power [*potestas*]' (Negri 1991: 192) that decrees an impossible but effective closure. For Spinoza instead, no juridical genesis of *potestas* can be given as the latter has always ultimately to do with war. The discourse of civil rights from Hobbes to Hegel ideologically hides the horizon of war that ceaselessly expresses the irruption of *potentia*. The task is to restore the centrality of this dimension by demystifying the genealogy of *potestas* from the perspective of the fullness of being and its *potentia*.

Spinoza's starts this process of deconstruction with an analysis of God and divine power, which the thought of *potestas* has always conceived as source of legitimation for constituted political power and order. If modern thought has based the legitimation of human *potestas* on the parallelism with God as king and legislator, then divine power needs to be analysed in order to verify this hypothesis.

> By God's power (*potentia*) ordinary people understand God's free will and his right over all things which are, things which on that account are commonly considered to be contingent. For they say that God has the Power (*potestas*) of destroying all things and reducing them to nothing. Further, they very often compare God's power with the power of Kings. But we have refuted this ... and we have shown that God acts with the same necessity by which he understands himself .... And then we have shown ... that God's power is nothing except God's active essence. ... I could also show here that that power which ordinary people fictitiously ascribe to God is not only human (which shows that ordinary people conceive God as a man, or as like a man), but also involves lack of power ... For no one will be able to perceive rightly

the things I maintain unless he takes great care not to confuse God's power with the human power or right of Kings.

(Spinoza, Ethics, II, proposition 3, quoted in Negri 1991: 63)

The product of the mystification is the erroneous coupling of God's power (which is *potentia* rather than *potestas*) and human *potestas*. Instead, God's power is understood as the active essence of a unique being. Each thing that belongs to being is therefore animated by that same divine essence. God's power needs therefore to be understood in its radical difference with human *potestas* which is 'only human' in virtue of its partiality, a constituted thing that cannot account for the excessive constituent process that is, in turn, the only true divine totality. Whereas being was supposed to be proving the necessity of human *potestas*, Spinoza's God exposes the contingency of constituted power. Spinoza's metaphysics depicts 'a dimension of the world that is not hierarchical but, rather, flat, equal: versatile and equivalent. The absolute essence, predicated univocally, refers as much to the divine essence (the existence of God) as it does to all the things that descend from its essence' (Negri 1991: 62). Any abstraction or mediation that poses the idea of hierarchy and order does not reflect the constitutive structure of being. It functions, in turn, as an obstacle for its development by denying the univocal and therefore horizontal structure of being.

Yet this horizontal configuration of being is not given as immediately actualized and *potestas* presents itself in the materiality of its reality. Once deprived of its metaphysical foundation, human *potestas* does not disappear but is maintained by the solidity of the structure that supports it: corrupted imagination, superstition and fear. The reality and materiality of *potestas* lie not only in its practices and institutions, but also in the ideological and mystified discourse that reinforces its reproduction. Imagination plays a crucial role in Spinoza's politics. It is conceived as a material force that contributes to the construction and, as we will see, the reconstruction of reality. Yet its outcome is open. On the side of *potestas*, imagination is corrupted as it effectively imposes a metaphysical framework of legitimation (God as king or legislator – metaphysical order and human *potestas*).

This corrupt imagination effectively constructs the world! The imagination is as strong as tradition, it is as vast as Power, it is as destructive as war and it is the servant of all this, so that human unhappiness and ignorance, superstition and slavery, misery and death are grafted onto the imaginative faculty itself.

(Negri 1991: 90)

We are once again in a scenario a la La Boétie, where servitude is constructed in praxis through the active contribution of the subjects based on habit and short-sighted interests (La Boétie) or on superstition and corrupted imagination (Spinoza). It is ethical action – the refusal of servitude, the process of demystification – that is invoked in order to supersede this predicament. Yet whereas in La Boétie this process takes the form of a restoration of the true imperatives of nature (companionship), in Spinoza no restoration can be given. Nature (or being) is given in its fullness and its materiality. The existent, despite its inadequateness to being, is always a necessary product of being. No misfortune can interrupt its continuity. Servitude is at once the result of *potentia* and of the affirmation of being, and, at the same time, the obstacle that *potentia* needs to overcome in order to continue its affirmation. The unity of being cannot tolerate a divide between a pre-historical time of natural companionship and the historicity of servitude. In Spinoza, the refusal of servitude (*potentia*) and its government (*potestas*) coexist and their encounter determines the progression of being. Liberation is neither a lost state, nor a past to restore. Liberation is given in praxis: it is the same *potentia*, which creates *potestas* through corrupted imagination and superstition, that in turn progresses in its affirmation through a movement of opposition and supersession.

The self-organization of the multitude

Potestas cannot be understood in its independence and autonomy, but only as the historical product of *potentia* at a given time. Deprived of its divine foundation, *potestas* can only be given as contingent. It does not appear as a necessity imposed by the order of being, but only as necessitated by the contingent and accidental affirmation of conflicting singularities. Its contingency is the evidence of the real possibility of its supersession. This possibility is materially inscribed in its very constitution. As *potestas* is the subordinated product of *potentia*, its institution and reproduction depend entirely on how *potentia* is effectively converged and canalized within its structure. But the constitutive expansiveness of *potentia* and its excess always decree the inadequateness of *potestas* for this role.

Potestas is always incapable of containing this eruption. Potestas is constitutively impotent: 'There is no singular thing in nature than which there is not another more powerful and stronger. Whatever one is given, there is another more powerful by which the first can be destroyed' (Spinoza, Ethics, IV, axiom 1, quoted in Negri 1991: 158); 'No one can ever so utterly transfer to another his power [*potentia*], and consequently his right, as to cease to be a man; nor can there ever be a Power [*potestas*] so supreme that it can carry out its every possible wish' (Spinoza, Theologico-political treatise, Chapter XVII, quoted in Negri 1991: 112); 'power [*potestas*] which ordinary people fictitiously ascribe to God is not only human (which shows that ordinary people conceive God as a man, or as like a man), but also involves lack of power [*potentia*]' (Spinoza, Ethics, II, proposition 3, quoted in Negri 1991: 63). Potestas is never powerful enough, it is never endowed with enough *potentia* as the expansion of the latter always exceeds the limit that *potestas* determines. Therefore, its contours are defined as negativity through a radical inversion: *potestas* is not the positivity of affirmation, it is expressed only in terms of lack. Excess over lack, *potentia* over *potestas*.

Nevertheless, as *potentia* displays the urgency of this excess, the constitutive moment affirms itself posing the conditions for a truly democratic *potestas*. This is the moment of reconstruction in which Spinoza traces the lines of how human power should be organized in order to express the adequateness with being. Imagination returns once again but this time it is immediately deployed in tune with *potentia*. Spinoza's project consists of the ethical choice to set this positive coupling of imagination and *potentia* in opposition to the line of superstition and servitude: 'On the other side, the cupiditas is developed in libertas and securitas, which is to say philosophy-productive imagination-republic .... [Spinoza's] political decision founds, conditions, and moves the metaphysical project' (Negri 1991: 121). This is the moment of re-construction. After the demystification of politics and the radical inversion that poses *potestas* as transient and subordinated to *potentia*, now *potestas* has to be reconstructed in line with its immediate source: 'Potestas, Power, from this point of view, can mean only one thing: *potentia* toward constitution, a reinforcement of meaning that the term Power does not represent itself but merely alludes to, since the power [*potentia*] of being identifies it and destroys it, poses it and surpasses it, within a real process of constitution' (Negri 1991: 192). The positivity of the affirmation lies not only in the contingent constitution of a *potestas*, but, perhaps even more cogently, in the openness towards its own supersession. In order to be in tune with being, *potestas* needs to leave *potentia* in its free development, in its radical capacity of expressing its needs and the necessity of change and modification. The horizon of liberation that *potentia* reveals has to be served and accommodated through a *potestas* that is fluidly open to its own modification. *Potentia* sets the condition for a legitimate *potestas*:

> only the power of the many, by making itself collective constitution, can found a Power. In this framework, Power is not seen as a substance, but rather as the product of a process aimed at collective constitution, a process that is always reopened by the power of the multitude.
> (Negri 2004: 15)

The republic needs to be organized according to its constitutive force: the *potentia* of the multitude. Democracy takes the form of a self-organization of the multitude. But in virtue of its elusive and excessive character, what is crucial for the institution and reproduction of power is its capacity to adequate itself to the affirmation of *potentia*, that is its openness. At the basis of democratic *potestas*, there must be 'a continuous process of legitimation that traverses the multitude' (Negri 2004: 17). The legitimate exercise of *potestas* can only be given as active consensus, the material participation and contribution to the republic. It is a radical project of constitution from below that does not admit final closures. The preservation of this openness is the necessary condition for a praxis of liberation.

Yet no *potestas* can ever be democratic enough. No democracy can ultimately satisfy completely the affirmation of *potentia*. A final democracy would consist of an effective closure: being would become static. The spontaneity of being is therefore embedded in this dynamic of constitution that is always already democratic, but never democratic enough. We are very close to the conceptual line encountered in Rancière: every police regime is a regime of perception in which equality is de facto already actualized. It is politics that introduces (or reminds) the miscount or the disagreement. Each police is already democratic (for police itself), but not democratic enough (according to politics). Likewise, Spinoza sees any *potestas* as already democratic (in virtue of the necessary active consensus that supports *potestas*), but also as not democratic enough from the perspective of *potentia* or, as we will see in the next section, from the perspective of *potentia qua* resistance.

Potentia: Resistance – counter-power – constitution

So far *potentia* has been presented in its positive and affirmative sense that Spinoza attaches to the productivity of being. The purpose of this section is to show how Negri poses *potentia* as immediately related to resistance. This coupling or even identity of *potentia* and resistance can display that positive and active character that confers to resistance the primacy over power. The terrain in which the dynamics develops is 'an explosive reality' insofar the singularities of *potentia* determine 'the critical being, the conflictual being, the antagonistic being' (Negri 1991: 153). 'His metaphysics is, in effect, the clear and explicit declaration of the irreducibility of the development of productive forces to any ordering' (Negri 1991: 138). Here the idea of irreducibility resonates immediately with Foucault's definition of resistance: '[resistances] are inscribed in [power relations] as an irreducible opposite' (Foucault 1978: 96). No power relation, ordering or *potestas* can exhaustively act upon the capacity of action of other subjects or singularities preventing completely the possibility of resistance and the supersession of the contingent *potestas*. The two definitions start tracing their assonance. The irreducibility of the development of productive forces is the irreducibility that productive forces deploy as resistance. It is the irreducibility of the *potentia* of a singularity that does not contribute to the constitution of the power relation or of a specific *potestas* and affirms itself in opposition to power. What expresses the irreducible character of *potentia* is that aggregation of cupiditates that do not converge within the circuits of *potestas*, what remains outside from the mystified totality of *potestas*: an 'excess' (Negri 1991: 122).

The development of productive forces necessarily proceeds through situated resistances against a constituted power that is not able to manage them, a *potentia* that exceeds the limits posed by the materiality of the existent. The present constitutes the physical limit that *potentia* encounters in the form of *potestas*: 'The totality of Spinozian power [*potentia*], as a basis of the constitution of reality by means of the form of politics, can be defined in only one way: against Power [*potestas*]. It is a savage definition, a subversive determination, a materialistic foundation' (Negri 1991: 191). The existent as a physical limit needs to be transgressed posing *potentia* against *potestas*, that is, *potentia qua* resistance against *potestas*. Therefore, what brings about the transformation of the existent and aliments the dynamic expansion of being is a process of subversion, rebellion, revolt against *potestas*: 'It is power against Power [potenza contra potere]. That is, power against, or counter-Power [contropotere]' (Negri 2004: 97). *Potentia* (*qua* resistance) corresponds to counter-power (as *potestas*). This correspondence is furthermore specified by Negri introducing a series of distinction within the process of resistance and constitution:

> [what] constitutes political society [is] the self-organization of the power [*potentia*] of the individualities, the active resistance that is rationally transformed into a counter-Power [*potestas*], the counter-Power that is collectively developed in active consensus, the consensual praxis that is articulated in a real constitution.
>
> (Negri 1991: 112)

Resistance – counter-Power – active consensus – real constitution: the sequence links together the phases of the affirmation of *potentia*, the successive dislocations of being. A political and ontological dynamic that proceeds from destruction to re-construction or creation. But how to understand these distinctions? What happens between these phases? The different moments might as well be distinguished according to their respective intensity: to each phase corresponds a certain level of aggregation of resistant *potentiae*. In line with the ascending path of being, more and more *potentiae* converge forming a singularity up to the point in which the praxis of this singularity attains the level of a real constitution. Yet the problem becomes apparent once we approximate the threshold, the moment of passage in which singularities pass, for instance, from resistance to counter-Power.

Approximating the limit, we realize that no limit can be given: counter-Power looks still a bit like resistance and already smells of consensus and constitution. Resistance is the affirmation of an initial eruptive and excessive force. Resistance is both a process of constitution and a process of opposition. But its oppositional stance is only secondary to the fullness of being it expresses. The creative character of resistance in fact might as well not be completely exhausted and absorbed into counter-Power, whose *potentia* in turn will probably not be entirely transformed into an active consensus and real constitution. The process through which *potentia* affirms its development is primarily a process of resistance. Within the unity of this process, the various moments interact in a complex simultaneity that projects the present onto the future while discovering the future already in the present. 'Emancipation is a transition not because it intuits the future but because it permeates and animates the present' (Negri 1991: 221).

De-stat-ic-ization: The real urgency of the inexistent

The complexity of the relation between present and future in the unity of being and its dynamic tendency towards the supersession of the existent constitute the horizon of resistance and its possibility. 'Spinoza's disutopia is a revolt, a rebellion, only to the extent that it is, first of all, wealth. The tension between limit and tendency that constitute it, the metaphysically appropriative and constitutive thrust that form it – all of this is wealth; it is a liberation of productive force' (Negri 1991: 221). This wealth of *potentia* is its capacity to transgress the limit and impose a transition towards the future through an excess that is already given in the immediacy of the present under the guise of possibility that is already real and constitutive. Political imagination intercepts this process of material affirmation of the possible. Imagination is given in the materiality of its effects that actively constitute reality mobilizing the possible within the existent: 'this process ... raises illusion to the level of truth .... The instrumental paradox of the "libertine" critique of religion is accepted here (imagination is illusion) in the inverted form that really constitutes it (and illusion constitutes reality)' (Negri 1991: 95).

Yet reason and ethical action intervene in this project 'liberating the truth [imagination] contains' (Negri 1991: 106), differentiating it from the falsity of the corrupted imagination that becomes superstition and asserts *potestas*. Positive or constitutive imagination instead mobilizes the possible within the existent. It accommodates the dynamism of being and the spontaneity of its flow in a process of demystification that is also *de-stat-ic-ization* (against the static pretence of *potestas*/state, against the state). Being cannot be static: political imagination active follows the dynamic paths that exceed the physical limit of the existent. But in guiding this subversive transition towards the future, political imagination poses itself not only as politically constitutive but also as ontologically necessary. We are firmly 'on the terrain of the possible. It is this surpassing that essence effects on existence, it is the reality of the inexistent posed as a scheme of development from the ethical individuality toward the ethical world' (Negri 1991: 160). The necessary dynamism of being is given as supersession of the existent. Essence surpasses the existent by opposing against the latter 'the reality of the inexistent', the possible that haunts the present as a nagging reminder of the impossibility of its persistence. The present cannot persist because *potentia* keeps pushing through its interstices, affirming itself as resistance and its material possibility. Resistance and its possibility are real and necessary.

How far are we from Foucault's insistence on 'the reality of possible struggles' (Foucault 1996)? We are definitely approaching or even intersecting that territory in which Foucault has started formulating the primacy of resistance in virtue of the reality of its possibility and the possibility of struggle. But here, perhaps beyond Foucault, the possible is not only posed in its material reality, but, even more cogently, in its constitutive necessity. The inexistent necessarily pushes for its affirmation as dynamic transition towards a future that is already immanent in praxis. The necessary tension of being towards its dynamic development is not only real, but also inexorable, urgent.

> The imagination extends the tension from essence to existence on a terrain that is as vast as can be and decisively corporeal – it is material, possible. The nothingness that (presently) constitutes the nexus between essence and existence becomes fluid, phantasmagoric. This is the real urgency of the inexistent, posed as an expansive scheme of ethicalness.
>
> (Negri 1991: 160)

The real urgency of the inexistent marks the passage from ontological necessity to ethical decision. The drive towards supersession that *potentia qua* resistance expresses at the ontological level traces the path that ethical action has to follow within a process of constitution that is immediately political and ontological. The ontological demand for dynamic transformation is immediately the ethical demand of resistance: 'Spinozian being is the being of revolution, the ontology of revolution' (Negri 2004: 96). It is the very essence of being that poses resistance as the necessary element that drives the transition towards future 'scenarios of liberation' (Negri 2004: 6). A tendency that is arguably anti-teleological as it expresses nothing but the ontological pressure towards expansion, supersession and constitution realized in collective praxis. This revolutionary tendency of being marks 'the triumph of the untimely and the counter-factual – and here the subject rediscovers itself as collective subject … on the flattened presence of a world that is always reopened to absolute possibility' (Negri 2004: 91). Resistance expresses the urgency of this superabundant being and constitutes that share of *potentia* that is responsible for the necessary supersession of the existent. Imagination, when it is adequate to the truth of being, sets up this subversive dynamic. Political imagination is immediately resistant imagination that constitutes the world resting upon the open richness and wealth of being. Resistance actualizes itself by appealing to the 'inexhaustible virtuality of being' (Negri 2004: 96) that haunts the present and pushes for its supersession.

The primacy of *potentia* qua resistance

The primacy of *potentia* that Negri's Spinoza clearly outlines necessarily implies the radical subordination of *potestas*. Potestas is *potentia* without its dynamic impulse. It is defined in terms of lack as it does not have the capacity to contain the excess that *potentia* continuously affirms. Political constitution proceeds through the antagonism of *potentiae* that is dislocated at the level of a confrontation between *potentia* and *potestas*. But if the latter is nothing but a static and crystallized closure of *potentia*, then the constitutive struggle is between two expressions of the same material: *potentia*, being. Does it still make sense to speak of primacy within a monist ontological edifice? Yes, because the primacy is not attributed to *potentia* as such. There is an internal differentiation that has to do with two distinct modalities. On the one hand, *potestas* is static and coagulated *potentia*. On the other hand, *potentia* as such consists of the contingent coagulated *potentia* (*potestas*) and the dynamic real virtuality of the inexistent. As the *potentia* projected towards this virtuality is necessarily posed as a subversion of the present and therefore as resistance, Spinoza's primacy of *potentia* needs to be specified as the primacy of *potentia qua* resistance. Spinoza's politics inverts that classic tradition that has relegated resistance to a mere rebound to power, a passive reaction.

It is the tradition of Hobbes and the social contract theory, but also of neoliberalism and biofinancialization that contribute to this conceptual subordination of resistance in the form of the exploitation of productive forces. A tradition that is as well hegemonic despite its strategical mystification of the materiality of being. Therefore, an attack to this tradition is contingently given as inversion, as a 'true Copernican revolution' (Negri 2004: 40). The inversion is contingent upon the historical fact of the hegemony of this tradition. But at the level of ontology, no inversion is needed: resistance has always been prior to power. It is the discourse of power that presents itself at the very outset of its emergence as the strategic inversion of the ontological dynamic. The positivity of Spinoza's project and of the conceptual lines of the primacy of resistance in general is implicit in the inversion of the historically prior mystified inversion. The inversion of the inversion traces the affirmative trajectory of revolutionary constitution.

Therefore, there is a distinction between the historical and the ontological understanding of Spinoza's Copernican revolution: it is an inversion when we consider the historical plane and the hegemonic affirmation of a conceptual line over the other; at the ontological (and political) level, it is a restoration, the liberation of a dynamic obstructed by power-*potestas*. It is *potestas* that attempts to invert or arrest the spontaneity of *potentia*. Resistance intervenes to liberate a flux that has been contingently restrained. In short, the idea of inversion here represents a negative moment (as against something) only in the contingency of a hegemonic thought that is not adequate to the reality of being. But the process in itself is purely affirmative and constitutive, it is full positivity. Once again, we are confronted with the problem of securing the series of attributes active-positive-constitutive on the side of resistance, refusing the sequence reactive-negative-oppositional historically traditionally attributed to resistance. In Rancière, this has emerged as the problematization of the relation between politics and interruption that, despite a seemingly negative and oppositional understanding sedimented in the idea of interruption, needs still to be understood in its constitutive tendency (the creation of new worlds, new regime of aesthetics). Now, mixing the two, it is police, insofar it determines a contingent *potestas*, that interrupts the spontaneous and excessive flow of *potentia* that resistance and Rancière's politics express.

The positivity of resistance, on which its primacy is radically grounded, corresponds immediately to the creative and constitutive capacity that the dynamic transition of the existent towards the future requires. The development of being is a matter of continuous and dynamic flux where the present is always already on the verge of being surpassed. But this passage of supersession is not so much about the destruction of the present. The transition to the future is a matter of modification and transformation of the existent. Yet this is not a mere temporal succession in which instants press upon each other in an inexorable linearity. The future that marks the development of being is not that of the following instant as this expresses only a mere reproduction of the existent. For *potestas*, future has to be an eternal present notwithstanding its biological processes. Instead, the dynamic of the development of being is constituted of successive dislocations, discontinuities that radically transform the present and constitutively decree its transition towards the future. *Potentia qua* resistance is the element that activates this dynamic where the present is truly surpassed, where *potestas* is obliged to change: 'Political constitution is always set in motion by the resistance to Power [*potestas*]. It is a physics of resistance' (Negri 1991: 226).

Resistance becomes so central in the political model that Negri elaborates through Spinoza up to the extent that the whole dynamic that animates the world and simultaneously constitutes the world is named after itself: a physics of resistance. All the movements of being, its transitions and dislocations are a matter of resistance. If being is dynamic, this is due exclusively to resistance. Being is given as the horizon of liberation in virtue of this exuberant resistance that *de-stat-ic-izes* the crystallization of being into *potestas*, obliging to change with it and according to the constitutive lines that resistance determines. The proximity with Foucault's foundation of the primacy of resistance could not be more intense: 'So resistance comes first, and resistance remains superior to the forces of the process; power relations are obliged to change with the resistance' (Foucault 1997a). Resistance is the motor ('set in motion') of this forced process of change, of transformation, imposed upon something (power relations or *potestas*) that is reluctant to this change, something that would not have changed if not obliged to by a heteronomous force. Resistance, in contrast, expresses the autonomy of being given as the constitutive collective praxis of the multitude.

Constitutive affirmation and accidental opposition

The autonomy of resistance can be given only as affirmative practice. But in order to maintain this autonomy, the relation of resistance with power needs to be considered as subordinated to the constitutive process that the autonomy implies. By imposing a change upon power, resistance might seem to operate with a precise concern of the other pole of the relation. The objective of resistance would accordingly be placed somehow outside itself as the determination of an effect upon its other (i.e. power). And this would imply a sort of heteronomy by return to be cast upon resistance: its action would be driven by the transformation of the other. Instead, the constitutive process that Negri's Spinoza ascribes to resistance needs necessarily to be understood in the absoluteness of its affirmation. The relation to power in form of opposition is not discarded but subordinated to the positivity of the constitutive process. The opposition is accidental. The autonomy of resistance corresponds to the necessity of its affirmation and the contingency of its oppositional character. 'By a Desire arising from reason, we directly follow the good, and indirectly flee the evil' (Spinoza, Ethics, IV, propositions 63, quoted in Negri 1991: 166). Resistance (in the nexus imagination-desire-reason) directly follows the good and only indirectly flees or fights the evil that *potestas* deploys. For resistance, direct confrontation is only an unpleasant hustle, an inconvenience in the urgency of the affirmation of being. Positivity is what is more cogently at stake in resistance. The traditional reduction of resistance to its negative moment concretely succeeds in the sabotage of the constitutive potential of the primacy of resistance. The theoretical reduction is in a relation of mutual reinforcement with the material practices of power that try to embank (as with a dyke that limits and puts to work) the flow of resistance.

Besides its strategic material effects, the fault of the traditional theoretical reduction of resistance to its oppositional stance lies in the orientation of the comparison of the elements that compose the relation. Using for once Spinoza without the explicit aid of Negri, it is interesting here to refer to what the former says of privation and negation:

> it is impossible to absolutely degrade being toward privation and negation, because privation is not the act of depriving, but only the pure and simple lack, which in itself is nothing. Indeed, it is only a ... mode of thinking, which we form when we compare things with one another. We say, for example, that a blind man is deprived of sight because we easily imagine him as seeing.
>
> (Spinoza, letter 21, quoted in Negri 1991: 88)

Now, with a delicate process of translocation, there is the possibility of attempting to outline the underlying genealogy of the traditional attribution of negativity to resistance. When a certain mode of thinking poses illegitimately *potestas* as prior in relation to resistance, the emergence of resistance signals a situation of deprivation. As the blind is said to be deprived of sight insofar is expected to be able to see, *potestas* appears to be deprived of its *potentia* insofar it pretends or expects that the totality of *potentia* has to converge and coagulate in its unity. Once the active participation to the contingent *potestas* (voluntary servitude) is reduced in virtue of resistance, the political scenario becomes a matter of negativity and opposition, deprivation and lack. Yet if the blind is expected to see is only for a previous contingent mystification of the attributes that pertain to the nature of every single human being. *Potentia* is expected to contribute indefinitely to power in the form of voluntary servitude, only in virtue of the malicious mystification through which *potestas* claims its necessity despite its constitutive contingency and subordination. But with the Copernican revolution that Spinoza and the other conceptual lines of the primacy of resistance bring about, *potentia* can no longer be expected to contribute to constituted power.

The hegemonic philosophical tradition and their relative understanding of negation and deprivation are inverted: resistance is expected only to affirm itself in a process of creation and constitution. Pure positivity with some accidental stains of negative opposition: 'Expansiveness is also destruction, but it is so in the growth and overabundance of the vital process, in the continuous movement of self-definition toward higher levels of being. Dynamism is dislocation, and therefore it is a sudden reversal, a systematic redefinition of the affects and their ontological determinateness, continually reaching higher levels of ontological complexity' (Negri 1991: 152). This is where resistance irrupts as the force that destroys accidentally while concerned with affirming and expanding being. There is destruction but that is subordinated to the process of constitution of which that destruction is only an accidental moment in comparison with the creative tension towards 'higher levels of ontological complexity'. What resistance primarily determines is this progression where being is deployed in always higher and more complex forms of self-organization.

Yet this progression cannot be given as a transcendental drive as Spinoza's ontology is strictly anti-teleological. Therefore, the progression is measured upon the material praxis of the multitude in a given moment and upon the magnitude of the freedom that the multitude has won. The crescent accumulation of being reaches higher levels of perfection through dislocations that are not given in advance in a linear progression, but are given only in the materiality of the constitutive praxis that actualizes them. But higher complexity and development can be reached only through the convergence of a growing set of multiple *potentiae*.

Convergence (companionship?) functions as a connective modality that maximizes potentiality by canalizing the whole of the intensity of a singular *potentia* towards a specific direction. In pure affirmation, horizontality represents the maximum of efficiency as no *potentia* is dispersed for confrontational purposes. The immanent tendency towards higher levels of being is a tendency towards horizontality: '[the continuous incursions of power (*potentia*) toward constitution] are described on the surface of the univocal being, which presses for more, not satisfied with the horizontality that it has achieved, with its beautiful and animated flatness' (Negri 1991: 119). The freedom that has already been won and that is deployed in praxis is exceeded by the potentiality of *potentia* (the possibility of resistance) in the form of a contestation of the achieved horizontality. As for democracy, any configuration of the existent shows already some horizontality, but the horizontality achieved is never enough. Within the horizon of liberation, no level of horizontality can ever satisfy the development of productive forces.

Resistance never contents itself with a horizontality that is positively doomed to be never horizontal enough.

In Spinoza, this principle of contestation that continuously irrupts and transforms the existent is never, so to speak, a principle. It is a praxis, the immediate result of the encounter of *potentiae* (or, of powers insofar they display the possibility of resistance and therefore the possibility of struggles and of a re-opening of the horizon of being). Horizontality, as the possibility of aggregation and convergence of singularities are in fact the necessary ontological condition for the expansion and growth of *potentia*. Perfecting being is a collective process in which only a positive aggregation of powers (the singularity composed of many multiplicities) multiplies power and being. And such an aggregation is maximized when horizontal, as no power is dispersed in the (management of) antagonism that each verticality immediately implies.

An eternal age of resistance

In Spinoza, there is only the materiality of praxis that constitutes history immediately through its affirmation. Being is given as an immediate unity, a totality with no mediation and no reference to any transcendence – pure immanence. By extension, the dimension of time needs to reflect this radical ontological interconnectedness. The present and the future are immediately arranged upon the tension between the limit of crystallized *potentia* (the existent) and the excess of *potentia qua* resistance (potentiality of the present in seek of actualization). The inexistent materially presses already upon the existent. The two are given in a tense and dynamic relation of simultaneity. The inexistent is existent, but not existent enough: 'the future ... permeates and animates the present' (Negri 1991: 221). The untimely, the urgent inexistent, the anomaly: a future to come insofar is already here – but not here enough.

The reality of virtuality is the sign of a pregnant present that is already projected towards a future whose actualization simply reiterates this dynamic: a new present and new potentialities towards the next future. Yet Negri underlines that this sequence is not linear but proceeds through successive dislocations. But dislocations are ontological and are absorbed in the totality of being that reaches differentiated levels of being with progressive higher complexity. But, as discussed in relation to the possibility of isolating the different phases of the constituent process (resistance – counter-power – active consensus – political constitution), the fluidity of the process seems to lose its centrality when we attempt to introduce temporal caesurae within the dynamic. This necessarily problematizes Douzinas's (2013) idea that the 2011 wave of uprisings constitutes the basis for defining ours as an age of resistance. With Spinoza, our age of resistance has started long time ago and does not seem to be approaching its end. In fact, the age of resistance is the age of being: through its multiple transformations and dislocations, resistance never stops casting its mark over time and history. Every age is therefore an age of resistance.

Therefore, as Negri puts it, Spinoza´s politics becomes a ceaseless call for the affirmation of the primacy of *potentia qua* resistance. A call that is not given as proper of a specific age, but that is radically attuned to the endless affirmation and development of being. In the positive and constitutive character of collective praxis, Spinoza's politics is both a method of analysis (a physics of resistance) and at once an ethical attitude towards the existent: 'here we merely propose a method, with neither a model nor an instrument – perhaps not even a method, or rather a method embedded in a state of mind [spirito]. Spinozism is a state of mind: it allows existence to be considered as the possibility of subversion' (Negri 2004: 99). This is a revolutionary disposition towards the future that the possibility of resistance and its creative excess already express in the present. Revolutionary praxis explores the reality of this virtual territory in the continuous attempt to enhance being by affirming higher levels of horizontality. Every possibility bears the hope for revolutionary transformation: Every world can be experienced as 'a world to be rebuilt … every singular emergence of life as an act of resistance and creation' (Negri 2004: 117).

5

Re-existence: The materialist ontology of resistance and becoming

In the previous chapters, the emergence of the primacy of resistance has been the result of a meticulous search for fragments, undeveloped intuitions, hints and untold logical implications. In Deleuze's *Foucault*, by contrast, the primacy of resistance is outlined in detail. Its presentation draws a precise conceptual line that somehow cuts through all the other planes (human nature, labour, politics) in which the primacy of resistance has so far emerged. In fact, Deleuze presents the primacy of resistance in relation to elements that, although quite marginal in Foucault's work, place it on an ontological level. The primacy of resistance, that is to say, lies in the specific relations with the diagram, on the one side, and with the outside, on the other:

> the final word on power is that *resistance comes first,* to the extent that power relations operate completely within the diagram, while resistances necessarily operate in a direct relation with the outside from which the diagrams emerge.
>
> (Deleuze 2006a: 89)

Power relations and resistance are put in a sequence whose ordering is based upon their respective operational modality. Power relations are completely exhausted by the diagram. They do not operate outside the diagram. Power relations in fact constitute the diagram itself. Resistance is not captured by the diagram; it stands outside the diagram. It is its direct relation with the outside that confers to resistance its primacy over power.

This claim can only be understood by unravelling the complex ontological edifice that is immediately evoked by the reference to the diagram and the outside. The problematization of these two concepts is a necessary step in order to draw an ontology around the primacy of resistance. In *Foucault* (2006a), Deleuze maps these concepts in a comprehensive model that transforms the historical evolution of Foucault's work into an ontology. Archaeology corresponds to the analysis of historical formations or 'strata'. These strata are constituted through the integration or actualization of a microphysical network of power relations (as per the idea of power/knowledge developed in *Discipline and Punish* and *The Will to Knowledge*). The outside is where the interplay of forces, which is constitutive of power relations, takes place. This interplay results in the continuous mutation of diagrams provoked by the affirmation of resistance. The relations between strata, diagrams, resistance and the outside determine the emergence of a self-standing ontological model.

It is difficult to decipher whether this can be held as a Foucauldian ontology. Neither would it be fruitful to attempt such an enterprise, which ultimately reduces the potential of a conceptual line to a matter of authorship. What we need instead, as Deleuze himself suggests, is a 'transversal line' that crosses both their works in an eruptive process of creative hybridization: 'I'm not, in this book [his Foucault], trying to speak for Foucault, but trying to trace a transversal, diagonal line running from him to me (there's no other option)' (Deleuze 1995a: 88). But this transversal line is not simply the image of the way in which Deleuze connects his thought with Foucault. It is a line that is compelling precisely in virtue of its ontological status. It is a line of flight, the line of thought, the line of the outside. But this is also a line of resistance. The transversal in fact is the hallmark of what Nietzsche calls the untimely, or more precisely, of the untimely that is incumbent for Deleuze and Foucault.

In 'Subject and Power', Foucault refers to the forms of resistance that have characterized the 1960s and the 1970s and, trying to isolate what is common to those struggles, calls them 'transversal' as 'they are not limited to one country. ... [T]hey are not confined to a particular political or economic form of government' (Foucault 1982: 211). And it is no coincidence that Deleuze comments this excerpt in his lectures on Foucault, relating this idea of 'transversal struggles' in particular to the experience of the Italian Autonomist Marxism and to the work of Tronti. And it is obviously not accidental that Tronti's idea of the primacy of workers' struggle was already presented in this project as a substantial contribution to the conceptual lines that draw the primacy of resistance in relation to labour. In short, the primacy of resistance seems to have an intimate relationship with the idea of transversality,[1] where transversal lines reconfigure the existent and maintain the dynamicity of becoming. It is not a stylistic choice to install the trajectory of the primacy of resistance on this transversal line. Rather, it is a necessity that comes directly from the ontological model that this line simultaneously attempts to draw.

A transversal line

This transversal line needs to be understood immediately in ontological terms. What Deleuze does with his book on Foucault is to actualize the transversal line. It cannot be but an actualization as the line is encasted between two points ('running from him to me'). This chapter destratifies that line, prolonging its extremities, drawing a new trajectory. This requires a double task: tracing a line through history and inscribing it into a becoming – a conceptual creation. This historical line is not linear. Deleuze's view on Foucault changes over time. I propose to analyse their relationship or (how Deleuze changes this relationship) through the problematization of the primacy of resistance. In particular, this line connects the moments in which the relation between Deleuze and Foucault is directly articulated upon the problem of the primacy of resistance. As such, its emergence is located in the aftermath of the publication of the first volume of the *History of Sexuality* (1976).

The first part of this line is fairly well-known. It connects a series of moments where Deleuze is critical of how Foucault presents his own resistance. Deleuze's problem with Foucault at this stage is the status of phenomena of resistance, understood as a counter-attack against power which in turn seems to be held as constitutive. Deleuze's critique targets the role of resistance in relation to its location: as it remains outside the diagram of power, Foucault's resistance cannot be but secondary. This segment of the line contains a letter addressed to Foucault in 1976 and published later under the title of *Desire and Pleasure* (1977), and Deleuze's chapter 'Many Politics' published in *Dialogues* (1977) together with Claire Parnet. This segment in which Deleuze is critical of Foucault's resistance is condensed in the famous note in *A Thousand Plateaus*, published in 1980 with Felix Guattari.

We then approach a point of modification in which Deleuze seems to display a more conciliatory view: although outside the diagram, Foucault's resistance is necessarily prior to power. There is a mutual contribution. Foucault's work on subjectification provides Deleuze with those elements that he would have liked to find in Foucault earlier on. Before subjectification, Foucault's resistance appears charged with an oppositional role that Deleuze cannot reconciliate with his own thinking. After that point, Deleuze can finally liberate what Foucault already had all along: the primacy of resistance. This transformation is triggered by Foucault's later work on subjectification. With subjectification, Deleuze finally detects a point in Foucault's work in which to anchor the primacy of resistance. And, in addition, this seems to renew Deleuze's perspective also on Foucault's previous work. This point of modification emerges through his course on Foucault at Université Paris VIII, Vincennes in 1985/1986 and is then disseminated through the book published in 1986 and in some interviews released by Deleuze immediately after the publication of the book and then collected in *Negotiations* (1995c). 'What Is a Dispositif?' (presented in 1988) also belongs to this segment of the line.

The creative combinations of these two segments make their opposition superfluous: rather than two distinct Deleuzian understandings of Foucault, a hybrid encounter that allows us to install on this transversal line a series of heterogeneous concepts – resistance, lines of flight, diagrams, abstract machines. Retrospectively, we can claim that already in the first segment Deleuze is more Foucauldian than what he thinks to be. The same holds for Foucault: perhaps, the day has come that his resistance rather than last century 'will be known as Deleuzian' (Foucault 1998: 343).

In tracing this extended transversal line, it is necessary to resist the temptation of shifting the trajectory on the plane of a traditional understanding of the history of philosophy. The purpose of this enquiry is not to define the evolution of Deleuze's thought or of his relation with Foucault. That is the problem of history, which is only incidentally encountered in this path. Instead, the aim is to sketch the becoming of the line of the primacy of resistance. The trajectory of this line needs to be understood as a mapping of the process of creation of the concept in its ontological horizon. This transversal line attempts to constitute the primacy of resistance in its autonomous affirmation. A line that is in fact not drawn by Deleuze and/or Foucault. Instead, it is a matter of install ourselves on this transversal line. This move is crucial in order to move away from history and approach the dimension of becoming. With this orientation, what is at stake here is not so much to explore and experiment with the potentiality of the concept of the primacy of resistance. This would immediately imply an actualization, a reterritorialization that somehow blocks the ontological proliferation of potentialities. Instead, the challenge is to tune thought with becoming, to preserve the creative aspect that the thought of the primacy of resistance implies and therefore imposes. The aim is to draw the conditions for the ontological emergence of the new: a radical opening towards creation. This transversal line escapes history and traces its path at the hearth of becoming, pure matter. A conception of matter that is necessarily 'anti-hylomorphic', as put by John Protevi. Turning towards matter implies a move away from the human, from the stratifications of an anthropocentric ontology.

But how can we trace a transversal line without plotting an end point ('from him to me')? How can we leave this line open while not falling into the sterile banality of repetition? If, for Deleuze, the problem was to preserve a body without organs from turning into a fascist or suicidal body (Deleuze and Guattari 1987), here the question concerns directly the status of this work. The problem here is to prevent the riding of this transversal line from turning into an arid report of someone else's work. In short, the problem is to tune thought with becoming, to preserve the creative aspect that the thought of the primacy of resistance implies and therefore imposes. To say it with Alberto Toscano, this chapter attempts to respect the fact that confronting the problematic character of the topics at stake 'demands the creativity of commentary rather than the sterile tedium of exposition' (Toscano 2004: xxv).

The emergence of the first segment of this transversal line is located right after the publication of the first volume of the *History of Sexuality* (1976). In comparison with Foucault's previous book *Discipline and Punish*, one of the great novelties of the *History of Sexuality* is the appearance of the idea of resistance. But the status of this resistance in Foucault's model is understood by Deleuze as problematic. Resistance becomes the problem around which Deleuze sees Foucault's thought drifting away from his. Deleuze writes a letter to Foucault in which he expresses a series of criticisms on the status of resistance, on the constitutive character of power relations and on the relation between dispositifs of power and assemblages of desire. According to Miller, this moment marked a moment of profound separation: 'Shortly afterward, Foucault abruptly decided that he would see no more of Deleuze. ... In the years that followed, the two philosophers would occasionally exchange ideas by mail. But they would never again meet face-to-face' (Miller 1994: 297). This letter has been published under the title of *Desire and Pleasure* and expresses a position that lasts up to *A Thousand Plateaus*.

> It seems to me, then, that Michel confronts a problem that does not have the same status for me. For if *dispositifs* of power are in some way constitutive, there can only be phenomena of 'resistance' against them, and the question bears on the status of these phenomena. ... Lines of fight and movements of deterritorialization, as collective historical determinations, do not seem to me to have any equivalent in Michel. For myself, the status of phenomena of resistance is not a problem; since lines of flight are primary determinations, since desire assembles the social field, it is rather the dispositifs of power that are both produced by these agencements and crushed or sealed off by them.
>
> (Deleuze 1997: 188–9)

At this stage, Deleuze sees Foucault's power relations as primary in relation to resistance. Dispositifs of power come first and resistance is limited to a phenomenon of counter-attack. This deprives resistance of any possibility of creation as it becomes bound to a purely reactive role. Furthermore, within this understanding resistance can be given exclusively against something, that is to say, it is essentially reactive. It becomes flattened to its oppositional or confrontational aspect. And this has also another crucial consequence. If dispositifs of power are constitutive, how are we to understand their transformation? Why should a dispositif of power change or mutate? This characterization of resistance is completely at odds with Deleuze's lines of flights. This understanding of Foucault's resistance as secondary, reactive and exclusively oppositional persists in Deleuze's collaboration with Guattari. A note in *A Thousand Plateaus* exhaustively summarizes their points of disagreement:

> Our only points of disagreement with Foucault are the following: (1) to us the assemblages seem fundamentally to be assemblages not of power but of desire (desire is always assembled), and power seems to be a stratified dimension of the assemblage; (2) the diagram and abstract machine have

lines of flight that are primary, which are not phenomena of resistance or counterattack in an assemblage, but cutting edges of creation and deterritorialization.

(Deleuze and Guattari 1987: 531)

Here the problematization of Foucault's resistance is confronted at an ontological level. What Deleuze and Guattari contest is the effect of that characterization of resistance as secondary and oppositional on the nature of the diagram and of the abstract machine. Resistance as a phenomenon of counter-attack remains excluded from the abstract machine. It does not participate to the constitution of abstract machines but operates outside them. Lines of flights instead are constitutive of the abstract machine and this determines their primacy.

This understanding of Foucault's resistance as secondary, reactive, exclusively oppositional and confined outside the abstract machine is not necessarily the unique interpretation that can be extracted from his works. As already discussed in Chapter 1, it is possible to detect fragments in Foucault's whole work (including interviews, courses and conference papers) that somehow hint towards a characterization of resistance as primary and creative. Nevertheless, Deleuze's interpretation remains legitimate to the extent that, on the one hand, it is hard to define the amount of material available to him at that time, and that, on the other hand, the concise way in which Foucault presents resistance in the *History of Sexuality* allows for a multiplicity of possible understandings. What is interesting though is that the line drawn by Deleuze upon this specific characterization of Foucault's resistance later reaches a point of decisive transformation. After this point, Deleuze finally finds in Foucault's resistance that creative and constitutive aspect that he could not find earlier. This point of modification is triggered by Foucault's later work on subjectification and the aesthetics of existence. In this third axis, distinguished both from the archive and from power, Deleuze finds Foucault finally dealing with lines of flight. Subjectification concerns both creation *and* resistance. It is through the aesthetics of existence that Deleuze re-evaluates Foucault's account of resistance so as to draw that transversal line he actualizes in his book on Foucault. This process is quite evident especially in the course given by Deleuze at Université Paris VIII Vincennes in 1985/1986. Here that transversal line seems to be suppler, more open to creative conjunctions and ambitious experimentations. On this transversal line, the earlier disagreements seem almost to vanish.

It is striking comparing two fragments respectively belonging to the two segments of Deleuze's view of Foucault's resistance. In *Desire and Pleasure*, Deleuze denounces the primacy of strategies as constitutive of a social field:

> another great novelty of Michel's conception of power would be: a society does not contradict itself, or rarely. But his response is: it is strategized, it strategizes. I find that very beautiful; ... But I am not completely at ease with this idea. I would say, for my part, that a society, a social field, does not contradict itself, but what is primary is that it takes flight; it first of all flees in every direction; it is lines of flight that are primary (even if *primary* is not chronological). ... if the first given of a society is that everything takes flight, then everything in it is deterritorialized.
>
> (Deleuze 1997: 187)

In the lectures of 1986 instead, after the decisive point of modification, Deleuze arrives to the opposite conclusion. There is an internal necessity that somehow emerges from Foucault's whole work that blocks any understanding of resistance that does not attribute to it a primary and creative character. Deleuze seems to present the primacy of resistance as a necessary premise of Foucault's thought. Resistance, even in Foucault, *must* come first. There is a radical inversion in comparison with the above fragment. And this is even more evident and amplified by the striking similarity between the ways in which Deleuze phrases his positions in the two excerpts:

> can Foucault maintain his definition of the social field, 'it strategises'; that it is constituted as strategy? I mean: is it not that, one way or another, he will end up being forced into saying (which is bizarre): the points of resistance are primary in relation to power; they are not vis-à-vis, they have to be primary. From this moment a social field must be defined by this: *it resists everywhere*.
>
> (Deleuze 2018d)

Before the turning point, Deleuze claims that, for Foucault, society is what strategizes everywhere; in the lectures instead, Deleuze concludes that for Foucault necessarily ('he will end up being forced into saying') society is what resists everywhere. The primacy of resistance becomes an internal necessity of Foucault's model and this puts also the previous fragment under a different perspective. It is not only Foucault's work on subjectification that shows the primacy of resistance. This retroactively transforms the concept of resistance as developed in the *History of Sexuality*. Or better still, it does not literally transform that concept but imposes on it a necessary transformation. Independently on the work on subjectification, resistance in the *History of Sexuality* is discovered as already primary. Among the possible interpretation that its concise presentation allows, resistance in Foucault can only be understood as primary. But this opens up to a correspondence between resistance and Deleuze's ontology that was previously denied. Through this move, resistance places itself in continuity or perhaps even in identity with the idea of lines of flight ('what is primary [in a social field] is that it takes flight; ... it is lines of flight that are primary' – 'points of resistance are primary in relation to power ... ; a social field can be defined as what resists everywhere'). By prolonging this transversal line, resistance and its primacy can be deployed on an ontological horizon.

How many diagrams?

The trajectory of this line is drawn upon the problematization of the relation between resistance and the diagram. Between the two extremities of the line, between the Deleuze against Foucault's resistance and the Deleuze that (re-)discovers the primacy of Foucault's resistance, there is an interesting series of minor shifts and slight modifications particularly focused on the idea of diagram and the status of resistance in relation to it. Foucault mentions the idea of diagram only once. He uses it to explain the role that the Panopticon plays in relation to a number of different disciplinary institutions (schools, hospitals, prisons, warehouses, etc.):

> the Panopticon must not be understood as a dream building: it is the diagram of a mechanism of power reduced to its ideal form; its functioning, abstracted from any obstacle, resistance or friction, must be represented as a pure architectural and optical system: it is in fact a figure of political technology that may and must be detached from any specific use.
>
> (Foucault 1995: 205)

In comparison with its concrete actualizations, the Panopticon represents an ideal or abstract configuration of power relations. It maps the way in which a number of power relations should be (or are already to a certain extent) organized in order to produce a concrete disciplinary institution. This shift from the concrete assemblages to its ideal figure is produced via an abstraction: all the potential elements that might hinder or arrest the smooth functioning of the machine are excluded from the diagram. In a word, the diagram expresses the way in which a specific set of power relations operates in the ideal case in which there was no resistance. Power relations are instable by definition, but, abstracting their interplay from the potential resistances that might disrupt them, we obtain a figure of the diagram that seems to express stability. The diagram represents the ideal of a stable system of distribution of power relations, whose functioning is ideally projected towards infinite reproduction. Abstracting resistance, the mechanism displays the stability that makes transformation and creation superfluous, affirming an operative cycle that can be reiterated indefinitely.

The diagram nevertheless expresses a double movement. On the one hand, we depart from concrete disciplinary institutions (schools, prisons, hospitals, etc.) and through a process of abstraction we arrive to this pure figure. On the other hand, though, there is another movement that follows this same trajectory but in an opposite sense. The pure figure of the Panopticon also becomes a model for establishing disciplinary institutions. The diagram is not only descriptive, but also constitutive and normative. It is not only an abstraction: the diagram functions also as a prescription to the extent that provides a program for the organization of specific concrete disciplinary institutions. Does this constitutive capacity of the diagram suffice to relegate resistance to a secondary and merely oppositional character?

Deleuze, perhaps more than Foucault, appreciates the richness of the notion of the diagram. He uses it to detach politics (and ontology) from the traditional submission to the idea of the state: 'the diagram, which is irreducible to the global instance of the State, perhaps, brings about a micro-unification of the small dispositifs' (Deleuze 1997: 191). But at the same time, as already seen above, the acknowledgement of the constitutive character of the diagram seems to end up with a model in which phenomena of resistance are secondary to power relations. Beyond Foucault's diagram then, Deleuze seems to extend and rethink this notion with the underlying objective of preserving the primacy of his lines of flight. In *Desire and Pleasure* and in 'Many Politics', Deleuze doubles the notion of diagram and attaches it to the idea of abstract machine. Not just one diagram for each society, but at least two. The first one does not go much further than that sketched by Foucault:

> It is by discovering this segmentarity and this heterogeneity of modern powers that Foucault was able to break with the hollow abstractions of the State .... It is not that the apparatus of the State has no meaning. ... The apparatus of the State is a concrete assemblage which realizes the machine of overcoding of a society. This machine in its turn is thus not the State itself, it is the abstract machine which organizes the dominant utterances and the established order of a society, the dominant languages and knowledge, conformist actions and feelings, the segments which prevail over the others. The abstract machine of overcoding ensures the homogenization of different segments, their convertibility, their translatability, it regulates the passages from one side to the other, and the prevailing force under which this takes place. It does not depend on the State, but its effectiveness depends on the State as the assemblage which realizes it in a social field.
>
> (Deleuze and Parnet 1987: 129)

The apparatus of the state is posed in an immediate relation with an abstract machine that somehow presides to its functioning. The state corresponds to the assemblage that realizes this abstract machine in a given society. But this is not yet the same abstract machine that Deleuze ultimately develops with Guattari in *A Thousand Plateaus*. This is an abstract machine of overcoding. It is a specific kind of abstract machine. And it is the kind that better approximates Foucault's diagram. An abstract machine of overcoding functions exactly as the Panopticon for disciplinary societies: it presides to its organization, being effectuated at varying degrees in a number of different concrete institutions or 'small dispositifs'. But this abstract machine of overcoding does not suffice to define a social field on its own (as it would seem to be the case in Foucault according to Deleuze at this stage). As much as power relations or dispositifs of power are mapped within a diagram or an abstract machine of overcoding, Deleuze needs to find a figure that maps the other components of a social field: lines of flight.

> But on the side of lines of resistance, or what I call lines of flight: How should we conceive of the relations or conjugations, the conjunctions, the processes of unification? I would say that the collective field of immanence in which agencements are made at a given moment, and where they trace their lines of flight, also have a veritable diagram.
>
> (Deleuze 1997: 191)

Lines of flight cannot be reduced to scattered and isolated points of resistance. As much as power relations manage to create a fairly stable system of connections, lines of flight need to be thought capable of forming conjunctions. Even lines of flight participate in a process of unification that brings them together. For Deleuze, there is a diagram of lines of flight and this marks a departure from Foucault's notion of the diagram and from the risk of attributing primacy to it. And this diagram of lines of flight cannot be given in a direct relation to the apparatus of state but needs to find its own machinic assemblage: the war machine.

> It is necessary then to find the complex agencement capable of actualizing this diagram, by bringing about the conjunction of lines or points of deterritorialization. It is in this sense that I spoke of a war machine, which is completely different from a State apparatus and from military institutions, but also from dispositifs of power. We would thus have, on the one hand, a State-diagram of power (the State being the molar apparatus that actualizes the microelements of the diagram as a plane of organization); on the other hand, the war machine-diagram of lines of flight (the war machine being the agencement that actualizes the microelements of the diagram as the plane of immanence).
>
> (Deleuze 1997: 191)

From diagram to diagrams: a doubling that concerns two series that immediately appeal to a differentiation of the ontological horizon. On the one hand, we find the series state – diagram of power – plane of organization. On the other hand, there is a distinct series that includes the war machine, the diagram of lines of flight and the plane of immanence. These two series are in a relation of mutual presupposition that revokes the primacy of power relations expressed by the constitutive character of Foucault's diagram. At the same time, these two series necessarily impose a modification of the idea of the abstract machine. The diagram of lines of flight cannot by any means be considered an abstract machine of overcoding. If there has to be an abstract machine that expresses this specific kind of diagram, it also needs to have its own specific operational modality. Coding and overcoding are by definition a process that contrasts and opposes lines of flight to the extent that their primary characterization is their irreducibility to be coded or formalized. In turn, the abstract machine that is adequate to express the diagram of lines of flight needs to be driven by a radical opening to the new, to creation and therefore to transformation rather than to an operation of coding or overcoding. This is the radical difference that distinguishes abstract machines of overcoding from this new emerging type of abstract machines.

> The status of the other type of lines [lines of flight] seems to be completely different. The segments here are not the same, proceeding by thresholds, constituting becomings, blocs of becoming, marking continuums of intensity, combinations of fluxes. The abstract machines here are not the same, they are mutating and not overcoding, marking their mutations at each threshold and each combination.
> (Deleuze and Parnet 1987: 130)

The diagram of lines of flight defines an abstract machine of mutation. What cannot be included within a diagram of power relations is precisely the possibility of its transformation. Going back to Foucault's definition, the abstraction of power relations from any resistance or friction defines a stable system which has no tendency whatsoever towards its own mutation. Why should a system change at all if it shows stability? This is why Deleuze needs a different type of abstract machine that presides at the preservation of mutation. By adopting mutation as its operational modality, this new abstract machine that pertains to lines of flight comes to perform a crucial ontological function: it preserves the fluidity of becoming, the continuous variation of intensities. There is no becoming without mutation, there would be no becoming without abstract machines of mutation, there would be no becoming if only abstract machines of overcoding were given. However, this emerging primacy of the abstract machine of mutation cannot be postulated without a relation of mutual presupposition with the abstract machine of overcoding:

> There is no dualism between abstract overcoding machines and abstract machines of mutation: the latter find themselves segmentarized, organized, overcoded by the others, at the same time as they undermine them; both work within each other at the heart of the assemblage.
>
> (Deleuze and Parnet 1987: 132)

The two abstract machines, although opposed in their operations, work simultaneously in the assemblage. It is their functions that allow a distinction but, as we will see later on, such a distinction does not need to be substantialized into two different machines. This represents an intermediate step towards the 'unified' abstract machine in *A Thousand Plateaus*.

In as much as this trajectory is traced by Deleuze in order to respond to what is, for him, Foucault's limited and reductive conception of the diagram, this line cannot be thought as a radical rejection of Foucault. What drives Deleuze is the necessity to overcome Foucault's conception for the sake of postulating a diagram for resistance. This Deleuzian move, for its part, is not entirely Deleuzian. There are points in Foucault that already engage with Deleuze's question on how to conceive a diagram of the conjunctions and possible unification of the lines of flight. This problem does not seem to be extraneous to Foucault's work.

> Just as the network of power relations ends by forming a dense web that passes through apparatuses and institutions, without being exactly localized in them, so too the swarm of points of resistance traverses social stratifications and individual unities. And it is doubtless the strategic codification of these points of resistance that makes a revolution possible, somewhat similar to the way in which the state relies on the institutional integration of power relationships.
>
> (Foucault 1978: 96)

Foucault also hints towards an analogy between the diagram of power relations and a process of conjunction between dispersed points of resistance. The terminology he adopts is inadequate for highlighting the difference in nature between the two kinds of lines and their respective modality of conjunction. In revolutions, Foucault detects a strategy that codifies points of resistance. This, however, is not the same process at work in Deleuze's abstract machine of overcoding. Nor, with Deleuze, can we talk of a strategy for as long as it is deemed the result of a state-diagram. To what extent, then, can we separate what Foucault here calls codification and strategy from the processes that Deleuze attributes to the war machine? Foucault struggles to conceptualize this war machine but this does not mean that the conceptual line of the war machine is not present in his attempt to define a moment of strategization and of codification proper to resistance.

The unified abstract machine

Deleuze's war machine seems to be presented as what determines his difference from Foucault. But through the excerpt above, his war machine seems more to be a solution to a problem common to both authors. From its outset, the war machine is already more Foucauldian than Deleuze realizes. The war machine is virtual in Foucault's intuition of a strategy constituted exclusively by points of resistance. And this also provokes a conceptual detachment of the idea of strategy from its exclusive relation with power. If strategy is somehow doubled up and opens to two different modalities (a strategy of power relations on the one hand, and a strategy of resistance towards revolution on the other hand), then to say that 'a social field is what strategizes everywhere' becomes less problematic from a Deleuzian perspective. A social field is what shows a strategy of power and simultaneously a strategy of resistance (or war machine). The primacy of this strategy of resistance is not explicit yet, but neither is it excluded.

This standpoint sheds light on a possible conceptual tension that drives Deleuze to formulate a further definition of the concepts of diagram and of abstract machine in his work with Guattari. In *A Thousand Plateaus* (published in 1980), there is no longer a sheer separation between overcoding abstract machines and abstract machines of mutation. This 'new' abstract machine seems to incorporate both without reducing its overall complexity. On the contrary, the complexity of the concept of abstract machine as developed in this work sets into play a wider ontological horizon that needs to be attentively unravelled. 'Abstract machines consist of unformed matters and nonformal functions. Every abstract machine is a consolidated aggregate of matters – functions (phylum and diagram)' (Deleuze and Guattari 1987: 511). Abstract machines appeal to the informal dimension or ontological domain in which matter is given in its pure state, transcending and exceeding its historical formations. The diagram is now more specifically circumscribed to only one of the two aspects that the abstract machine comprises (non-formal functions). The diagram is related but distinguished from the phylum, unformed matter. Nevertheless, the diagram is primary as it sets the way in which the abstract machine operates. The diagram is what characterizes the abstract machine. To a certain extent, there is an identity between the two and the two terms are often used interchangeably.

The informal dimension of abstract machines (unformed matter and non-formal functions) logically implies the existence of a distinct yet related formal domain: the strata. Strata are the formalization or actualization of the abstract machine. This marks a distinctive character of the abstract machine: it is always virtual, although real. Against the breaks, rigid distributions and sedimented ruptures of the strata, the informal dimension of the abstract machine is expressed by continuous variation of unformed matter and non-formal functions: 'only continuous variation brings forth this virtual line, this virtual continuum of life, the essential element of the real beneath the everyday' (Deleuze and Guattari 1987: 110). On the one hand, the strata, the everyday, the actual, forms of expression and forms of content; on the other hand, abstract machines, the virtual continuum of life, the essence of the real, continuous variation of unformed matter and non-formal functions. This constitutes the scheme of an ontology dynamically organized upon the relation of two domains. In this ontology, abstract machines preside to the whole process of interaction between the virtual and the actual. They operate at the intersection and attend to the process of constitution of the real. As such, abstract machines are not limited to the informal domain of the virtual. They are also somehow present in the strata.

> Abstract machines do not exist only on the plane of consistency, upon which they develop diagrams; they are already present enveloped or 'encasted' in the strata ... Thus there are two complementary movements, one by which abstract machines work the strata and are constantly setting things loose, another by which they are effectively stratified, effectively captured by the strata.
>
> (Deleuze and Guattari 1987: 144)

Abstract machines exist in two modalities or 'complementary movements', distinguished according to the ontological regions in which they operate. On the one hand, there is the informal domain which it is more specifically labelled as the plane of consistency, the virtual continuum of life. Upon the plane of consistency, abstract machines develop diagrams. On the other hand, there is a second movement of abstract machines that occurs directly on the strata. The latter capture the abstract machine, formalizing or stratifying its unformed matter and non-formal functions. The abstract machine exists also in the strata as enveloped or encasted. There is a process of capture that determines the constitution itself of the stratum: 'strata could never organize themselves if they did not harness diagrammatic matters or functions and formalize them from the standpoint of both expression and content' (Deleuze and Guattari 1987: 144). It is a process of capture that simultaneously implies a subordination of the stratum to the abstract machine to the extent that the very organization of the stratum is not primarily operated by the stratum itself: 'every regime of signs, and even significance and subjectification, is still a diagrammatic effect (although relativized and negativized)' (Deleuze and Guattari 1987: 144). Although it operates its relativization by capturing or harnessing it, a stratum is still somehow the effect of the diagram. This is the negative or relative modality of the diagram: encasted in a stratum, its destratified and deterritorialized nature (unformed matter and non-formal functions) is stratified and reterritorialized.

At the same time though, there is a complementary movement through which the abstract machine operates directly on the plane of consistency. This movement constitutes an absolute deterritorialization insofar it inverts the other path: no longer from the plane of consistency to the stratum, but from the stratum to the plane of consistency. What the abstract machine does along this axis is disrupt the organization of the stratum by 'setting things loose' in virtue of its 'power or potentiality to extract and accelerate destratified particles-signs (the passage to the absolute)' (Deleuze and Guattari 1987: 144). This movement is presented as absolute or positive in opposition to the negative and relative movement towards the strata. Therefore, the abstract machine operates simultaneously in two opposed modalities: on the one hand, organizing the strata and provisionally determining their homeostatic equilibrium; on the other hand, disrupting the organization of the strata by accelerating and conjugating the constitutive processes of deterritorialization towards the plane of consistency. This double movement of the abstract machine is ultimately connected to the constitution of concrete machinic assemblages that mediate the relation between the plane of consistency and the strata. Nevertheless, this internal configuration of the abstract machine resembles without completely corresponding to the idea of distinguishing an overcoding abstract machine and an abstract machine of mutation encountered above. Deleuze and Guattari do not need two distinct kinds of abstract machines: the functions that each abstract machine was specifically supposed to perform are attributed to the two axes of a singular abstract machine.

There is no primacy of abstract machines of mutation over abstract machines of overcoding. Rather, there is the overall primacy of the abstract machine over the strata and the primacy of lines of flights and movements of destratifications (the axis of the abstract machine oriented towards the plane of consistency – planomenon) over the segments of an encasted or stratified abstract machine (its axis oriented towards the strata – ecumenon). The primacy of lines of flight is therefore based on their constitutive character. They are fully internal to the abstract machine insofar they define its primary function (destratification, drawing of a plane of consistency, opening to becoming).

> Lines of change or creation are fully and directly a part of the abstract machine. Hjelmslev remarked that a language necessarily includes unexploited possibilities or potentialities and that the abstract machine must include these possibilities or potentialities. 'Potential' and 'virtual' are not at all in opposition to 'real'; on the contrary, the reality of the creative, or the placing-in-continuous variation of variables, is in opposition only to the actual determination of their constant relations.
> (Deleuze and Guattari 1987: 99)

Lines of change or creation are immediately included within the abstract machine. The diagram is constituted primarily by those points that lead towards its own transformation. It is inherent to the very functioning of the abstract machine that it has the potential to change and create. And this is because the abstract machine is nothing but unformed matters and non-formal functions: their mixing is by definition a dynamic state of continuous variation. On the plane of consistency, there is nothing that halts the free interaction of these particle-signs. What is opposed to the continuous variation of the abstract machine is not present on the plane of consistency itself. The only opposition that lines of change encounter is at the level of assemblages insofar they transform variable relations into constant through their actualization or the stratification of the abstract machine.

Deleuze's lectures on Foucault

The segment of the line that connects the aftermath of the publication of the *History of Sexuality* (1976) to *A Thousand Plateaus* (1980) is polarized towards an ontology that poses lines of flight as primary as they are constitutive of abstract machines. The latter are defined more through their primary movements of destratification and deterritorialization along the axis oriented towards the plane of consistency (in correspondence with the series abstract machine of mutation – diagram of lines of flight). These movements are primary as they bring about mutation and creation in contrast with what the abstract machine does when encasted in the strata (in correspondence with the series overcoding abstract machines – state-diagram).

But as anticipated above, after this segment we find a point of transformation in which the primacy of lines of flight can be finally posed in immediate correspondence with the primacy of resistance. In Deleuze's lectures on Foucault in 1985/1986, the understanding of diagram changes again by incorporating the tensions that have animated its evolution in the previous segment. What happens to the abstract machine at this stage? Nothing, at least in the lectures. In fact, although the idea of diagram is discussed at length during the course with a frequency that is quite bizarre if confronted on the times in which the diagram actually appears in Foucault (once!), Deleuze never mentions the abstract machine. Even more surprisingly, in the book that follows and ultimately condenses the lectures, the abstract machine pops up again immediately as a synonym for diagram. To be more specific, rather than a mere coupling here there is a complete identity which is fixed from the outset: 'The diagram is no longer an auditory or visual archive but a map, a cartography that is coextensive with the whole social field. It is an abstract machine' (Deleuze 2006a: 40). Although this difference is arguably quite striking, it is hard to propose an explanatory hypothesis. But somehow this difference can be taken as an accidental invitation to truly draw a transversal line in a tense and conflictual creative process. It can serve to reinforce the idea of creating a line instead of merely discussing two authors. Thus, in these lectures Deleuze identifies the diagram with power.

> the diagram is power ... we call 'diagram' the exposition of a relation of forces or a set of relations of forces. ... we call 'diagram' every distribution of the power to affect and the power to be affected, that is, every emission of singularities. In this sense, the diagram goes from one point to another. It goes from some point to some other point, these points being determinable as singularities.
>
> (Deleuze 2018a)

Resistance plays no role yet in this definition. The diagram maps a series of points or singularities distributed in relations in which one affects and the other is affected. Here power is understood as an ontological domain whose nature is distinctively discerned through a microphysics of force. This microphysics is concerned with the interplay of forces deployed in relations that determine a set of points. This distinguishes power as a domain from knowledge. The latter consists of forms that emerge through a concrete interlacement of discursive and non-discursive multiplicities. Points instead express a pure abstraction: the ontological material of power as a domain is informal. Forces are 'unformed matter' whose interplay (affecting and being affected) expresses 'non-formalized functions' (Deleuze 1986). In this sense the diagram selects a whatsoever multiplicity (a set of forces as unformed pure matter) that is organized and distributed according to a function whatsoever ('imposing a task or conduct' in the disciplinary diagram, or 'making something probable' in the diagram of biopower). The informal dimension of the diagram determines therefore a distinction in nature with the concrete forms that are actualized (a school, a hospital, a warehouse) and the specific tasks that will be imposed. The diagram is abstract in relation to the formal dimension of the archive or historical formations.

This definition of the diagram comes closer to Foucault's original account, while it starts slightly deviating from the segment that goes from *Desire and Pleasure* to *A Thousand Plateaus*. What Deleuze adds at this stage though is a series of considerations on the status of forces within the diagram. He anchors the discussion of power relations to the distinction between active and reactive forces. There is an evident Nietzschean inspiration in this move that borders Spinoza's idea of affects. This move is absolutely crucial in order to appreciate the primacy of resistance between Foucault and Deleuze. In fact, the absence of resistance within the diagram/abstract machine that Deleuze criticizes in the previous works is resolved in the lectures precisely through this discussion on the distinction between active and reactive forces. Here the absence of resistance within the diagram becomes the necessary step that Deleuze takes in order to bridge the initial distance from Foucault's work. More than a deviation from his previous works then, this passage needs to be understood as a creative re-composition that prolongs the transversal line between Foucault and Deleuze.

Active and reactive singularities

According to Deleuze, underneath Foucault's idea of power relations there is an obvious reference to the idea of force. A relation of forces occurs when one force is exerted upon another. The point of application of one force upon another constitutes a singularity, a singular point and the distribution of these points constitute or can be represented as a diagram.

> Every power, Foucault says to us, goes from one point to another. ... points as singular points will be the points of application of a force upon another force. The result is that I can distinguish two sorts of points or two sorts of singularities. The points that mark or the singularities that mark the way in which a force is affected by another, and the singularities that mark the way in which one force affects others. For convenience sake, let us place what we can call 'active points' on the one side, points of application of the affecting force, and on the other what we can call 'reactive points', 'points of reaction', or 'singularities of reaction', points of application on the affected force.
>
> (Deleuze 2018d)

These two distinct types of singularities constitute the two poles of a power relation. Power operates through this double capacity of force: the capacity to affect and the capacity to be affected. There is a power relation not simply because one force affects another, but also because the other force is affected by the former. Deleuze distinguishes these two types of points or singularities respectively as active, which affect, and reactive, which are affected, points.

What matters here is to underline the necessity of the mutual correspondence of affective and affected singularities and the exclusion of resistance within the relation. The constitutive aspect of a relation of power is the pairing of two points that can be distinguished according to their function or to the capacity that is contingently actualized. The constitutive pair of any power relation does not consist of one singularity of power and one singularity of resistance. The singularity that is affected in no way exerts resistance as its unique operation is the actualization of its capacity of being affected. The actualization of any of the capacity that pertains to each singularity occurs through the exclusion of the others: at a given moment, each singularity can either affect or be affected. If this pair is ideally abstracted from what surrounds it, there can be no trace of resistance as the latter is excluded by definition. If resistance took the place of the affected singularity, the relation at stake would no longer be a power relation. Taken in the abstract isolation of the diagram, a relation of power has nothing to do with resistance and implies exclusively two singularities that are complementary as they reciprocally necessitate the other (any affective singularity can affect only upon an affected singularity). These two points are bounded to each other in a manner that makes them inseparable. They can be separated, but they do not separate themselves out of their own initiative. As it is evident from the relative longevity of power relation in virtue of their constitutive tendency to indefinite reproduction and crystallization (or staticization), 'relations of power put all these points, or all the singularities, into relation with each other in such a way as to compose a stable whole' (Deleuze 2018d). Stability is the inner characteristic of a pair whose peculiar disposition is to reproduce itself indefinitely in virtue of the intrinsic correspondence of its singularities.

Does the stability of a single power relation suffice to attribute stability to the diagram as well? The relation between stability and the diagram is quite ambivalent. There are multiple levels on which this question can be answered. In Foucault's definition, the abstraction of resistances, frictions and obstacles leaves an unhindered mechanism of power. The functioning of this mechanism is necessarily expected to be smooth. The diagram consists of a map of relations of forces that determine a number of points through which power circulates. As this represents an abstraction that can be actualized in different concrete institutions or assemblages, the resulting mechanism needs to be reliable in delivering the same outcome indefinitely.

It is no surprise that many authors could not find any trace of resistance in *Discipline and Punish*. The nightmare of a carceral society feeds upon this image of the inescapable Panopticon, tremendously effective, widespread throughout the whole of society, producing docile and efficient bodies. When Foucault explores the emergence of this disciplinary power, whose traits are effectuated by a number of very different institutions, what he is tracing is not the full portrait of power relations in a given society and at a given time. He seems to present just the diagram of that society. And, insofar it is a diagram, it is given *as if* there was no resistance. The diagram is the result of a work of abstraction that maps relations of power without taking into account either resistance or its possibility. The process of abstraction that eliminates resistances and frictions from the deployment of power relations seems to be a cognitive artifice. It serves the purpose of outlining a differentiation within the domain of power by distinguishing forces that are actually taken from power relations and those which remain outside these relations. As such the diagram needs to be taken as substantially stable. If resistance is abstracted from the concrete functioning of institutions in which the diagram is actualized, how can the diagram display elements of instability? What is left to determine an instability that is intrinsically inherent to the diagram? In their abstract isolation, power relations match two points which are somehow complementary in the functions they operate. A relation of power is established once a point affects another: both forces need to perform a specific function (to affect or to be affected). A reactive point has no reluctance in joining this relation: no instability can be given in such a scenario. If taken in its absolute isolation, a diagram on its own is completely stable.

However, a diagram is never given in its abstract isolation but in a complex relation both with the strata and with the frictions and obstacles that hinder its alleged stability. In this complex relation, the diagram appears always on the verge to change: 'The diagram is fundamentally unstable ... the diagram never stops going through [*traverser*] mutations. The diagram is fundamentally mutant, and Foucault will several times spell this out, speaking of a site of mutation'

(Deleuze 2018a). What seems to happen in this section of Deleuze's lectures is a confusing overlap between the diagram and the domain of power as a whole. At this stage, his target seems mainly to distinguish strata and power: the diagram is somehow embarked in this journey too and benefits from a treatment that seems to go beyond the initial expectation and beyond its actual role in this ontology. This is quite evident when Deleuze emphasizes the instability of the diagram in relation to the (relative) stability of the strata and promotes the diagram as the key element in the dynamic. In particular, the diagram drives the transition between one stratum, or historical formation, to another:

> Diagrams are always intermediary between a social field in the process of disappearing and a social field in the process of emerging. Why? … It is something that will concern a fundamental instability of the diagram. The relations between forces in a social field are fundamentally unstable. What is stable? You will see right away what is stable, namely, the strata, yes, the very formation, but the diagram that is like the motor of the formation is itself fundamentally unstable.
>
> (Deleuze 2017b)

The diagram becomes not just one element among others but the cornerstone of the whole ontology, its motor. It seems also to close off all the efforts to look for what determines the overall instability of the system as the diagram seems to have taken up this function. The risk is in fact that the diagram effectively swallows up the entire construction as it alone provides all the necessary elements: it determines the creation of historical formations, it decrees the end of their (relative) stability and replaces them with new creative arrangements. Such a system though would say nothing about why a mutation needs to occur at all. What is the turning point that convinces this diagram to change and project a social field towards a new configuration? What complicates things even more is that we have a plurality of diagrams (for instance, disciplinary, biopower, pastoral, etc.): how to account for their succession?

Diagrams and mutation

There are different levels in which we need to understand the diagram in relation to stability. There is an internal stability of the diagram based on the fact that a power relation matches an active singularity with a reactive one. At the same time, this stability is shown only if the diagram is taken in its isolation. In this sense, the diagram is a cognitive artifice that allows to see a structure that tends to last over time. On the other hand, diagrams are instable because they do not last over time. Does this mean that diagrams are instable on their own or in virtue of an element that is external to them? The problematization of the succession of diagrams paves the way for the emergence of resistance in this ontological edifice.

In the lecture of 15 April1986, Deleuze focuses on the continuous succession of diagrams. Any society at a given time displays a strategic distribution of power relations that define a system with fairly stable (or relatively stable but fundamentally unstable) regularities. The diagram displays the complexity of this system. Yet diagrams are contingent to a specific society and to a specific time: the diagram of disciplinary power in European societies around the nineteenth century differs from that of biopower of the following centuries (and most probably even of today). There are definitely consistent continuities between the two diagrams, power relations that survive the passage from one diagram to the other. Yet their difference is manifest and it cannot be argued that the diagram that follows is the natural or necessary evolution of the one that preceded it. There is no endogenous line of transformation that lets the disciplinary diagram make room for biopower. Rather, we find the solidity and robustness of quasi-isolated blocks that function smoothly for relatively long period of time expressing stability. Against the rigid stability of power networks, there is the fact of their transformation that cannot but sounds enigmatic and somehow mysterious. Mutations from one diagram to the other do exist. The mere fact of their existence and their continuous occurrence throughout history alone constitutes a contradiction of the stability that each system claims and concretely displays. Mechanisms of power function smoothly and are, so to speak, engineered to reproduce themselves indefinitely: why do they change then?

> Good, that's all fine to say 'mutation, mutation, mutation', but it seems a bit easy. What are these mutations? The word 'mutation', okay, Foucault employs it ... Foucault invokes mutation, and at the level of relations of forces. Fine, but does he just leave us with that? He abandons us, he says nothing more.

How to take account of these mutations? How to explain the passage from one diagram to another diagram? And what relation is there between diagram B and diagram A?

(Deleuze 2018d)

There is no component or mechanism that induces the diagram to mutate. Therefore, in relation to the diagram, change must be accounted for as driven by a heterogeneous element. We cannot look at the diagram, but outside of it: with this orientation, the trajectory proceeds towards the creation of the concept of the primacy of resistance. It is resistance that determines the continuous occurrence of mutations. A diagram changes with resistance, in virtue of its affirmation. Its primacy is built upon this dynamical function. The ideal indefinite reproduction of a given diagram determines a static scenario in which mutation and creation are obstructed. But continuous mutation demonstrates that no attempt of crystallization can actually revoke the dynamic nature of becoming. Resistance is prior to power insofar it makes sure that this dynamism is preserved and fostered by determining the continuous and creative transformation of the existent.

At the level of forces, this imposes the acknowledgement of a third capacity, a third type of point or singularities. Deleuze critically discusses one by one all the sentences that compose the brief account of resistance given by Foucault in the Method section of the *History of Sexuality*. His problem is similar to that encountered here in Chapter 1: how to understand this ambiguous location of resistance in comparison with power relation, remaining not external but neither internal to the very relation. In particular, Deleuze targets a precise clause of that excerpt: '[Resistances] are the odd term in relations of power; they are inscribed in the latter as an irreducible opposite (vis-à-vis)' (Foucault 1978: 96). It might seem, and perhaps this has often been the dominant interpretation or misinterpretation of Foucault's resistance, that, as resistance is said to be inscribed in power relations, it might coincide with the second pole of the relation itself. But that point has been so far identified as a certain capacity to be affected, which is necessary if we want to account for the actual effectiveness of power relations and diagrams of power. Yet if resistance has to be nevertheless irreducible to power relations, how could it possibly play a role that is vital for the power relation itself? We need to bear in mind that the problem of the whole enquiry has been to account both for the fact of change and transformation of diagrams, but also for the fact of the stability of power relations. And resistance as an irreducibly opposite is not what guarantees this stability.

A third kind of singularity

The problematic quotation at stake can only be explained if we clearly distinguish the novelty of these points of resistance from those points that display their capacity to be affected. Even though the latter seem to be the perfect candidate to embody these points of resistance that Foucault introduces in the *History of Sexuality*, their distinction is crucial to tackle the problematic coupling of change and stability. And for Deleuze this distinction is crucial as it decisively inaugurates the process of creation of the concept of resistance:

> One must understand: power relations put two vis-à-vises into relation, the force of affecting and the force of being affected, that is to say, the point of action and the point of reaction. That's the first thing. But more importantly there is a vis-à-vis of the relation of power, and the vis-à-vis of the relation of power involves points of resistance. This is because points of resistance are not at all the same thing as points of reaction.
>
> (Deleuze 2018d)

Power as the force to affect is vis-à-vis a singularity that is affected and, as a whole, they constitute a power relation. In turn, this power relation (the pairing of an affecting point vis-à-vis an affected point) is vis-à-vis resistance. The other within power is a reactive affect, a force that is affected. The other within power is not resistance. Resistance is the other to power, that is, to a force that affects and a force that is affected. Resistance neither affects nor is affected. Resistance is a kind of affect on its own, a third kind of affect. It is somehow inscribed within the diagram under dissemination, but not within the single power relation. It confronts the power relation but it does not participate to its own reproduction. Resistance is not always already co-opted into power, as it conserves its irreducible otherness and peculiarity. This possibly resolves Deleuze's earlier problem of placing lines of flights within the abstract machine: although resistance is not internal to the diagram, it is nevertheless constitutive as it determines its mutations. If in the segment between *Desire and Pleasure* and *A Thousand Plateaus* Foucault's resistance was problematic as, for Deleuze, it had the status of a secondary phenomenon of counter-attack in virtue of its exclusion from the diagram, here in the lectures this perspective is inverted: resistance is outside the diagram, but it is also constitutive and primary.

We have still a multiplicity of forces that ceaselessly interact with each other determining points distributed in a fashion contingent to the specific evolution of a given society. But this multiplicity finally offers a principle of differentiation that divides these various points or singularities according to their specific capacity. What Foucault decisively adds to this analysis of points is the crucial discovery of this third type:

> I can no longer say, as I was happy to do up until now, that there is a fundamentally a double power in relation, namely, a power to affect and a power to be affected. Now I must link it up with a third power: the power to resist. The power to resist is a third sort of affect, irreducible to the active affects and to reactive affects. It is a third kind of singularity.
>
> (Deleuze 2018d)

This discovery serves exactly the purpose to respond to the initial problem of the mutation of diagrams. If neither the power to affect nor the power to be affected is able to determine the change of the diagram, only this third power, the capacity to resist must necessarily perform this function. Resistance imposes the transformation of power relations and their distribution within the diagram. When resistance or, better still, a multiplicity of points of resistance, attains a certain consistency (Foucault's codification? An abstract machine of mutation? A war machine?), the contingent diagram is obliged to change. The fact of transformation and continuous mutation of diagrams can be explained exclusively through these points of resistance and their primacy.

Resistance as the third possibility of force is precisely what disrupt the stability of diagrams and the predictability of the actualizations it produces. Resistance is what preserves change within the ontological edifice. Against predictability, it immediately relates with chance. In this sense, the diagram is a place of mutation because, in virtue of resistance and the element of chance implied by its creative character and its orientation towards novelty, the diagram can be understood as 'the casting of a dice throw [*l'émission d'un coup de dés*]' (Deleuze 2017b). This is typically a Nietzschean theme that Deleuze already explores in his *Nietzsche and Philosophy*. But the idea of emission is also often used to describe the work of the abstract machine on the plane of consistency in *A Thousand Plateaus*. Here Deleuze sees the succession of diagrams as a succession of dice throws in which each diagram vanishes to let a new one emerges in an open and undetermined relation of dependence.

> Every diagram comes from a preceding diagram. ... There are successive drawings [*tirages*]. There are successive drawings. ... you give yourself a first roll of the dice, you call it 'diagram 1', and then you give yourself a second roll of the dice, which yields 'diagram 2'. In what relation is diagram 2 to diagram 1? ... the preceding dice throw fixes the conditions under which the following dice throws are cast. This does not remove chance. But it makes a mixture that we will call a mixture of chance and dependency.
>
> (Deleuze 2017b)

The succession of diagrams defines according to Deleuze a sort of 'Markov chain', a sequence in which there is only a certain degree of dependence between two successive states. We might think of Escher's *Metamorphoses*: a continuous variation that as soon it seems to be stratified into a citadel on the sea is immediately destratified for a new reterritorialization that transform the tower of the citadel into a rook on a chessboard. This undecided element which is in the process to differ from what it is and already in the process of becoming other (a tower? A rook?) revokes any possibility of determinism: the new is always already coextensive without being predictable. The rook looks like the natural evolution of the tower, while at once its emergence remains completely aleatory in virtue of the creative excess it implies (what were the other potentialities, the other becomings of the tower?). This is the ontological mixture of what Deleuze, quoting Nietzsche, calls 'the iron hand of necessity that shakes the cup of chance' (Deleuze 2017b). And it is precisely resistance, or matter insofar it deploys its third capacity, that forces that iron hand to shake again that dice-box. Resistance imposes a new dice-throw, affirming necessity and chance at once. And becoming is precisely this material interplay of dice-throws and resistances that keep playing the game: 'there always come the dawns, when one perceives that a new roll of the dice is possible' (Deleuze 2017b). Stratified matter is happy with the last emission of dices; resistant matter wants to throw the dices again and again.

Resistance as the outside of the outside

This continuous reshuffling of the existent that resistance imposes shows its privileged relation with becoming and in particular with that informal dimension of the outside:

> The outside attests to its irreducibility, which is to say, to its irreducibility to the diagram itself, by inspiring irreducible points of resistance in each diagram. ... It is the points of resistance that force and bring about a mutation of the diagram, which is to say, a second drawing that comes from the outside, no less than the preceding one, which will also have its points of resistance, and a third drawing, etc.
>
> (Deleuze 2018c)

The concept of the outside comes from Blanchot and plays a very relevant role in Foucault's early work. For Deleuze, Blanchot's outside is translated into an ontological region. Whereas the strata create a sort of interiority at different levels, the outside seems to represent the complement to historical formation. These two regions stand in a relation of mutual presupposition while being radically differentiated in nature and hierarchized according to their nature and function: 'where does the diagram come from? ... The diagram always comes from outside' (Deleuze 2017b). Outside what though? Outside the strata.

Paradoxically though, there is an outside to this outside! Deleuze adds up another layer to his bipartition of the real: 'Resistances ... are the outside of relations of power. The relations of power are the outside of the stratified formations, yet there is still an outside of relations of power' (Deleuze 2018c). Whereas power relations are completely captured within the diagram, resistance emerges outside of it. Both the diagram and resistance belong to a shared outside in relation to the strata. The outside of strata consists of power as a domain. This is not constituted only by relations of power (which are mapped in the diagram), but also by the resistance exerted against them. The outside accounts for the interplay of forces, which in turn is somehow distributed between power relations, on the one hand, and resistances, on the other. The outside constitutes a domain on its own as opposed to strata or historical formations.

This domain is often labelled as power but needs to be carefully distinguished by power relations as they do not constitute the entirety of the ontological material of the domain. In fact, the material of the outside is unformed matter, that is forces. Forces have two capacities (to affect or to be affected) that account for their entering into a power relation. But resistance is qualitatively different from the forces at stake: neither active, nor reactive – a third kind of affect. When forces exert resistance, by definition they do not enter into power relations and, by extension, they do not enter into the diagram either. The primacy of resistance rests upon this obstinate relation with the outside: 'the final word on power is that *resistance comes first*, ... resistances necessarily operate in a direct relation with the outside' (Deleuze 2006a: 89).

As for the other concepts, the outside does not to be understood as one concept in Blanchot's work, but as a line which Blanchot and others have installed themselves on. The transversal line of the primacy of resistance starts showing its affinity or perhaps even its overlapping with this line that marks the outside: 'the terrible line of the outside. This is Melville's whale line in Moby Dick. ... the line that throws the dice, then in this sense, it will be the line of Nietzsche' (Deleuze 2018c). And this is the line that preserves the continuous variation of becoming, its creative chaos, its opening to change: 'This capacity to transform [the diagram] can only be explained by the line of the outside' (Deleuze 2018c).

In short, in the segment extracted connecting the points emitted by Deleuze in his course on Foucault, the diagram is defined as the map of power relations and is continuously immersed in a process of mutation in virtue of resistance. The latter remains outside the diagram but is nevertheless primary. In the segment that goes from *Desire and Pleasure* to *A Thousand Plateaus*, a diagram including no resistance was intolerable as it was held as constitutive while incapable of transformation. Here, resistance is not part of the diagram, does not necessarily form a diagram on its own, but this in no way dismisses its creative and not exclusively oppositional character. This is a very interesting shift that retroactively poses resistance and its primacy firmly at the hearth of ontology. Whether resistance belongs to the diagram (which diagram?) or remains outside of it, becomes almost irrelevant as it can easily be bypassed by referring to those intermediate points which we found in the first segment: we might argue for instance that resistance remains outside the state-diagram or outside the abstract machine of overcoding, while specifically operating in the abstract machine of mutation. However, the importance of these series of shifts for the definition of an ontology is more cogently the affirmation of the primacy of resistance through its affinity with mutation, creation and becoming.

From history to becoming

'The forms are subject to history. Forces are instead subject to a mutation, subject to the diagram; ... forces are taken up in a becoming' (Deleuze 2017b). The transversal line of the primacy of resistance in its ontological understanding traces a movement of evasion in which thought tries to liberate itself from forms and to reach the informal dimension and the outside. It is a move that goes from history to becoming, from historical formations or strata to pure matter in continuous variation, to the creative chaos of becoming. This might at first seem a move away from Foucault, the historian, towards Deleuze, the philosopher. But again we need to resist the problematization of the concepts at stake as a matter of authorship. The line from history to becoming designs a trajectory that needs to be ridden continuously back and forth. Or better still, even when becoming as the locus of creation is posed as the focus of our concerns, history cannot be wiped out all at once. There is a history that is completely subservient to stratification, but there is also a history that is functional to becoming: '[Foucault] was always dealing with historical formations (either short-term or, toward the end, long-term ones), but always in relation to us today' (Deleuze and Parnet 1995: 105). But the present ('in relation to us today') is what is on the verge of mutating, what opens up to creation, to becoming. For Deleuze, the lines that history surveys are lines of stratification or sedimentation. But next to these lines, we find 'lines leading to the present day or creativity' (Deleuze 1992: 165). And this bipartition is posed in correlation with the entirety of Foucault's work, beyond the canonical appreciation of an author through his or her 'official' production. Foucault's books are ultimately histories (of the clinic, of prison, of sexuality, of modes of subjectification, etc.). There are only traces or 'distant roars' that take us away from history in these books.

> But that is one half of his task. For, through a concern for rigorousness, through a desire not to mix things up and through confidence in his reader, he does not formulate the other half. He formulates this explicitly only in the interviews which take place contemporary with the writing of each of his major books: what can be said nowadays about insanity, prison, sexuality? What new modes of subjectification can be seen to appear today which, indeed, are neither Greek nor Christian? ... These interviews are diagnostics. ... The complete work of Foucault ... cannot separate off the books which have made such an impression on all of us from the interviews which lead us towards a future, towards a becoming: the underlying strata and the present day.
>
> (Deleuze 1992: 165)

It is not accidental then that the only explicit reference to the primacy of resistance in Foucault comes in an interview (which Deleuze did not know of at that time as there is no mention of it in his course of 1985/1986).[2] The mutual presupposition of books and interviews in Foucault's work becomes immediately the figure of the mutual presupposition between history and becoming, which nevertheless does not reject the primacy of the latter. The objective is the definition of a transversal line that leads towards a destratified dimension that constitutes our present, our today inasmuch it is oriented 'towards a future, towards a becoming', which is necessarily the time of creation, the time of resistance and, to say it with Nietzsche, the time of the untimely.

Obviously, this trajectory is somehow barred. There is no direct access to becoming as historical formations constitute a material obstacle. History has got therefore a negative connotation because the recollection of the past can be as well an invitation to its reiteration. History says nothing about the new or about creation but expresses only what there was or what there has already been. If we take history as an exhaustive system, no modification or change can be conceived. The past that history installs in the present has the pretence of its eternal and static reiteration. In *A Thousand Plateaus*, Deleuze and Guattari write:

> The principal strata binding human beings are the organism, significance and interpretation, and subjectification and subjection. These strata together are what separates us from the plane of consistency and the abstract machine, where there is no longer any regime of signs, where the line of flight effectuates its own potential positivity and deterritorialization its absolute power (puissance).
>
> (Deleuze and Guattari 1987: 134)

But these strata are precisely historical sedimentations that have the negative function of separating us from the creative dimension of becoming. Almost the same expression is used by Deleuze in relation to Foucault's conception of history:

> History, according to Foucault, circumscribes us and sets limits, it doesn't determine what we are, but what we're in the process of differing from; it doesn't fix our identity, but disperses it into our essential otherness. ... History, in short, is what separates us from ourselves and what we have to go through and beyond in order to think what we are.
>
> (Deleuze 1995b: 95)

History as much as the strata are 'what separate us from ourselves' in the sense that it holds a static moment as the conclusion of a process of becoming rather than one intermediate state on the verge to vanish. History tries to impose the last word on this becoming (any story starts with 'once upon a time' and finishes with 'they live happily thereafter'). It constitutes a blockage upon becoming, upon the emergence of the new and upon these lines of creation that are drawn through experimentation. We are always more than we seem to be or what history held us to be (or what we have been). To think ourselves is to tap into what we could have been and what we could be. We are not what we are but we are already what we could be.

Therefore, history needs to be considered necessarily as a starting point for a movement of escape, of creative resistance, a movement beyond history: 'History isn't experimentation, it's only the set of conditions, negative conditions almost, that make it possible to experience, experiment with, something beyond history' (Deleuze and Parnet 1995: 106). This something beyond history is what cannot be anticipated in a form because forms are always historical. Its formalization can only be sketched without contours as its emergence is necessarily informal without being immaterial. The materiality of becoming is its insistence on a history that never manages to block it completely. As the existent or the present has always a double orientation: on the one hand, history, the archive, the strata, the negative conditions for experimentations, forms and historical formations; on the other hand, becoming, the primacy of resistance, the diagram, the plane of consistency, creation, a near future that is already present.

> The newness of an apparatus in relation to those which have gone before is what we call its actuality, our actuality. The new is the current. The current is not what we are but rather what we are in the process of becoming – that is the Other, our becoming-other.
>
> (Deleuze 1992: 164)

The irruption of the new is the hallmark of a process of becoming that cannot be arrested. And the present always offers already an opening of these lines, lines that have not been formalized yet. Transformation is incessantly on the verge of occurring. And this is immediately given in opposition to what there has been and what tries to persist somehow denying its obsolescence. Pursuing these tracks of becoming cannot but imply a moment of opposition. In *Desire and Pleasure* and in *Dialogues*, Deleuze seemed to perceive the oppositional character of resistance as problematic. But the problem arises only if its creative aspect is barred by the oppositional stance. Here instead, the opening to becoming is at once a fight and a moment of creation. But this oppositional stance is subordinated to creation:

> [Foucault] used history for the sake of something beyond it: as Nietzsche said: acting against time, and thus on time, for the sake of a time one hopes will come. For what appears to be the present-day or the new according to Foucault is what Nietzsche called the unseasonable, the uncontemporary [the untimely], the becoming which bifurcates with history, the diagnostic which relays analysis with other roads.
>
> (Deleuze 1992: 165)

Being against time means resisting against the stratification of the existent, against its obstinate persistence that cannot tolerate the untimely. The untimely is what should not belong to the present, but that still or already does belong to it. The untimely is the prefiguration of novelty, the 'other roads' that can lead us away from the strata and from history. In history, all roads are constrained within the boundaries of an enclosed territory. But that same territory is always fractured and traversed by lines that escape, potential roads that might or might not be taken, but that yet impose their material reality over the present under the guise of the untimely: 'This primacy of lines of flight must not be understood chronologically, or in the sense of an eternal generality. It is rather the fact and the right of the untimely' (Deleuze and Parnet 1987: 136). The primacy of lines of flights, of these roads that act against time, of these resistances that affirm themselves against history, rests immediately upon the untimely, understood in its ontological necessity. The fact of the untimely is its undeniable presence, its pressing existence against what tries to exclude it. The untimely as a fact is appreciated as that excess that escapes formalization, that cannot be formalized yet, that cannot be reterritorialized yet. An excess that is uncontainable for the structures that try to segregate it: 'nothing big has ever passed through these windows, but everything, always, through the triumphant demolition of these walls' (Foucault 2007: 180).

At the same time, its fact, its material existence, which is the reality of the virtual, constitutes already a right. This is a purely affirmative right that does not await recognition. It is an imposition that needs no approval. It is self-assertive. Becoming cannot stop becoming: a fact, a necessity, an absolute right. This passage from fact to right anticipates the idea of an ontology that is immediately ethical and political insofar it attributes normativity to the fact of resistance by affirming its primacy. An ontology of immanence in which each move defines the rule, an optional rule that, as it will be shown in the last part of this section, needs to resist its crystallization into a constant rule. The ethics of the ontological primacy of resistance consists of playing with continuous variation, with rules that change, that are optional and have to be continuously replaced, because 'everything is played in uncertain games' (Deleuze and Parnet 1987: 147).

Resistance, dice-throws and optional rules

An ontology of uncertain games, a mixture of necessity and chance: dice-throws. Resistance leads the game imposing new throws. There are rules for this game, but rules of a specific kind, of a specific nature. Which rules can account for this mixture of chance and necessity? In Deleuze's analysis of subjectification in Foucault's later work, the aesthetics of the self is presented as a line of flight in which force is not trapped into power relations but is directly exerted upon itself determining a fold. Disciplines can be thought as the specular inversion of the aesthetics of the self: imposing rules or conducts upon others. The aesthetics of the self has instead to do with a self-imposition or a self-constrain, which sets a relation not with others but with oneself. But inasmuch as the imposition is not external, this rule can be revoked at any time. It is valid as long it is enacted, making the rule almost superfluous.

> It's no longer a matter of determinate forms, as with knowledge, or of constraining rules, as with power: it's a matter of optional rules that make existence a work of art, rules at once ethical and aesthetic that constitute ways of existing or styles of life (including even suicide). It's what Nietzsche discovered as the will to power operating artistically, inventing new possibilities of life.
>
> (Deleuze 1995b: 98)

These optional rules attain to an ontological modality that has to do with creation and becoming, and that is radically distinguished from the specific modalities of the strata. At the level of strata, the existent constitutes a rule that promises to stay even after the existent where it came from fades away and leaves room to a new diagram. This is 'the domain of codified rules of knowledge (relations between forms), and constraining rules of power (the relation of force to other forces)' (Deleuze and Parnet 1995: 113). But this bifurcation between constant rules (codified rules of knowledge and constraining rules of power) and optional rules ('self-relational') is not restricted to the problem of subjectification, but it is what presides to the overall ontological dynamic.

The mutual presupposition and opposition between optional and constant rules are discussed more extensively with regards to the relation between abstract machines and concrete machinic assemblages:

> 'the abstract machine ... is not actual, but virtual-real; it has, not invariable or obligatory rules, but optional rules that ceaselessly vary with the variation itself, as in a game in which each move changes the rules. ... The abstract machine ... draws lines of continuous variation, while the concrete assemblage treats variables and organizes their highly diverse relations as a function of those lines. The assemblage negotiates variables at this or that level of variation, according to this or that degree of deterritorialization, and determines which variables will enter into constant relations or obey obligatory rules and which will serve instead as a fluid matter for variation. ... The abstract machine does not exist independently of the assemblage, any more than the assemblage functions independently of the machine'.
>
> (Deleuze and Guattari 1987: 100)

The optional rules, which the abstract establishes and expresses in its own diagram, function as the basis for the obligatory rules that organize the strata through concrete assemblages. At the level of the strata, assemblages transform those optional rules into the obligatory rules that define the organization of strata and decree their provisional equilibrium. On the plane of consistency, unformed matters do not form an undifferentiated chaos but are somehow distributed according to non-formalized functions. Functions are not formalized through the extent that they emerge as the contingent conjunction of singularities (unformed matters or particles-signs). Functions do not pre-exist the actual interplay of two singularities but they emerge precisely in virtue of that interplay or conjunction. A non-formal function can be said to constitute an 'optional' rule to the extent that it is the obedience to the rule that determines the rule itself. This rule is optional insofar it stands as long as it is obeyed. Paradoxically, no disobedience can be given as the rule does not hold when it is not obeyed. Disobedience to a 'previous' optional rule marks immediately the establishment of a new optional rule. Optional rules are the expression of functions in continuous variation. Deleuze and Guattari use the idea of a game in which each move defines through its very movement the rule that is being obeyed by that movement itself. An optional rule is more like the acknowledgement of the move as it is being performed. It draws a line between two points while leaving open the possibility that the following move might as well draw a different line. The diagram draws the lines that singularities express through their interplay at a given moment. In a way, the diagram can be said to express the rules that emerge on the plane of consistency at a given instant.

The assemblage operates a transformation of these optional rules into constant ones. Once encasted or enveloped in the strata, the diagram is effectuated by the assemblage as a set of obligatory rules. The homeostatic equilibrium that the strata partly display rests precisely upon the constant relations determined along these obligatory rules. The double articulation of a plane of expression and a plane of content in a given stratum is operated through the obligatory rules that the assemblage effectuates from the diagram. It is a process in which singularities are treated not according to their continual variation but according to the constant relation in which they need to enter. It operates a process of selection that determines which 'portion' of unformed matter will be actualized into forms of content and forms of expression. This formed matter enters in relations that are held to be constant. Each stratum forms a game defining its rules once and for all. In this sense, chess is a game that belongs to the strata. 'Chess is a game of State, or of the court: the emperor of China played it. Chess pieces are coded; they have an internal nature and intrinsic properties from which their movements, situations, and confrontations derive' (Deleuze and Guattari 1987: 352).[3] Chess consists of a machinic assemblage that determines a series of possible movements, interactions (capture) and transformations (the pawn reaching the other end of the chessboard) of pieces on a segmentarized territory. A complex of formed matter (a pawn, a queen, a king) and formalized functions (which movements, which captures, which transformations) displaying constant rules. But at the same time, what is nevertheless coextensive and primary to chess is the virtual potentialities that exceed the game itself. There are lines of flight that can be immediately reterritorialized. By following these tracks, we do not attain the domain of optional rules, but we simply see the consolidation of new constant rules. This movement of relative deterritorialization and reterritorialization is reified in the classic commercial set of chessboard. Not only kings, queens, bishops and pawns, but mere pieces. With these pieces on, the chessboard mutates into a new territory: a checkerboard. New movements, new interactions, new transformations, but still organized into constant rules: again, formed matter and formalized functions.

In order to reach the destratified, the domain of optional rules, the informal dimension of becoming, we need to look for a potentiality that inserts a hiatus in this succession of constant rules. The problem of the primacy of resistance is to change the rules without fixing them. And this starts immediately outlining a possible process of ethical and political selection. The imperative of this ethics represents an ontological necessity: how to stop playing chess, without playing checkers. Lines of creation are those that are able to repattern the system and restructure the virtual (Bogue 1994: 12). The novelty in becoming is what irrupts at the level of the abstract machine and affirms the obsolescence of constant rules by imposing the primacy of continuous variation in which rules become immanent to movement. The ethical challenge is to play with a frog on the chessboard (Checchi 2014). The possible movements, interactions and transformations are yet to be determined and can be determined only by playing. Because the frog on the chessboard obliges to regain the realm of unformed matter and non-formalized functions: when the frog irrupts, the king is no longer a king and might as well abandon the chessboard without that the game has to be deemed over. A complete reshuffle: the frog has installed itself on the line of the outside, the line of the dice-throw. Each step the frog (is it still a frog?) takes on (what is no longer) the chessboard is ontological experimentation. When none of these steps is taken as a program for the ones that follow, the frog attains to becoming and tunes itself with a process of eruptive creation: we still do not know what a frog can do.

Material openings

The idea to describe the primacy of resistance at ontological level through the frog on the chessboard corresponds to the deliberate attempt to destabilize hasty formalizations. A chessboard, a prison, a state, the world. What kind of frog? Dead or alive? Organic or plastic? Who has inserted the frog? God, me or a lobster? These inherent multiplicities serve the purpose of grasping becoming in its materiality, beyond any formalization, riding the line of the outside:

> the outside of the strata is the oceanic diagram. ... the non-stratified element: it is the global strategic element. Global strategy in the sense that it is not only human beings who have a strategy; things also have a strategy. It does not matter which things: particles, electrons, all that, all the fields of forces. What defines a strategy is a field of forces, whether it be human or not.
> (Deleuze 2018a)

The transversal line of the outside is where forms vanish and the human loses its self-illusionary ontological privilege: 'who does man think he is?' (Deleuze and Guattari 1987: 63). The continuous variation of variables consists exclusively of unformed matter (particle and signs) and non-formalized functions. Does it still make sense to talk of resistance then? Perhaps not after this point, although it is the primacy of resistance that has drawn us till here. It is not that resistance loses its primacy or its capacity to shake the dice-box. Rather, resistance becomes completely immersed into matter. The capacity to resist as third affect is fully internal to matter and its own dynamism. It is a matter of matter.

The ontology of the primacy of resistance results into a materialism that affirms 'an excess, force, vitality, relationality, or difference that renders matter active, self-creative, productive, unpredictable' (Coole and Frost 2010: 9). Through resistance, materiality is understood as affirmative and capable of transformation and creation without the intervention of a transcendental agent. Matter is chaotic but awaits no imposition of forms as it produces its own forms autonomously. The idea of a chaosmos renders this image of a chaos which is somehow organized nonetheless: a mixture of necessity and chance. And this constitutes a break with the traditional dualism between form and matter. Protevi highlights this shift presenting this materialist ontology as non-hylomorphic: 'Hylomorphism is thus the doctrine that production is the result of an (architectural) imposition of a transcendent form on a chaotic and/or passive matter' (Protevi 2001: 19). Matter organizes itself autonomously as it shows, at any given moment in time, a multiplicity of potentialities that can be actualized and that can determine its own transformation and (re-)ordering. The reality (and materiality) of the virtual as immanent to matter preserves this ontological materialism from any deterministic understanding. The virtual maps a set of potentialities that are distributed according to threshold of intensities: 'the flux of matter and energy is self-ordering at various singularities or triggers – thresholds of temperature, pressure, velocity, density, connectivity, etc. – giving rise to patterns of self-ordering such as crystallization, turbulence, autocatalysis and so on' (Protevi 2001: 21).

In this ontological horizon of immanence, the primacy of resistance affirms itself in the materiality of its constitutive and transformational potential. The self-ordering of matter becomes an organizational principle that creates crystallizations and strata: closures? Constant rules? Accidentally perhaps. But resistance guarantees the continuous reopening of this creative dynamic. Because no closure can be a real closure. Resistance does not even have to be against this closure, as it is already beyond opposition: its creative task already defines a new self-ordering. Continuous variation, optional rules, new dice-throws. This is how the primacy of resistance affirms the radical openness of its ontology: 'a revolutionary scrambling of the codes that allows events of disorganization and creative novelty in a new ordering, but one in turn open to its own dissolution in time. The question … is then not how to last for a thousand years but how to connect with a thousand plateaus' (Protevi 2001: 203).

A conclusive opening: At last resistance comes first

The conceptual trajectory of this work has passed through a variety of lines and bodies of thought that are decisive to form a coherent and consistent concept. In these explorations, the primacy of resistance has been followed in the complex interplay between openings, closures and new re-openings. To each closure, a new re-opening, a re-existence that affirms itself through its eruptive and creative potential. Resistance claims its primacy in virtue of its capacity to transform, to impose change, to remove any closure, any attempt to make its flow static. Movement, movement, movement: de-static-ize, dynamize becoming. This creative character becomes the hallmark of its conceptualization. 'Prefer what is positive and multiple, difference over uniformity, flows over unities, mobile arrangements over systems. Believe that what is productive is not sedentary but nomadic' (Foucault 2000: xiii). This is the ethical, conceptual and methodological principle of the primacy of resistance. An injunction to understand, decipher and invent resistant practices following its dynamic paths of creation. Resistance is to be appreciated in its autonomy, in its spontaneous affirmation: for what it creates, rather than for what it opposes. To think the primacy of resistance means redirecting the focus on its creative paths of innovation, its techniques, its successful tactics, its conjunctions, the transformations it provokes.

This does not mean that resistance is no longer exerted *against* power. The primacy of resistance does not do away with an oppositional stance. It revokes the privilege that was traditionally accorded to it. What I have tried to demonstrate is that resistance's oppositional stance is the accidental and contingent result of a misfortunate closure. What defines resistance is not its opponent, but the thickness of its processes of creation and transformation.

In the midst of becoming, opposition occurs but this occurrence is not constitutive of or essential to resistance. Resistances are oppositional only when power opposes them. But resistances are never exhausted from this oppositional moment. That opposition is the peak of an iceberg.

Why focus on it? Is it not power itself that invites us to understand resistance only in its reactive and oppositional stances? Is it not functional for power to strategically impose a reductive view that deprives resistance of the plenitude of its creative potential? Paraphrasing Fanon, resistance is treated as inferior but is not convinced by its inferiority.[1] The traditional subordination of the creative side of resistance in favour of its oppositional stance has required a radical inversion. Such an inversion constitutes the basis for a further inversion that turns the relation between power and resistance upside down. If we still want to adopt the categories of active and reactive, affirmative and repressive, superior and inferior, we need to invert these series in relation to resistance and power. Power can only be reactive as it is obliged to change with resistance and the possibility of resistance. On the other hand, resistance affirms its radical difference through a posture that is always active (or more than active – a third kind of affect) as it does not have to concern itself with its opponent: creation is its primary task. Power disrupts resistance's creative processes, it interrupts its affirmation. Power imposes closures to this eruptive movement, it arrests the creative flow by crystallizing it into constant and rigid assemblages for an indefinite and static reproduction of the existent.

From this perspective, the primacy of resistance imposes new ways for understanding power and the powerlessness of power. Each resistance was traditionally required to declare which one was its enemy. The primacy of resistance does not answer this question anymore. It is a question for power: to each power we will ask to which resistance it is against. Power is counter-resistance: it exists only in its reactive posture. The existence of power is nothing but the material result of a concession emanating from resistance. Only when resistance is suspended can power emerge: not as a matter of obedience, but as a matter of suspension.

Becoming over opposition, resistance over power: these inversions have to be understood as a radical opening in its positivity. This would seem to lead thought away from its familiar grounds, from the traditional ways in which resistance and power have been presented. Yet what seems familiar did not have to be familiar: it is accidentally familiar, it could have been otherwise. It should have been otherwise. It should have been forever extraneous. The inversion operated by the primacy of resistance adopts the spirit of a Copernican revolution. It is an inversion of something already inverted. It turns upside down something that was already upside down: the inversion of a previous inversion. It is neither the aim of this book to inaugurate the primacy of resistance over power, nor the conceptual lines that have been explored to arrive to this conclusion. Resistance *is* prior to power. Even when resistance is conceptualized as secondary, as reactive, as oppositional, resistance is already prior to power. The conceptualization of the primacy of resistance turns upside down what has been traditionally inverted.

It can be said that the inversion of a previous inversion restores an original order. But no nostalgic restoration can be given in a dynamic horizon. The inversion operated by traditional accounts of resistance has its historical and strategic value. It needs to be understood as a reactive closure, a stratification that holds us apart from becoming. The primacy of resistance inverts this stratified inversion and opens up a new horizon of creation and experimentation: we still do not know if we can become frogs, we still do not know if a frog on a chessboard can play something different than chess. The Copernican revolution of the primacy of resistance cannot be a restoration, but a new opening.

This does not exclude the emergence of new closures to the affirmative trajectory of the primacy of resistance. New accidental oppositions will pop up again and again. We will have to oppose power, awaiting to march over its ashes. We will have to occupy streets, picket our workplaces, form barricades, throw tear gas canisters back at police. And we will enjoy that too. What changes though is that when power will try to impose its closures, their reactive character will be unmasked. We have seen historical examples of these closures and the way in which they strategically attempt to close the potential of the primacy of resistance. We have seen Hobbes and the tradition of modern sovereignty almost annihilating the discourse on human nature through the appeal to the idea of individual rights. We have seen how the neoliberal discourses of human capital and the financialization of life have managed to close off the potential of the primacy of resistance qua worker's struggles by incorporating its tension towards an expansive conception of labour. History is marked by these interruptions. These closures persist today and continue to produce an obstacle, a deviation to the affirmation of the primacy of resistance. Yet there have been even more powerful openings and more will come! From La Boétie to Tronti, from Spinoza to *operaismo*, and also the openings we have seen between Rancière and Negri, and between Deleuze and Foucault. Hybrid lines of creation on which we can only try to install ourselves.

Is this attempt a creative opening? Is it not just another closure? Any research that deals with resistance is reductive from the outset and cannot be otherwise. Hegel suggests that philosophy is like Minerva's owl that waits for the night before starting its flight (Hegel 2001). But the night for resistance never comes: when is an age of Resistance over? When can resistance be considered terminated so that we can start engaging with its philosophical conceptualization? The primacy of resistance has to impose its own idea of philosophy: a philosophy of becoming. Any attempt to draw a conclusion to a conceptualization of resistance must preserve its allegiance to what is positive, multiple and creative. This work wants to be seen as an ongoing strategy that sets up the most temporary and flexible closure, the least closed of the closures, craving to be reopened by new lines, new flows, new trajectories. The primacy of resistance demands to look at this conclusion as a new beginning, a renovated existence: re-existence. There is a radical orientation towards the expansion and the prolongation of this conceptual trajectory. There is a projection towards all the other conceptual lines of the primacy of resistance that this book has ignored, forgotten or excluded. There is an opening towards the continuation of this trajectory with other bodies of thought, other researchers, other struggles, other deviations. The concept of the primacy of resistance aspires to be a generator of de-stat-ic-izations.

Ideally, the primacy of resistance could constitute a strategic and conceptual tool for contemporary struggles. What is the effect of understanding empirical practices under this inverted lens? What kind of struggles can emerge departing from resistance and subordinating power to a secondary and reactive function? Resistances today already do that though. There is no closure that can stop the continuous flourishing of new resistances, new transformations, new becomings: indigenous resistances against infrastructures, Ni Una Menos, guerrilla wars, Fridays For Future, recuperated factories, Black Lives Matter, squats and communes, No Tav, solidarity network of producers, craftivism,

Gilet Jaunes, social clinics, Capitol Hill Autonomous Zone, commons, Pride parades, wildcat strikes, the Resistencia Ancestral Mapuche, community organizing ... and then a myriad of others at any latitude, micro-subversions, lone comrades, small groups, structured actions, outbursts. They all converge in the affirmation of the primacy of resistance. Perhaps this is the hallmark of today's movements. But resisters have probably known it all along. In the midst of the roars of melancholic defeatist or utopian visionaries, you can still hear a voice, at times feeble, at others more vigorous, that says: resistance comes first!

It is through these lines that the primacy of resistance can prolong its trajectory. But it is not a matter of determining in advance which paths can actually be taken. A book would never be able to do that. After all, any conceptual elaboration is just a theoretical recombination of old words, old ideas: 'Words, however you choose them, always strike you as something bourgeois. But that is how things are. In an enemy society, we cannot freely choose the means we use to fight it. And the weapons of proletarian revolt have always been taken from the bosses' arsenals' (Tronti 2019: xxiii). I have tried to choose words from the arsenal of resistance, but the curse of still living in 'an enemy society' does not really allow us to craft our own words. Thus, these explorations serve more to illustrate how the primacy of resistance produces a horizon that is already fertile for the savage proliferation of other creative processes: a certain disposition towards a horizon that embraces the unknown in its joyful necessity. Avoid affecting and being affected: affirm becoming. It is an invitation to throw the dices again and again. An invitation to mobilize new re-openings against any closure, without being concerned for the closure. A radical celebration of openness, creation and becoming: resistances everywhere!

Notes

Introduction

1. 'Della mia infanzia a Genzano il ricordo che più di altri ha inciso nella mia mente è quello del cambio di abitazione […]. Questo fatto mi dette la possibilità di frequentar[e] spesso […] il Circolo per l'infanzia socialista, nel quale I giovani socialisti e gli adulti davano i primi insegnamenti di cosa era la lotta di classe e quali obiettivi si ponevano I socialisti per costruire una società migliore, senza classi e senza lo sfruttamento dell'uomo sull'uomo' (Capogrossi 2018: 9).

    'Una coppia di fidanzati non poteva andare a passeggio senza la presenza di qualche famigliare. […] [S]i facevano molte discussioni sull'arretratezza di questa consuetudine. Deliberammo di romperle […] [uscendo] per il paese con la fidanzata a braccetto' (Capogrossi 2018: 42).

    '[Dopo l'8 Settembre 1943] costituii un Comitato di Liberazione Nazionale, provvisorio, per i Castelli Romani del quale facevo parte io stesso come presidente' (Capogrossi 2018: 159–60). All subsequent translations are mine. The author and publisher gratefully acknowledge the permission granted to reproduce this copyright material in this book.

2. In his introduction to Capogrossi's book, Claudio Del Bello defines Genzano as 'an extremely distinctive microcosm' which radically expressed communist demands despite its agrarian context. Even Antonio Gramsci remained puzzled by this anomaly (Capogrossi 2018: 119). Today, that communist, rebel, agrarian Genzano does not exist any longer. I was born two miles away from Genzano and I learnt about Capogrossi only recently thanks to Paola and Peppe of the bookshop 'Le Baruffe'. I felt close to Capogrossi's story because he partly reminds of my grandparents (who worked in those same vineyards) and partly reminds me of comrades from my area, such as Paola and Peppe, with that attitude that is at once aggressive, impatient, obstinate, loud and often unwelcome. Even though my contribution to resistance is risible in comparison to their historical achievements, I have always felt bound to that way of resisting.

3   After the invasion of southern Italy by the allies, Nazis set up a series of military fortifications in Cassino (the Winter line), strategically situated on the main route north to Rome. The town was therefore the site of protracted fighting in the so-called battles of Monte Cassino.

4   'Come ho potuto dimostrare, la Resistenze al fascismo, a Genzano, e' cominciata nel 1919' (Capogrossi 2018: 246). This is highlighted also by Del Bello in his introduction who notes that this 'is not a book focused on the facts of the Resistance ... as, in Capogrossi's life story, the partisan struggle represents almost a minor time [un tempuscolo], a handful of months' (in Capogrossi 2018: 1–2).

5   Psychoanalysis has managed somehow to shelter its engagement with the concept of resistance from the experience of Resistance to Nazism. From Freud to Lacan, resistance has featured especially from a clinical perspective in the relation between analyst and patient: 'Whatever disturbs the progress of the work is a resistance' (Freud 2010: 520). Although there have been several attempts to integrate this psychoanalytic concept of resistance within a socio-political debate (see in particular Butler 1997, Žižek 1999), these accounts might be said to rely upon a reactive understanding of resistance (Trumbull 2012). As such, psychoanalysis does not seem to offer an appropriate trajectory towards the primacy of resistance.

6   Resistance affirms itself in a variety of different forms and practices. We regularly witness the emergence of novel forms of resistance. Some manage to mark the practices of entire generations. While it is worthwhile detecting these historical distinctions in terms of practices, at times this ends up erasing any thread of continuity. However, if we look at resistance strategically, practices of resistance converge towards a common conceptual trajectory. To what extent contemporary social movements can be said to refute the idea of resistance? Mark and Paul Engler emphasize the importance of the strategic turn in the practice of non-violence. They cite Gene Sharp's *The politics of nonviolent action* as a turning point where non-violent action is separated from its moral and spiritual dimensions and presented as an effective strategy of resistance. This is the troubling revelation that comes from Sharp's research on Gandhi's satyagraha: '[Sharp] found evidence that most participants ... did not embrace nonviolence out of a sense of moral commitment. Instead, they chose to employ nonviolent struggle because they believe it worked' (Engler and Engler 2016: 4).
On this premise, Engler and Engler elaborate their model of civil resistance or movement-based organizing. Notably, this model has inspired a number of experiences that, despite they might not explicitly refer to resistance (as in

the case of Extinction Rebellion), can definitely be subsumed under a wider understanding of resistance advocated in this book. This allows to place different forms of resistances (violent and non-violent, movements and organizations, traditional Marxist militants and LGBTQIA activists, etc.) in a creative continuum of diverse strategic practices.

7. 'Hence, the importance of this affair of the points of resistance, and, I say to you: a destiny! It is truly a destiny, a destiny must draw him to posit more and more the points of resistance as primary, because to say "the points of resistance are primary" is already to have crossed the line. But one cannot cross the line by simply saying something that arranges things in a different order – it must be necessary, it must be absolutely necessary in such a way that one cannot do otherwise' (Deleuze 2018d).

8. An earlier draft of this chapter has been published in the edited volume *Engaging Foucault* with the title 'Engaging with Foucault's Microphysics of Power through the Primacy of Resistance'. The author and publisher gratefully acknowledge the permission granted to reproduce the copyright material in this book.

Chapter 1

1. On the relation between Foucault's books and his public interventions, see the discussion on Deleuze's take in Chapter 5.
2. Dominations are actually presented as phenomena that somehow determined by the intertwinement and reciprocal appeal of power relations and relations of confrontation. As such, they do not really constitute a different kind of political relation. Rather, phenomena of dominations design a more complex scenario of interaction between two actual kinds of political relations.
3. To an extent, macro-events of resistance (occupied squares, barricades, etc.) could be coded not as resistance anymore, but as strategies of confrontation. When there are open confrontations in the streets, power relations are somehow suspended. What is the power relation that resistance is confronting? None. Because the control of the specific site of struggle is not in the hands of agent only (police for instance), but it is decisively contested. We are not just resisting there, we are on the verge of establishing new power relations radically different from those we had before the confrontation! This partly rejects Caygill's suggestion that Clausewitz's famous work had to be called *On Resistance* rather than *On War*. When resistance forces power relations

to engage in a relation of confrontation, we have indeed a relation of confrontation.

4 'Si [...] on veut faire valoir contre les prises du pouvoir, les corps, les plaisirs, les savoirs, dans leur multiplicité et leur possibilité de résistance' (Foucault 1976: 146). Robert Hurley's translation does not fully transmit the modality of this call for action in the original expressed by '*faire valoir*': 'if we aim ... to counter the grips of power with the claims of bodies, pleasures, and knowledges, in their multiplicity and their possibility of resistance' (Foucault 1978: 157).

5 The idea of superior forces evokes Nietzsche's famous dichotomies on forces and their will to power superior versus inferior, active versus reactive (see Deleuze 1983, Toymentsev 2010). Although these considerations somehow underlie the discussion on the primacy of resistance, here Foucault's quotation draws already a conceptual line that leads to the superiority of resistance without the need to take these dichotomies into account.

6 It is interesting to note how Foucault points to that same historical period that will be so central in the other discussions in Chapter 3 in relation to *operaismo*. The shift from the centrality of political parties to social movements is somehow at the centre of those theoretical reflections. This reinforces Deleuze's hypothesis on the influence of Tronti's Copernican revolution on Foucault's elaboration of the concept of resistance.

Chapter 2

1 The Payot edition of the *Discourse* was published in 1976, two years before Foucault's presentation. Despite the lack of explicit reference, according to Newman (2015), La Boétie 'forms the enigmatic background to Foucault's thinking, who is silently but reverentially intoned behind his words'. On the relation between Foucault and La Boétie, see also Schachter (2009) and Newman (2010).

2 The debate on the political outcomes of La Boétie's *Discourse* contains an interesting variety of positions that go from anarchism to the republican despise of the masses (see in particular Abensour 2011). The object of this project is not to take a precise position within this debate. Rather, the intention is to appropriate those conceptual traces in his text that show a certain propensity towards a specific narrative of anarchism, the absolute rejection of power and the affirmation of natural and cooperative social relationships.

3   In the original, the reference to a new people is given with even more emphasis. Instead of 'some newborn individuals', La Boétie says 'quelques gens tout à fait neufs'. If we accept Clastres's hypothesis, we might interpret La Boétie's remarks as a hope that these remote indigenous people (tragically) encountered by European colonisers know how to live without a tyrant. Or at least, they used to know that until that encounter. If so, we should conclude (or we should force La Boétie to say) that whereas his inevitably Euro-centric gaze does not allow him, as we will see later in the chapter, to locate the misfortune of power, for entire indigenous populations the tragic accident that produces subjugation and tyranny coincides with the start of colonialism.

4   Even the cover of 1978 Payot edition of the *Discourse* presents Abraham Bosse's celebre image.

5   Interestingly, centuries later an Otpor activist (a movement instrumental to the overthrow of Milošević in 2000) puts it in a very similar fashion: 'Even a dictator can't collect taxes on his own … He can't deliver the mail, he can't even milk a cow: someone has to obey his orders or the whole thing shuts down. The task is to convince them to disobey. When they change sides, the government starts to fall' (Collins 2007, cited in Engler and Engler 2016: 91).

6   'il ne faut pas faire doute que nous ne soions tous naturellement libres, puis que nous sommes tous compagnons'.

7   Sreedhar demonstrates that a certain right of resistance (both individual and collective) can be legitimately extracted from Hobbes's work. This definitely remains a delicate object of debate. Nevertheless, at the conceptual level, whether in Hobbes there are only vague traces of the right of resistance that will be then fully developed by other authors is not a question that is crucial to this project. Endorsing Sreedhar's position facilitates the continuity of the narrative deployed in this chapter.

Chapter 3

1   Although there are some conceptual or linguistic choices in the sentence that could be considered to be foreign to a Foucauldian context (in particular the idea of birth), this does not suffice to discredit the validity or the effectiveness of this ventriloquism.

2   Arendt nevertheless reserves an exception for the artist, who alone resists to this process conserving the traits of the *homo faber*.

3   Arendt's conception of labour as distinct from work and action does not seem to provide instruments to a political understanding of the capitalist mode of production. For this reason, *operaismo* remained quite impermeable to Arendt's insights:

> I must say that we've never – neither then nor later – been particularly intrigued by Arendt's weakening [debolista] tripartition of labour, work, action. The Italian version (by Bompiani) of *The human condition* is published in 1964 with the title of *Vita activa*. But it lacked what we were looking for, a thought of workers' struggle on labour [un pensiero di lotte del lavoratore sul lavoro].
>
> (Tronti 2008a: 43) [my translation]

4   All subsequent translation from this source are mine.
5   FIOM stands for *Federazione Italiana Operai Metalmeccanici* (Italian Federation of Metalworkers Employees). Traditionally, it has always represented one of the most radical trade union organizations for industrial workers in Italy.
6   All subsequent translation from this source are mine.
7   All subsequent translation from this source are mine.
8   This tension between the importance of the oppositional stance and the radical orientation towards building a communist horizon is reflected in Tronti's considerations on friendship: 'I say we, because I believe I can speak for a handful of people inseparably linked by a bond of political friendship, who shared a common knot of problems as "lived thought". For us, the classic political friend/enemy distinction was not just a concept of the enemy, but a theory and a practice of the friend as well' (Tronti 2012: 119).

Chapter 4

1   As traditional understandings of resistance have emphasized the role of opposition and condensed this opposition into the confinement of the event, what the primacy of resistance can add is a focus on the thickness of resistant practices and their continuity through varying intensities. The underlying idea is that resistance is essentially affirmative and therefore active, rather than exclusively oppositional. This might give the impression that I am trying to present a 'liberal and romantic' version of resistance. But this is absolutely not the goal of my argument! There is beauty in the struggle! Demos, pickets and clashes count as some of my dearest memories. Far from dismissing them, I want to shed light on the thickness of these mass resistances, the continuous flow of organizing

that makes them possible, the legacy of those resistances that preceded them. As the Commoners' Choir beautifully put it: 'We are the descendants of the striking miners and we're coming for you … We are the descendants of the history-makers … and we are coming for you' (Commoners Choir 2017).

2   In *Inventing the Future*, Nick Srnicek and Alex Williams note how an emphasis on the immediacy of resistance has progressively eroded those narratives of the left projected onto long-term goals. They reclaim the political importance of the future. Although my thesis seems to be in direct opposition with Srnicek and Williams, an emphasis on *potentia* and possibility does engage with the future although within the thickness of the present. Any future projection or narrative exerts an effect on the present.

3   This refers back to Claistre's argument on the logical character of La Boétie's discovery of an originary freedom derived from comradeship discussed in Chapter 2.

4   Engler and Engler show how resistance continuously engage with social and political change. Rather than isolated and inexplicable events of revolt, these 'moments of the whirlwind' happen all the time and are not as rare as they might seem. Furthermore, there is an art to harnessing them to wider moments of resistant organizing. Rejecting the rarity of resistance becomes therefore a strategic imperative: 'If we do not want to be perpetually blindsided by outbreaks of heightened political activity, a first step is recognizing that these are not odd flukes. Rather, they are common, and they play an important role in the ups and downs of social movements' (Engler and Engler 2016: 178).

Chapter 5

1   The idea of transversality would probably have deserved a chapter on its own. There is an interesting convergence between Guattari and Foucault on this idea. Both introduce transversality in their early writings: Guattari in a report presented to the first International Psychodrama Congress, held in Paris in September 1964; Foucault in a brief article which appeared in March 1973 in *Derrière le miroir*, No. 202, 1–8 to accompany a series of paintings by Paul Rebeyrolle. For Guattari, 'transversality is a dimension that tries to overcome both the impasse of pure verticality and that of mere horizontality' (Guattari 2015: 114). And he explains his idea imagining an assemblage of horses, blinkers and fences: 'Think of a field with a fence around it in which there are horses with adjustable blinkers: the adjustment of their blinkers is the "coefficient of

transversality." If they are so adjusted as to make the horses totally blind, then presumably a certain traumatic form of encounter will take place. Gradually, as the flaps are opened, one can envisage them moving about more easily' (Guattari 2015: 112). Likewise, Foucault refers transversality to Rebeyrolle's series of paintings where dogs confront the verticality of power:

> 'And the grand finale, the great last canvas unfurls and spreads out a new space, hitherto absent from the whole series. It is the charting of transversality; it is divided by halves between the black fortress of the past and the clouds of future colour. But, across its whole length, the traces of a gallop – "the sign of an escapee". It seems that the truth comes softly, in the steps of a dove. Force, too, leaves on the earth the claw-marks, the signature of its flight'.
>
> (Foucault 2007: 171)

For a more extensive discussion on transversality see also Genosko (2002) and Checchi (2018).

2   Deleuze never engages with Foucault's interview published in the Canadian magazine *The Stateman* with the title 'Sex, power and the politics of identity'. If he knew it, he would have definitely mentioned it during his lectures as it would have been the shortest way to discuss the problem of the primacy of resistance. As it does not, we have to conclude that Deleuze traces that line as it emerges as a conceptual necessity implicit to Foucault's work independently of that interview.

3   There is definitely some irony in this quotation. Deleuze and Guattari played chess as much as the emperor of China. In the picture published in 'Gilles Deleuze and Félix Guattari: Intersecting Lives', Deleuze's position implies a certain knowledge of the game. The occasion caught in the picture was definitely not the first time he played! Yet it also tells us something more about: in the picture, Deleuze has a substantial advantage over the opponent. That game should have stopped way earlier with either the opponent abandoning or Deleuze suggesting his opponent to abandon and start a new game!

Conclusion

1   'Confronted with a world ruled by the settler, the native is always presumed guilty. But the native's guilt is never a guilt which he accepts; it is rather a kind of curse, a sort of sword of Damocles, for, in his innermost spirit, the native admits no accusation. He is overpowered but not tamed; he is treated as an inferior but he is not convinced of his inferiority' (Fanon 2001: 41).

References

Abensour, M. (2011). 'Is there a proper way to use the voluntary servitude hypothesis?' *Journal of political ideologies* 16(3): 329–48.

Abensour, M. and M. Gauchet (2002). Les Leçons de la Servitude et Leur Destin. *Le discours de la servitude volontaire*. É. d. La Boetie. Paris, Editions Payot: 7–44.

Adorno, T. W. (2005). *Minima moralia: Reflections on a damaged life*. London; New York, Verso.

Adorno, T. W. and M. Horkheimer (1997). *Dialectic of enlightenment*. London, Verso.

Arendt, H. (1998). *The human condition*. Chicago, the University of Chicago Press.

Aristotle (1981). *The politics*. Harmondsworth, Penguin Books.

Ashcraft, R. (1968). 'Locke's state of nature: Historical fact or moral fiction?' *The American political science review* 62(3): 898–915.

Badiou, A. (2007). 'The event in Deleuze.' *Parrhesia* 2: 37–44.

Barnett, R. E. (1986). 'A consent theory of contract.' *Columbia law review* 86(2): 269–321.

Barrère, J. (1923). *L'humanisme et la politique dans le Discours de la servitude volontaire: Étude sur les origines du texte et l'objet du Discours d'Estienne de la Boétie*. Paris, Librairie Ancienne Edouard Champion.

Baumgold, D. (1993). 'Pacifying politics. Resistance, violence, and accountability in seventeenth century contract theory.' *Political theory* 21(1): 6–27.

Baumgold, D. (2010). *Contract theory in historical context: Essays on Grotius, Hobbes, and Locke*. Leiden; Boston, Brill.

Becker, G. S. (1976). *The economic approach to human behavior*. Chicago; London, University of Chicago Press.

Bensaïd, D. (2001). *Résistances: essai de taupologie générale*. Paris, Fayard.

Bensaïd, D. (2004). Alain Badiou and the miracle of the event. *Think again: Alain Badiou and the future of philosophy*. P. Hallward. London, Continuum: 94–105.

Bentouhami, H. (2009). 'Discours de la servitude volontaire de La Boétie et Désobéissance civile de Thoreau. Regards croisés.' *Erytheis* 4: 86–102.

Beran, H. (1977). 'In defense of the consent theory of political obligation and authority.' *Ethics* 87(3): 260–71.

Beverungen, A., S. Dunne and C. Hoedemaekers (2013). 'The financialisation of business ethics.' *Business ethics: A European review* 22(1): 102–17.

Bloom, P. (2016). *Beyond power and resistance: Politics at the radical limits.* London; New York, Rowman & Littlefield.

Bogue, R. (1994). Foucault, Deleuze and the playful fold of the self. *The play of the self.* R. Bogue and M. Spariosu. New York, State University of New York Press: 3–22.

Bosteels, B. (2010). Archipolitics, parapolitics, metapolitics. *Jacques Rancière: Key concepts.* J. P. Deranty. Durham, Acumen: 80–92.

Branson, R. (2014). 'Why we're letting Virgin staff take as much holiday as they want.' Retrieved 30 February 2015, from https://www.virgin.com/richard-branson/why-were-letting-virgin-staff-take-as-much-holiday-as-they-want.

Burgess, G. (1994). 'On Hobbesian resistance theory.' *Political studies* 42(1): 62–83.

Burke, T. F. (2000). 'Rights revolution continues: Why new rights are born (and old rights rarely die).' *Connecticut law review* 33: 1259–74.

Butler, J. (1997). *The psychic life of power: Theories in subjection.* Stanford, CA, Stanford University Press.

Butler, J. (2001). What is critique? An essay on Foucault's virtue. *The political: Readings in continental philosophy.* D. Ingram. London, Basil Blackwell: 212–26.

Callinicos, A. (1982). *Is there a future for Marxism?* London, Macmillan.

Capogrossi, S. (2018). *Storia di antagonismo e resistenza.* Roma, Odradek.

Caygill, H. (2013). *On resistance: A philosophy of defiance.* London, Bloomsbury.

Chambers, S. A. (2010). Police and oligarchy. *Jacques Rancière: Key concepts.* J. P. Deranty. Durham, Acumen: 57–68.

Checchi, M. (2014). 'Spotting the primacy of resistance in the virtual encounter of Foucault and Deleuze.' *Foucault studies* 18: 197–212.

Checchi, M. (2015). Engaging with Foucault's microphysics of power through the primacy of resistance. *Engaging Foucault.* A. Zaharijević, I. Cvejić and M. Losoncz. Belgrade, Institute for Philosophy and Social Theory, Belgrade. 1: 96–111.

Checchi, M. (2018). Come regolare i paraocchi: la trasversalita oltre Guattari. *Guattari.* Greve in Chianti, Quaderni di Testalepre: 47–64.

Chin, C. B. N. and J. H. Mittelman (2000). Conceptualizing resistance to globalization. *Globalization and the politics of resistance.* B. Gills. Basingstoke, Palgrave: 29–47.

Clastres, P. (1994). Freedom, misfortune, the unnameable. *Archaeology of violence.* Pierre Clastres and Jeanine Herman. New York, Semiotext (e): 171–88.

Cleaver, H. (1992). 'The inversion of class perspective in Marxian theory: From valorisation to self-valorisation.' *Open Marxism* 2: 92–106.

Cleaver, H. (2000). *Reading capital politically.* Edinburgh, AK, Anti/Theses.

Commoners Choir. (2017). 'Singalong Protest.' Retrieved 23 October 2019, from http://www.commonerschoir.com/protest.php.

Coole, D. and S. Frost (2010). Introducing the new materialism. *New materialisms. Ontology, agency and politics*. Diana H Coole and Samantha Frost. Durham: Duke University Press: 1–43.

Copp, D. (1980). 'Hobbes on artificial persons and collective actions.' *The Philosophical review* 89(4): 579–606.

Dalla Costa, M. (1988). 'Domestic labour and the feminist movement in Italy since the 1970s.' *International sociology* 3(1): 23–34.

Dalla Costa, M. and S. James (1975). *The power of women and the subversion of the community*. Bristol, Falling Wall Press.

Deleuze, G. (1983). Nietzsche and Philosophy *New York*: Columbia University Press.

Deleuze, G. (1986). Foucault. Le pouvoir, http://www2.univ-paris8.fr/deleuze/rubrique.php3?id_rubrique=22.

Deleuze, G. (1992). What is a dispositif? *Michel Foucault, philosopher: Essays translated from the French and German*. T. J. Armstrong. New York, Routledge: 159–68.

Deleuze, G. (1995a). Breaking things open, breaking words open. *Negotiations: 1972–1990*. Gilles Deleuze. New York, Columbia University Press: 83–93.

Deleuze, G. (1995b). Life as a work of art. *Negotiations, 1972–1990*. Gilles Deleuze. New York, Columbia University Press: 94–101.

Deleuze, G. (1995c). *Negotiations: 1972–1990*. New York, Columbia University Press.

Deleuze, G. (1997). Desire and pleasure. *Foucault and his interlocutors*. A. I. Davidson. Chicago, University of Chicago Press: 183–94.

Deleuze, G. (2006a). *Foucault*. London, Continuum.

Deleuze, G. (2006b). *Nietzsche and philosophy*. London; New York, Continuum.

Deleuze, G. (2017a). Foucault: Lecture 9, 7 January 1986, https://purr.purdue.edu/publications/2865/1.

Deleuze, G. (2017b). Foucault: Lecture 11, 21 January 1986, https://purr.purdue.edu/publications/2869/1.

Deleuze, G. (2018a). Foucault: Lecture 10, 14 January 1986, https://purr.purdue.edu/publications/2943/1.

Deleuze, G. (2018b). Foucault: Lecture 12, 28 January 1986, https://purr.purdue.edu/publications/2949/1.

Deleuze, G. (2018c). Foucault: Lecture 13, 25 February 1986, https://purr.purdue.edu/publications/2684/1.

Deleuze, G. (2018d). Foucault: Lecture 19, 15 April 1986, https://purr.purdue.edu/publications/2690/1.

Deleuze, G. and C. Parnet (1987). *Dialogues*. New York, Columbia University Press.

Deleuze, G. and C. Parnet (1995). A portrait of Michel Foucault. *Negotiations*. G. Deleuze. New York, Columbia University Press: 102–17.

Deleuze, G. and F. Guattari (1987). *A thousand plateaus. Capitalism and schizophrenia.* Minneapolis, University of Minnesota Press.

Deleuze, G. and F. Guattari (1994). *What is philosophy?* New York, Columbia University Press.

Deranty, J. P. (2003). 'Jacques Rancière's contribution to the ethics of recognition.' *Political theory* 31(1): 136–56.

Derrida, J. (1998). *Resistances of psychoanalysis.* Stanford, CA, Stanford University Press.

Dews, P. (1987). *Logics of disintegration. Post-structuralist thought and the claims of critical theory.* London, Verso.

Douzinas, C. (2013). *Philosophy and resistance in the crisis: Greece and the future of Europe.* Cambridge, Polity.

Douzinas, C. (2014). 'Notes towards an analytics of resistance.' *New formations* 83: 79–98.

Dunn, J. (1982). *The political thought of John Locke: An historical account of the argument of the 'two treatises of government'.* Cambridge: Cambridge University Press.

Engler, M. and P. Engler (2016). *This is an uprising. How nonviolent revolt is shaping the twenty-first century.* London, Hachette UK.

Fanon, F. (2001). *The wretched of the Earth.* London, Penguin.

Fassin, E. (2014). Biopower, sexual democracy, and the racialization of sex. *Foucault now: Current perspectives in Foucault studies.* J. D. Faubion. Cambridge, Polity Press: 131–51.

Fishwick, A. and H. Connolly (2018). *Austerity and working-class resistance: survival, disruption and creation in hard times.* A. Fishwick and H. Connolly. London; New York, Rowman and Littlefield International: 1–16.

Foucault, M. (1976). Histoire de la sexualité. Tome I. *La volonté de savoir*, Vol. 1. Gallimard Paris.

Foucault, M. (1977). A preface to transgression. *Language, counter-memory, practice: Selected essays and interviews.* D. F. Bouchard. Ithaca, NY, Cornell University Press: 29–53.

Foucault, M. (1978). *The history of sexuality: An introduction.* New York, Pantheon Books.

Foucault, M. (1980). Power and strategies. *Power/Knowledge: Selected interviews and other writings, 1972–1977.* C. Gordon. New York, Pantheon Books: 134–45.

Foucault, M. (1981). 'Is it useless to revolt?' *Philosophy & social criticism* 8: 2–9.

Foucault, M. (1982). The subject and power. *Michel Foucault: Beyond structuralism and hermeneutics.* P. Rabinow and H. L. Dreyfus. Chicago, University of Chicago Press: 208–26.

Foucault, M. (1988). Power and sex. *Michel Foucault. Politics, philosophy, culture. interviews and other writings 1977–1984*. Alan Sheridan and Lawrence D Kritzman. London; New York, Routledge: 110–24.

Foucault, M. (1994). 'Le Sujet et le Pouvoir.' *Dits et écrits*. Paris, Gallimard. 4: 222–43.

Foucault, M. (1995). *Discipline and punish. The birth of the prison*. New York, Vintage Books.

Foucault, M. (1996). Clarifications on the question of power. *Foucault live. Collected interviews 1966–84*. S. Lotringer. New York, Semiotext(e): 255–63.

Foucault, M. (1997a). Sex, power and the politics of identity. *Ethics: Subjectivity and truth. Essential works of Foucault 1954–1984*. P. Rabinow. New York, New Press: 163–73.

Foucault, M. (1997b). What is critique? *The politics of truth*. S. Lotringer. Los Angeles, Semiotext(e): 23–82.

Foucault, M. (1998). Theatrum philosophicum. *Aesthetics, method, and epistemology. Essential works of Foucault 1954–1984*. J. D. Faubion. New York, the New Press: 343–68.

Foucault, M. (2000). Preface. *Anti-oedipus: Capitalism and schizophrenia*. G. Deleuze and F. Guattari. Minneapolis, MN, University of Minnesota Press: xiii–xvi.

Foucault, M. (2001). The subject and power. *Power. Essential works of Foucault 1954–1984*. J. D. Faubion. New York, New Press: 326–48

Foucault, M. (2004). *Society must be defended. Lectures at the Collège de France 1975–1976*. London, Penguin Books.

Foucault, M. (2007). The force of flight. *Space, knowledge and power: Foucault and geography*. J. W. Crampton, and S. Elden. Aldershot, Ashgate: 169–72.

Foucault, M. (2010). *The birth of biopolitics: Lectures at the Collège de France, 1978–1979*. New York, Palgrave Macmillan.

Fraser, N. (1981). 'Foucault on modern power: Empirical insights and normative confusions.' *Praxis International* 1(3): 272–87.

Freud, S. (2010). *The interpretation of dreams*. New York, Basic Books.

García-Alonso, M. (2013). 'La Boétie and the neo-Roman conception of freedom.' *History of European ideas* 39(3): 317–34.

Genosko, G. (2002). *Felix Guattari: An Aberrant introduction. Transversals: New directions in philosophy*. New York, Continuum.

Ghelfi, A. (2016). *Worlding politics: Justice, commons and technoscience*. PhD, University of Leicester.

Gibson-Graham, J. K. (2006). *A postcapitalist politics*. Minneapolis; London, University of Minnesota Press.

Greyl, L., H. Healy, E. Leonardi and L. Temper (2012). 'Stop that train! Ideological conflict and the TAV.' *Economics and policy of energy and the environment* 2: 193-218.

Guattari, F. (2015). Psychoanalysis and transversality : texts and interviews 1955-1971. South Pasadena, CA: Semiotext(e).

Guattari, F., G. Deleuze and A. Hodges (2015). *Psychoanalysis and transversality: Texts and interviews 1955-1971*. South Pasadena, CA, Semiotext(e).

Habermas, J. (1987). *The philosophical discourse of modernity: Twelve lectures*. Cambridge, MA, MIT Press.

Hampton, J. (1988). *Hobbes and the social contract tradition*. Cambridge: Cambridge University Press.

Hardt, M. (2010). 'Militant life.' *New left review* 64(1): 151-60.

Hardt, M. and A. Negri (1994). *Labor of Dionysus: A critique of the state-form*. Minneapolis, University of Minnesota Press.

Hardt, M. and A. Negri (2000). *Empire*. Cambridge, London, Harvard University Press.

Hardt, M. and A. Negri (2002). 'Marx's mole is dead.' *Globalisation and communication, Eurozine* 13: 1-14.

Hardt, M. and A. Negri (2004). *Multitude: War and democracy in the age of empire*. New York, the Penguin Press.

Hardt, M. and A. Negri (2009). *Commonwealth*. Cambridge, MA, the Belknap of Harvard University Press.

Hardt, M. and A. Negri (2012). *Declaration*. New York, Argo-Navis Author Services.

Harvey, D. (2005). *A brief history of neoliberalism*. Oxford, Oxford University Press.

Hegel, G. W. F. (2001). *Philosophy of right*. Kitchener, ON, Batoche.

Hobbes, T. (1998). *Leviathan*. Oxford, Oxford University Press.

Hoffman, M. (2014). *Foucault and power: The influence of political engagement on theories of power*. New York, Bloomsbury.

Hoy, D. C. (2004). *Critical resistance. From poststructuralism to post-critique*. Cambridge, MA, MIT Press.

Hürlimann, G. (2013). 'Hobbes, Foucault et la peur de la révolte.' *Rue Descartes* 1: 52-68.

Kann, M. E. (1978). 'The dialectic of consent theory.' *The journal of politics* 40(02): 386-408.

Kantorowicz, E. H. (1997). *The king's two bodies: A study in mediaeval political theology*. Princeton, NJ, Princeton University Press.

Keohane, N. O. (1977). 'The radical humanism of etienne de La Boétie.' *Journal of the history of ideas* 38(1): 119-30.

Kusch, M. (1991). *Foucault's strata and fields: An investigation into archaeological and genealogical science studies*. Dordrecht; Boston, Kluwer Academic Publishers.

Labban, M. (2014). 'Against value: Accumulation in the oil industry and the biopolitics of labour under finance.' *Antipode* 46(2): 477–96.

La Boétie, É. d. (2008). *The politics of obedience: The discourse of voluntary servitude*. Auburn, Ludwig von Mises Institute.

Lapavitsas, C. (2013). *Profiting without producing: How finance exploits us all*. London; New York, Verso.

Lazzarato, M. (2002). 'From biopower to biopolitics.' *Pli: The Warwick journal of philosophy* 13(8): 99–113.

Lefort, C. (2002). Le Nom d'Un. *Le discours de la servitude volontaire*. É. d. La Boétie. Paris, Éditions Payot: 269–335.

Lessnoff, M. H. (1990). *Social contract theory*. New York, New York University Press.

Lilley, S. and D. Papadopoulos (2014). 'Material returns: Cultures of valuation, biofinancialisation and the autonomy of politics.' *Sociology* 48(5): 972–88.

Locke, J. (1980). *Second treatise of government*. Indianapolis, IN, Hackett Pub. Co.

Malos, E. (1980). *The politics of housework*. London, Allison and Busby.

Margel, S. (2009). 'De la résistance volontaire. La Boétie et le corps politique du pouvoir.' *Erytheis* (4): 48–56.

Marx, K. (1959). *Economic and philosophic manuscripts of 1844*. Moscow, Foreign languages publishing house.

Marx, K. (1977). *Capital: A critique of political economy*. New York, Vintage Books.

Marx, K. (1994). *Selected writings*. Indianapolis, Hackett Pub. Co.

Mason, P. (2012). *Why it's kicking off everywhere: The new global revolutions*. London; New York, Verso.

May, T. (1993). *Between genealogy and epistemology: Psychology, politics, and knowledge in the thought of Michel Foucault*. University Park, PA, Pennsylvania State University Press.

May, T. (2009). 'Thinking the break: Rancière, Badiou and the return of a politics of resistance.' *Comparative and continental philosophy* 1(2): 253–68.

May, T. (2010). Wrong, disagreement, subjectification. *Jacques Rancière: Key concepts*. J. P. Deranty. Durham, Acumen: 69–79.

McGushin, E. (2010). Arts of life, arts of resistance: Foucault and Hadot on living philosophy. *A Foucault for the 21st century: Governmentality, biopolitics and discipline in the new millennium*. S. Binkley and J. Capetillo Ponce. Newcastle upon Tyne, Cambridge Scholars: 46–61.

McNay, L. (1994). *Foucault: A critical introduction*. Cambridge, Polity Press.

Miller, J. (1994). *The passion of Michel Foucault*. New York, Anchor Books.

Mincer, J. (1991). Job training: Costs, returns, and wage profiles. *Market Failure in Training?*. David Stern and Jozef M.M. Ritzen. Berlin, Heidelberg, Springer: 15–39.

Mincer, J. (1993). *Studies in human capital*. Aldershot, Hants, England; Brookfield, VT, E. Elgar.

Nail, T. (2015). *The figure of the migrant*. Stanford, CA, Stanford University Press.

Negri, A. (1991). *The savage anomaly: The power of Spinoza's metaphysics and politics*. Minneapolis, University of Minnesota Press.

Negri, A. (1999). *Insurgencies. Constituent power and the modern state*. Minneapolis, University of Minnesota Press.

Negri, A. (2004). *Subversive Spinoza*. Manchester, Manchester University Press.

Negri, A. (2005). Domination and Sabotage: On the Marxist method of social transformation. *Books for burning: Between civil war and democracy in 1970s Italy*. A. Negri. London, Verso: 231–90.

Newman, S. (2010). 'Voluntary servitude reconsidered: Radical politics and the problem of self-domination.' *Anarchist developments in cultural studies* 1.

Newman, S. (2015). 'Critique will be the art of voluntary inservitude': Foucault, La Boétie and the problem of freedom. *Foucault and the history of our present*. S. Fuggle, Y. Lanci and M. Tazzioli. London, Palgrave Macmillan UK: 58–73.

Nozick, R. (1974). *Anarchy, state, and utopia*. New York, Basic Books.

O'Hearn, D. and A. Grubačić (2016). 'Capitalism, mutual aid, and material life: Understanding exilic spaces.' *Capital & Class* 40(1): 147–65.

Orwin, C. (1975). 'On the sovereign authorization.' *Political theory* 3(1): 26–44.

Panzieri, R. (2008). Separare le strade. *L' operaismo degli anni sessanta da 'Quaderni rossi' a 'Classe operaia'*. G. Trotta and F. Milana. Rome, Derive e Approdi: 312–14.

Papadopoulos, D. (2018). *Experimental practice: Technoscience, alterontologies, and more-than-social movements*. Durham, NC, Chesham, Duke University Press.

Paras, E. (2006). *Foucault 2.0: Beyond power and knowledge*. New York, Other Press.

Patton, P. (2000). *Deleuze & the political*. London; New York, Routledge.

Philp, M. (1983). 'Foucault on power: A problem in radical translation?' *Political theory* 11(1): 29–52.

Poulantzas, N. (1978). *State, power, socialism*. London, NLB.

Protevi, J. (2001). *Political physics. Deleuze, Derrida and the body politic*. London, the Athlone Press.

Proust, F. (2000). 'The line of resistance.' *Hypatia* 15(4): 23–37.

Rancière, J. (1999). *Dis-agreement. Politics and philosophy*. Minneapolis; London, University of Minnesota Press.

Rancière, J. (2010). *Dissensus. On politics and aesthetics*. London; New York, Continuum.
Rawls, J. (1999). *A theory of justice*. Cambridge, MA, Harvard University Press.
Rawls, J. (2005). *Political liberalism*. New York, Columbia University Press.
Riboud, M. and F. Hernandez-Iglesias (1977). La théorie du capital humain: Un retour aux classiques. *L'économie retrouvée: Vielles critiques et nouvelles analyses*. J. Rosa and F. Aftalion. Paris, Economica: 226–49.
Roggero, G. (2019). *L'operaismo politico italiano: genealogia, storia, metodo*. Rome, Derive e Approdi.
Rose, N. S. (1990). *Governing the soul: The shaping of the private self*. London; New York, Routledge.
Rothbard, M. N. (2008). The political thought of Étienne de La Boétie. *The politics of obedience: The discourse of voluntary servitude*. É.d. L. Boétie. Auburn, Ludwig von Mises Institute: 7–35.
Said, E. W. (1986). Foucault and the imagination of power. *Foucault: A critical reader*. D. C. Hoy. Oxford; New York, Basil Blackwell: 149–56.
Schachter, Marc. (2009). "'Qu'est-ce que la critique': La Boétie, Montaigne, Foucault.' *Montaigne after Theory, Theory after Montaigne*: 122–41.
Schultz, T. W. (1971). *Investment in human capital: The role of education and of research*. New York; London, Free Press.
Simmons, A. J. (1983). 'Inalienable rights and Locke's treatises.' *Philosophy & public affairs* 12(3): 175–204.
Simmons, A. J. (1989). 'Locke's state of nature.' *Political theory* 17(3): 449–70.
Simmons, A. J. (1993). *On the edge of anarchy: Locke, consent, and the limits of society*, Cambridge: Cambridge University Press.
Simons, J. (2003). *Foucault & the political*. London; New York, Routledge.
Smart, B. (1985). *Michel Foucault*. Chichester; London; New York, Ellis Horwood; Tavistock Publications.
Sreedhar, S. (2010). *Hobbes on resistance: Defying the Leviathan*. Cambridge: Cambridge University Press.
Stirner, M. (1995). *The ego and its own*. Cambridge, Cambridge University Press.
Strauss, L. (1953). *Natural right and history*. Chicago, the University of Chicago Press.
Taylor, C. (1984). 'Foucault on freedom and truth.' *Political theory* 12(2): 152–83.
Teixeira, P. (2014). 'Gary Becker's early work on human capital – collaborations and distinctiveness.' *IZA journal of labor economics* 3(1): 1–20.
Terrel, J. (2009). 'Républicanisme et droit naturel dans le Discours de la servitude volontaire: Une rencontre aporétique.' *Erytheis* 4: 35–60.

Thompson, K. (2015). The final word on power: Deleuze and Foucault on resistance. *The political philosophy of Michel Foucault and Gilles Deleuze*. Purdue University. 13–14 November 2015.

Toscano, A. (2004). The coloured thickness of a problem. *The signature of the world, or, what is Deleuze and Guattari's philosophy?* É. Alliez. New York; London, Continuum: ix–xxvi.

Toscano, A. (2009). 'Chronicles of insurrection: Tronti, Negri and the subject of antagonism.' *Cosmos and history: The journal of natural and social philosophy* 5(1): 76–91.

Toymentsev, S. (2010). 'Active/reactive body in Deleuze and Foucault.' *Journal of Philosophy: A Cross-Disciplinary Inquiry* 5(11): 44–56.

Tronti, M. (1980). The strategy of refusal. *Autonomia: Post-political politics*. S. Lotringer and C. Marazzi. New York, Semiotext(e): 28–35.

Tronti, M. (2008a). Noi operaisti. *L' operaismo degli anni sessanta da 'Quaderni rossi' a 'Classe operaia'*. G. Trotta and F. Milana. Rome, Derive e Approdi: 5–58.

Tronti, M. (2008b). Tronti a Panzieri 30.6.61. *L' operaismo degli anni sessanta da 'Quaderni rossi' a 'Classe operaia'*. G. Trotta and F. Milana. Rome, Derive e Approdi: 118–19.

Tronti, M. (2008c). Tronti, la rivoluzione copernicana. Riunione 27 maggio 63. *L' operaismo degli anni sessanta da 'Quaderni rossi' a 'Classe operaia'*. G. Trotta, and F. Milana. Rome, Derive e Approdi: 290–301.

Tronti, M. (2009). *Non si può accettare*. Roma, Ediesse.

Tronti, M. (2012). 'Our operaismo.' *New left review* (73): 119–39.

Tronti, M. (2019). *Workers and capital*. London; New York, Verso.

Trumbull, R. (2012). *Derrida, Freud, Lacan: Resistances*. Santa Cruz, University of California.

Tuck, R. (1981). *Natural rights theories: Their origin and development*. Cambridge, Cambridge University Press.

Virno, P. and M. Hardt (1996). Glossary of concepts. *Radical thought in Italy: A potential politics*. P. Virno and M. Hardt. Minneapolis, MN; London, University of Minnesota Press: 261–4.

Walzer, M. (1984). 'Liberalism and the art of separation.' *Political theory* 12(3).

Walzer, M. (1986). The politics of Michel Foucault. *Foucault: A critical reader*. D. C. Hoy. Oxford; New York, Basil Blackwell: 51–68.

Weber, M. (2001). *The Protestant ethic and the spirit of capitalism*. London, Routledge.

Weeks, K. (2011). *The problem with work. Feminism, Marxism, antiwork politics, and postwork imaginaries*. Durham and London, Duke University Press.

Worth, O. (2013). *Resistance in the age of austerity nationalism, the failure of the left and the return of God*. Halifax, Canada; London, Fernwood; Zed Books.

Žižek, S. (1999). *The ticklish subject: The absent centre of political ontology*. London; New York, Verso.

Žižek, S. (2012). *The year of dreaming dangerously*. London; New York, Verso.

Index

abstract machine 182-3, 187-95, 208, 214
accidentality 12, 16, 18-19, 47, 53-4, 56-8, 137, 143-6, 171-3, 221
action 10, 15, 18, 32-9, 72-4, 85, 88, 114-15, 133, 143-4, 203
actualization 31, 33, 36-7, 39, 41, 105, 111-12, 174, 188, 198-9
Adorno, Theodor W. 9, 68
adversary 6, 10, 18, 36-7, 41
aesthetics of the self 27, 183, 213
affect 15, 153, 196-9, 202-4, 207, 217, 220, 223
affirmation 9-14, 16-19, 47, 68, 80-1, 104, 108-11, 137-8, 154, 161-6, 171, 217-18, 223
aganaktismenoi 3, 135
Alquati, Romano 99, 100
anarchism 52, 80-2, 137, 141
antagonism 11, 33-4, 39-40, 64, 87, 98, 103-4, 127, 155-8
Arab spring 3, 135
Arendt, Hannah 86-97
Aristotle 51, 65-6, 88
armed struggle 2-4
assemblage 182-3, 187, 190, 214-15
autonomist Marxism 3, 8, 87, 98, 100, 110, 130-1, 178

Badiou, Alain 4
battle 28, 37, 64, 72, 133
Becker, Gary 123, 126
becoming 4, 13, 17, 19, 32, 46-8, 107, 110-11, 148, 181, 189, 205-12, 216, 220-3
Bensaïd, Daniel 4, 21
biofinancialization 86-7, 98, 123, 128, 130-1, 169
biopower 196, 200-1
Black Lives Matter 222
Blanchot, Maurice 206-7
Bloom, Peter 4, 12
Butler, Judith 2, 27

capacity of resistance 15, 18, 35, 39-40, 204, 217
capital, capitalism 7, 11, 83-7, 92-3, 98, 100-13, 116, 121, 123, 129, 132
  human capital 87, 98, 123-4, 126-7, 133, 221
Capogrossi, Salvatore 1-2, 4-5, 9, 16
Caygill, Howard 3, 10-11, 18, 25
centralization 7-8, 98
chance 57, 204-6, 213, 217
change 12, 16-18, 27, 41, 43-4, 170-1, 182, 194, 200-4
chaosmos 217
civil resistance 225 n.6
civil state 7, 51, 58-9, 68-70, 73-4, 76, 80-1, 155, 159
class, class struggle 1, 84, 87, 99, 101-10, 112, 119
Clastres, Pierre 57-8, 67
closure 7, 19, 21, 54, 70, 110, 123, 154, 158, 218-19, 221-3
colonialism 8-9, 16, 228 n.3
command 142-4
Communism 98-100
community economy 86-7, 94, 117, 119-20
companionship and comradeship, 53, 62-4, 66, 68, 70-3, 144, 161
composition 99, 112
conflict 6, 28, 70, 103, 105, 151, 155
concept and concept formation 2-3, 20-2, 26, 100, 179
confrontation 6, 11, 44, 68, 72, 122, 132, 168, 171. *See also* relations of confrontation
consent 53, 60, 68-70, 80-1, 112, 139, 163-6
conservation 9, 10, 18, 103, 140
constitution, constitutive 7, 12-14, 19, 23, 35, 54-5, 69, 73-5, 80, 104, 136-7, 153-7, 162-6, 170-1, 183, 194
contract 23, 53-4, 56, 58, 62, 67-71, 73, 155, 169

Copernican revolution 5, 15, 24, 84, 100, 106, 136, 169, 172, 221
counter-resistance 11
creation, creative, creativity 5, 8, 11–14, 19, 26–7, 46–7, 49, 72, 94, 104, 111, 125, 137–8, 147–9, 175, 181–4, 194, 209–11, 216–19
   political creation 42, 48, 136
critique 2, 10, 27, 52, 63, 128
crystallization 17, 19, 40, 98, 157–8, 170, 198, 202, 212, 218
culture of valuation 123, 125, 129, 131. See also value

danger 41–2, 80, 154, 156
death 37, 45, 59, 76, 91
Deleuze, Gilles 8, 17, 23, 83, 178–81, 184, 187–9, 200–6, 211–13
   Deleuze and Felix Guattari, *A Thousand Plateaus* 16, 182–3, 191–4, 210, 214–17
   Foucault 15, 177, 195–7, 207
   Nietzsche and philosophy 9
democracy 55, 135, 162–4, 173
Derrida, Jacques 2
desire 18, 33, 46, 57, 61, 105, 130, 171, 181–2
destratification 193–5, 205, 209, 216. See also strata, stratification
destruction 13, 37, 55, 75, 90, 165, 172–3
diagram 177–80, 185–208, 215
dialectic 137, 140, 158
dice-throw 205–6, 213, 216, 218
difference 7, 29, 47–8, 51, 58, 64–5, 72, 217, 219
dislocation 158, 165, 170, 173–5
disobedience 14, 77, 143–4, 214
dispositif 180–2, 186–8
dispossession 9, 13
disruption 4, 16, 36, 137, 139–40, 193, 204, 220
Djilas, Milovan 8
domination 6, 10, 33–4, 57, 63, 136, 139–41, 148, 152
Douzinas, Costas 4, 10, 14. 135–7, 175
dynamism 17, 95, 137, 140, 158, 167, 173, 202, 217

echo 23, 83–5, 120
emancipation 10, 86, 89, 93, 113, 137–8, 166

enclosure 9, 80–1
enemy 3–4, 6–8, 18–19, 71, 103–4, 220, 223
energy 19, 218
equality 37, 51, 71–2, 98, 139–42, 145–7, 151–2. See also inequality
escape 35–6, 39, 80, 84, 210, 212
ethics 41, 47, 49, 129–30, 138, 152, 161–2, 167–8, 175, 212, 216. See also work ethics
excess 30, 85, 104, 153, 158, 162–4, 166, 174–5, 205, 212, 217
exchange 68, 71, 81, 102, 109, 111, 125–6
event 4, 45, 57–8, 98, 106, 135–6, 147, 218
evil 54, 58, 65, 171
existence 6, 17, 24, 44, 66–7, 93, 98, 127, 150, 167, 175, 213, 219, 222. See also non-existences
expansion, expansiveness 4–5, 23, 82, 85–6, 96–7, 110–15, 122, 124, 154–5, 162, 165, 172
exploitation 1, 43, 84, 87, 98, 108–13, 121, 125, 169
extensification 23, 86, 97, 123, 130, 132, 150
exteriority 28–9
extinction 6, 81, 85, 87, 94, 98, 104, 110–11, 113, 132–3

Fanon, Frantz 16, 220
Fascism 1–4, 16, 98, 181
fear 55, 71–4
feminism 86, 112–13, 118
field of possibilities 22, 32–3, 35–7, 39, 64, 76
flow 24, 40, 136–7, 148–9, 167, 170–1, 219–20
force 5, 9–10, 27, 39, 43–4, 47, 59, 73–5, 99, 132–3, 137, 196–9, 203, 207–8, 213, 217
   productive forces 100, 105, 153, 164
Foucault, Michel 2–5, 15, 20, 25–6, 31–2, 34–8, 41, 43–9, 52–3, 83, 136, 167, 178–80, 182–4, 197–9, 204
   Discipline and Punish 27–8, 181, 185
   History of Sexuality 19, 27–30, 42, 164, 190, 202
   The Birth of Biopolitics 124–8
freedom 27, 51–4, 60–2, 72–4, 79–82, 88–9, 130, 141, 152, 173
future 11, 14, 19, 33, 58, 126, 129, 138, 154, 166–7, 170, 174, 209, 211

Gibson-Graham, J. K. 13, 23, 86, 113–20
government 7, 35–6, 39, 52–3, 74, 77, 80, 161, 178
Gramsci, Antonio 224 n.2, 6
Guattari, Felix 16, 24, 179, 182–3, 191, 210, 214

Hardt, Michael 3, 7, 25, 27, 101, 111
Hegel, G. W. F. 154, 158–9, 222
hierarchy 9, 51, 55–7, 63, 84, 139–42, 145, 160
history 4, 19, 24, 45–6, 67, 95, 100–1, 136, 181, 208–12
hylomorphism 181, 217
Hobbes, Thomas 7, 19, 23, 53, 62, 69–76, 80, 82, 154, 158–9, 169, 221
human nature 51, 56, 59–60, 63, 66, 70, 80, 153

imagination 58, 61, 135, 138, 153, 157, 160–2, 166–8
immanence 7, 29, 174, 188, 212, 218
indignados 3, 135
inequality 27, 29, 63–4, 66–7, 96, 118, 142, 144–5. *See also* equality
initiative 10–11, 72, 84, 105
injustice 10, 65, 73, 117
inservitude 53, 55
instability 35–6, 199–200
insurgency 13, 99
intentionality 33, 41–2
interruption 46, 91, 135–6, 139–41, 146–9, 151–2, 170, 222
invention 47, 61, 101, 111, 213
inversion 9, 14–15, 17, 24, 56, 92, 100, 107, 124, 148, 157, 162, 169, 220–1
irreducibility 15, 22, 30, 164, 189, 202–3, 206

Kant, Immanuel 70, 159
kinopolitics 17
Kropotkin, Peter 13

La Boétie, Etienne de 7, 21, 52–62, 64–9, 77, 111, 144, 161, 222
labour 23, 83–6, 103, 109, 114–16, 120–4, 132–3, 153
  Arendt on labour 87–97
  domestic labour 113

labour power 102–4, 125–6
labour movement, *see* working-class movement
living labour 104–8, 110–12, 125–6
law 52, 72–4, 78, 80, 159
Lazzarato, Maurizio 25, 49
Lefort, Claude 66
Lenin, V. I. 101
Leviathan 7, 59–60, 69, 75
liberalism 55, 62, 80–2. *See also* neoliberalism
liberation 93, 111–12, 116, 126, 155, 161, 163, 168–70
life 1, 12–3, 42, 47, 79–80, 84–9, 104, 115, 123, 129, 153, 175, 192–3, 213
lines of flight 16, 178, 180, 182–5, 188–9, 194–5, 212
Locke, John 53, 70, 76–7, 80, 82
love 63–4, 79, 81, 115

management 8, 22, 32–3, 73–4, 174
Marx, Karl 10–11, 95–6, 99, 101–2, 104–5, 124, 126–7
Marxism 8, 83–4, 99, 100–1, 112, 120, 130
materialism 138, 217–18
materiality, matter 13, 15, 20, 59–60, 75, 98–9, 105, 115, 129, 153, 160–3, 174, 181, 192, 211, 217
microphysics 13, 27, 43, 136, 196
misfortune 16, 53–4, 56–8, 63, 66–9, 82, 143–4, 146, 161
modernity 7, 87, 154, 159
movement 6, 16–17, 19, 157, 170, 173, 193–5, 210, 216, 219
multitude, multitudo 7, 14, 55–6, 59, 156–7, 163, 173
mutation 27, 178, 189–91, 194–5, 200–2, 204–8
mutualism 55, 64, 82

nature 22, 30, 51–3, 61–2, 64, 78, 81, 89–91, 148, 161. *See also* right of nature
necessity 17, 44, 54, 77–9, 81–2, 84, 88–9, 91–5, 106, 108, 130, 167–8, 184–5, 205–6, 213, 223
negation 10, 16, 24, 136–8, 147, 172
Negri, Antonio 3, 19, 100–1, 104, 111–12, 136–8, 152, 222

Subversive Spinoza 153, 157, 163, 168–9, 175
The Savage Anomaly 14, 19, 153–6, 158–62, 164–7, 170–4
neoliberalism 73, 86–7, 117, 123–9, 133, 221. *See also* liberalism
Nietzsche, Friedrich 9–11, 15, 178, 197, 205, 207, 209, 211, 213
non-existences, the inexistent 19, 138, 147, 149–50, 166–8, 174. *See also* existence
non-resistance 4, 73–6
non-violence 225 n.6
Nozick, Robert 53–4, 70, 82

obedience 43, 45–6, 55–6, 59, 69, 141–6, 214, 220
occupation 3–4, 9, 13, 135–6
ontology 15, 17, 136–8, 152–3, 168, 173, 178, 181, 192, 200, 208, 212, 217–18
opening 5, 19, 27, 35, 99, 154, 189, 194, 211, 216, 219–23
operaismo 84, 99–101, 103, 105, 107, 109–10, 222
opposition 5–8, 12–18, 26, 47, 53, 60, 72–3, 107–10, 116, 136–8, 147–8, 166, 171–2, 180, 182–3, 211, 218–21
optional rules 212–16
organization 14, 19, 48, 51, 55, 57, 77, 81, 100–1, 105–9, 139, 161–3, 173, 188, 218
outside 7, 177–8, 206–8, 216–17

pacification 7, 79, 137, 154, 158–9
Panzieri, Raniero 100–1, 105, 107
passivity 27, 34, 39, 47, 53, 98–9, 105, 107, 217
past 14, 19, 58, 61, 161, 209–10
people, the 7, 70, 141
philosophy 15, 19, 24, 52, 100, 144, 154, 162, 180, 208, 222
plane of consistency 192–5, 205, 210–11, 214–15
Plato 88, 147
points of resistance 29–31, 35, 37, 41–2, 46, 184–5, 188, 190–1, 203–4, 206
police 137–41, 144, 146–52, 164, 170, 221
politics 12, 17, 48, 111, 113, 116, 135–41, 146–51, 153–6, 164, 175, 186

possibility 5, 12–13, 18–19, 27, 31–6, 39, 41–2, 46, 61, 64, 67–8, 99, 138, 166–8, 175, 194, 213
potentia 138, 153–9, 162–5, 168–70, 172–5
potential 20, 23, 47–8, 72–3, 76, 103–8, 111, 125–6, 137, 173–4, 194, 216–18
potestas 154, 157–65, 168–72
power 7, 9, 14, 19, 33–5, 42, 51, 59–60, 68, 74–5, 136, 150, 163–6, 171, 177, 182, 191, 213, 219–21
  constituted power 154, 157, 160, 165, 172
  domain of power 196, 199–200, 207, 213
  legitimate power 54, 70, 77, 79
  necessity of power 69, 78–82
  network of power 29–31, 46, 151, 178, 190, 201
  power to affect 14, 197–9, 203–4
  primacy of power 8, 10–12, 14, 26, 159, 188
  stability of power 4, 13, 32, 36–40, 186, 188
primacy of resistance 5, 17–19, 25, 29, 35, 40, 42–9, 52, 60, 68–70, 75, 83–5, 132, 136–8, 141, 177–81, 184–5, 207–9, 216–19, 221–3
prison 185–6, 209, 216
production 43, 84–6, 89–95, 102–3, 111–13, 124, 127, 129–31, 138, 158, 217
program 48, 186, 216
proletariat 11, 99, 111, 149, 223
proliferation of rights 23, 79, 81
protest 14, 65, 135
psychoanalysis 225 n.5

Rancière, Jacques 24, 136–7, 145–6, 170, 222
  Dis-agreement 138–9, 142, 147, 149–52
  Dissensus 140–1, 144
rarity 4–5, 45, 152
Rawls, John 23, 53, 70
reaction 9–11, 37, 44, 72, 106, 128, 169, 197, 203
rebellion 65, 77–8, 112, 165–6
Red Army Faction (RAF) 3
Red Brigades 3

refusal of work 23, 85, 109–11, 130–1
relationality 4, 31, 47, 116, 120–1, 136–7, 213, 217
relations of confrontation 34, 36–41
resistance 6–9, 11–16, 26–8, 30–1, 39, 41, 104, 109, 129, 146, 151–2, 164–9, 171–3, 182–3, 186, 197–9, 202–6, 213, 220
 age of resistance 4–5, 24, 135–6, 174–5, 222
 animal resistance 61, 65
 art of absolute resistance 53
 forms of resistance 13, 178
 futility of resistance 26
 physics of resistance 152, 154, 170, 175
 practices of resistance 2, 4, 47, 151, 219
 pure resistance 11
 resistance to Nazi-fascism 1–4, 9, 16, 98
reversal 36, 39, 44–5, 63, 92, 173
revolt 45–6, 58, 101, 109, 135, 151, 165–6, 223
revolution 13, 99–100, 105–7, 113, 168, 175, 190–1, 218
right of nature 72–4, 76, 81, 154–5
riot 3, 135
Rousseau, Jean-Jacques 7, 67, 70, 144, 154, 158–9

sabotage 2, 31, 105, 117, 171
Sartre, Jean-Paul 8
Scott, James C. 6
self-defence 76
self-valorization 85, 111–12. *See also* value
servitude 53–8, 61–4, 66–8, 77, 111, 155, 161–2, 172
singularity 7, 15, 25, 153, 156–7, 161, 164–6, 174, 196–8, 201–4, 214–15, 218
slavery 35, 55, 58, 77, 89, 161
social movements 3, 12–13, 47–8, 112, 223
socialism 107
solidarity 14, 53, 61, 64, 82, 108, 111, 222
sovereignty 7, 12, 59, 73–8, 120–2, 132–3, 221
Spinoza, Baruch 7, 14, 19, 136–7, 153–5, 159–62, 169–75, 197, 222
spontaneity 80, 105, 107, 135–6, 154–6, 158, 163, 167, 169–70, 219

Stalinism 8
state of nature 7, 23, 54, 57–9, 66–71, 76, 80, 155–6
staticization. *See* crystallization
Stirner, Max 115
strata, stratification 29, 178, 181, 192–4, 200, 206–10, 213–15
strategy 13, 15, 34, 40–2, 45, 83, 152, 184, 190–1, 217, 222
strikes 105, 223
struggle 1, 3, 5–6, 8, 11–12, 34, 36–8, 42, 84, 99–102, 105–8, 110–12, 137, 167, 178, 222
subject of rights 54, 72–3, 76
subjectivation 8, 27, 61, 102–5, 108, 111, 146–7, 149, 180, 183, 185, 209–10, 213. *See also* aesthetics of the self.
surveillance 130

Tito 8
transgression 25, 147, 149, 165–6
transversality 8, 13, 178–81, 183–5, 196–7, 207–9, 217
Tronti, Mario 3, 8, 83–5, 100–3, 105–8, 110, 178, 222–3
truth 4, 88, 166–8
tyranny 8, 52, 55–6, 59–60, 81–2

unions 98–9, 102, 105
untimely 168, 174, 178, 209, 211–12
uprising 4, 135, 175

value 85, 87–8, 103, 109–12, 123, 127, 129–31, 141. *See also* culture of valuation
victory 6, 86, 89, 91–2, 133
violence 4, 33–5, 38–40, 77
virtuality, the virtual 18, 22, 31, 42, 132, 168–9, 174–5, 191–4, 212, 216–18

war 1–2, 7–8, 62, 68, 71–3, 79–80, 151–2, 155, 159, 161
 war machine 16, 188, 191, 204
Weber, Max 118
work 88–93, 95–8, 104, 109–10, 116–18, 122, 129–32
 work ethics 86, 109, 116–19
working-class movement 98–9, 105, 107–9. *See also* class

www.ingramcontent.com/pod-product-compliance
Lightning Source LLC
Chambersburg PA
CBHW072141290426
44111CB00012B/1940